Dalit and Backward Women
Fear and Discrimination

Satish Chandra

AMIGA PRESS. INC
Delhi -110051

AMIGA PRESS. INC

H.O :- 28-A, Indra Park,

Chander Nagar, Delhi :- 110051 (India)

Tel :- 011-22504028, +91-98736-57000

Email :- amigapress@gmail.com
amigaeditorial@gmail.com
amigapub@gmail.com

Website :- www.amigapress@co.in

This edition is published by Amiga Press Inc.

ISBN : 978-93-87295-43-8

First Published 2019

Printed and bound by Replika Press Pvt. Ltd.

Preface

The difficult lives of Dalit women are perhaps best revealed by studying the social, economic, educational, health and political conditions of Dalit women. India has celebrated its 62th year of Independence. The country is now recording 2-digit economic growth every year and successfully takes quite an important and dominant position in international politics and in the economic arena. The success of India is built up with the international reputation of well-educated human resources, "democratic and stabled" political circumstances, and promises of land, benefits and other resources to the foreign and national investors-which are all based on exploitation of Dalit women.

Though The Scheduled Castes and The Scheduled Tribes (Prevention of Atrocities) Act provides substantial protection to Dalits, the Act remains largely unenforced due to both ignorance and active obstruction on the part of Gujarat's law enforcement, judiciary and executive agencies. The CDHR organizes mass gatherings of victims of atrocities at the district level in order to help individual victims circumvent obstacles inhibiting their cases from moving forward and determine larger patterns of un-enforcement of Dalit-protective legislation.

The issue of cultural identity is a central question in the Dalit movement from its very inception. It has led to seeking different kinds of recognition by segments of Dalits at different times. They had sought recognition as Hindus, first settlers, laboring masses, depressed classes, untouchables, Indians, Buddhists, and simply as human beings at different phases of the movement and in different parts of the country, although such claims need not necessarily be exclusive. Socio-cultural discrimination of Dalits and their economic and political deprivation are indeed two sides of the same coin. The need for a multi-pronged approach to emancipation must therefore be a basic premise of any common ideology. The search for a common ideology must be rooted in the ideas, values, and perceptions of Dalits themselves, based on their own experiences of social reality in India. It is out of this that they can discover strategies for change.

Fear, insecurity, inferiority complexes, servility, hopelessness, and despair have enslaved millions of Dalits in India. They have been targets of frequent attacks of retribution and violence in the hands of upper castes. The emergence that Dalits as a "new people" out of the dregs of a history of being a "no people" is perhaps one of the major symbols of hope in our times. The search for a common ideology cannot ignore the existing linguistic, religious and cultural diversities or the geo-political reality that has scattered Dalits into the four corners of the country. But the unity within this diversity based on the sociocultural and politico-economic oppression of Dalits draws them together in a common quest for humanhood.

This is a reference book. All the matter is just compiled and edited in nature, taken from the various sources which are in public domain.

The book includes views of various communities on the status change of these people. The book is to tremendous use to students, teachers, social organisations and general readers.

—*Editor*

Contents

1

Introduction

The organization's concerns led it to carry out research into the area of violence against women in the community and the state's response to such violence. Under international standards states clearly have an obligation to act with due diligence to prevent, investigate and punish abuses of human rights even if not carried out directly by agents of the state. Amnesty International considers that acts of violence against women constitute torture for which the state is accountable when they are of the nature and severity envisaged in the definition of torture in international standards and the state has failed to fulfil its obligation to provide effective protection.

This report provides background information on the context of violence against marginalised groups of women in Uttar Pradesh and Rajasthan, demonstrating the vulnerability of certain groups of women to violence in the context of gender as well as caste and other forms of social and racial discrimination. It then looks in some detail at the problems these groups have in obtaining access to justice and sets the theory of safeguards and judicial process against practices of non-implementation, inaction and discrimination that are a reality for many victims. Presenting evidence of connivance by public servants in covering up crimes of violence against women and ensuring that perpetrators are not prosecuted as well as evidence of discrimination within organs of the criminal justice system, it argues that the state has failed to act with due diligence to prevent, investigate and punish many acts of violence against women which occur in the community. It recommends a series of actions which Amnesty International believes are necessary in order for India to fulfil its international human rights obligations towards women.

By raising its concerns about this aspect of torture within its Campaign against Torture, Amnesty International is seeking to broaden the debate about torture in India and the specific conditions— social, economic, legal and cultural — which allow the torture of women to occur and persist in India in many different contexts. By focussing on the situation of *dalits*, "backward caste", *adivasis* and women otherwise marginalised by their economic position, the report also seeks to highlight the role of discrimination within society and the state — also highlighted in its earlier recommendations — in not only increasing the vulnerability of women to torture but reducing their chances of obtaining justice.

While recognizing that violence against women in India takes many serious forms including trafficking and sexual exploitation, Amnesty International delegates limited their research to crimes of rape and other violent acts, such as assault (including stripping) which occur in the community. Amnesty International delegates also looked at the issue of violence against women in the home and the state's response. Amnesty International's intention is to address concerns arising from its findings on this issue in a separate submission to the Government of India at a later date.

In December 2000, Amnesty International delegates visited Uttar Pradesh and Rajasthan to conduct research into the torture and ill-treatment of women. A request had also been made to visit the state of Bihar. However, by the time delegates arrived in India the Bihar government had not yet responded to the Union Government concerning its willingness to cooperate with the visit so with regret this part of the visit was cancelled. The research carried out in Uttar Pradesh and Rajasthan focussed on the particular vulnerability of socially and economically disadvantaged women to torture and ill-treatment and problems of accessing justice that they face. An emphasis was placed on the situation of scheduled caste and scheduled tribe women, given the large populations of these communitiesin those two states and the existence of specific legislation designed to protect them; it is widely held that this legislation is not being fully implemented. Meetings were held with human rights organizations and victims of torture and ill-treatment, as well as lawyers and others involved in processing cases through the criminal justice system. Meetings were also held with officials in the Home and Women and Child Departments of the two state governments, as well as police officials in those states. Meetings were also held in Rajasthan with the State Commission for Women and the State Human Rights Commission. Amnesty International delegates were grateful to the Rajasthan government for open and frank discussions held with officials and for detailed information on crimes against women provided by the government. Unfortunately, despite requests prior to, during, and following meetings with officials in the Home department of the government of Uttar Pradesh, for details concerning government policy and figures in relation to violence against women and in relation to violence against members of the scheduled caste and scheduled tribe communities, it is regretted that no such information has been made available to Amnesty International to date. Prior to leaving the country, Amnesty International delegates met with officials in the Union Department of Women and Child Development in New Delhi to convey a preliminary impression of their findings and to hear of central government policies concerning violence against women.

Amnesty International does not claim that the situation in Uttar Pradesh and Rajasthan is representative of the whole of the country. Both have particularly feudal and patriarchal societies where caste divisions are strong and where landowning classes continue to wield significant power in many areas. However, the organization believes that many of the problems identified and the recommendations made will be applicable across the country and hopes that they will be fed into discussions concerning women's empowerment which are currently taking place at the government level in India and that they will support the numerous initiatives of the women's movement in the country.

VIOLENCE AND DISCRIMINATION OF DALIT, ADIVASI AND OTHER MARGINALIZED GROUPS OF WOMEN

Women in India are subject to discrimination not just on the basis of gender but on numerous other factors such as caste, community, religion etc. This report looks at the particular problems faced by *dalit*and other marginalised women who face this complex web of discrimination.

Amnesty International saw evidence of the intersection of gender inequality and other forms of discrimination throughout its visit to areas of Uttar Pradesh and Rajasthan. The concept of gender equality continues to be alien to many communities and many state institutions particularly at the local level. In the areas of Uttar Pradesh and Rajasthan visited, caste and land rights are crucial factors which impact on political, social and economic relationships. In Uttar Pradesh political parties representing *dalit*and lower-caste communities have played a role in recent years in empowering some of these groups in certain areas. While it is difficult to generalise about a situation in which caste groups and relationships between them are extremely complex, groups such as *dalits, adivasis*" backward castes" and others continue to be most socially and economically vulnerable as a result of lack of access to land ownership, meaningful political participation and free employment.

Estimates suggest that at least two thirds of the bonded labourers in India are *dalits* and that over half the *dalit* workforce are landless agricultural labourers. Sixty-six per cent of all women agricultural labourers are *dalits* earning between Rs.8-25 [$0.17-0.54] per day. *Dalit* women, and often children, dominate certain spheres of work, such as civic sanitation, scavenging and leatherwork.

Many of those who belong to *dalit* castes are expected to stay in the profession which they are born into. In Lucknow, Uttar Pradesh, Amnesty International delegates learnt of the situation of members of the *Balmiki* "sweeper" caste of whom there are around 10,000 in that city. The majority work as sweepers, often cleaning latrines and live in slum areas close to sewers and gutters as those are the only areas that they are able to obtain for habitation. *Dalit* activists from the Balmiki caste told of how they had struggled to set up an office in the city and how their neighbours while eventually accepting them socially, continue to refuse to eat or drink anything from the office. *Dalits* are also expected to marry within their own caste and relationships between *dalits* and other castes often result in punitive acts. In July 1999 it was reported that a *dalit* woman was gang-raped and burnt alive in front of villagers in Bhavanipur village in Kanpur district of Uttar Pradesh. 17-year-old Usha Yadav [a caste Hindu] had eloped with the woman's son, a *dalit* boy, in June. The girl's father detained the boy's mother and brother-in-law in his house where the mother is reported to have been gang raped and tortured. She was then burnt alive. Three policemen were suspended for negligence.

Discrimination on the Basis of "Descent"

India's caste system involves a social hierarchy and is a feature of Hinduism. Individuals are born into a particular caste and remain in that caste throughout their lives. Broad caste categories (varnas) separate caste groups according to occupation (although mobility between occupations seen in more recent times does not lead to changes in caste identity). Outside these caste categories are the "untouchables", now commonly known as dalits whose occupations — sweepers, tanners etc — were viewed as "polluting". Untouchability of dalits continues to be practised in India in many forms, reinforcing an iniquitous social hierarchy and allowing for the continuing disempowerment and humiliation of millions of people. Localities housing dalits are often segregated from those housing non-dalits, a segregation which often extends to the provision of separate wells, eating places and temples and restrictions on the use of land to defecate. These conditions of segregation were described by many of the victims of violence with whom Amnesty

International delegates spoke in Uttar Pradesh and Rajasthan in December 2000.

Adivasis are also subjected to forms of untouchability in some areas of India including Uttar Pradesh and Rajasthan where the economic and social differences between adivasis and dalits are often indistinguishable making them vulnerable to similar abuses and exploitation. In its 1996 examination of India's 10th to 14th periodic reports, the Committee on the Elimination of Racial Discrimination stated clearly that discrimination to which both communities are subjected falls within the scope of the Convention under its definition of racial discrimination set out in Article 1 which includes the notion of "descent". There are also castes in India not designated as scheduled castes but as "backward castes". While not "polluting" and therefore subject to untouchability, they are recognised as continuing to suffer from severe social and economic discrimination.

Article 17 of the Constitution of India states that the practice of untouchability is abolished and its practice in any form forbidden. It further prescribes that the enforcement of any disability arising out of "untouchability" shall be an offence punishable in accordance with law. Nonetheless, dalits and adivasis regularly suffer verbal and physical abuse at the hands of higher castes. Uttar Pradesh accounted for 25.4% of the total crimes committed against dalits in India during 1998 and Rajasthan 21.8%, both far higher than the next highest: Madhya Pradesh with 15.8%. Rajasthan accounted for 26.5% of the total crimes committed against adivasis in India during 1998, Uttar Pradesh accounting for 2.6% (its population of adivasis is significantly smaller). According to the 1999 Annual Report of the Rajasthan Police there was a significant increase in crimes recorded under the Scheduled Castes and Scheduled Tribes (Prevention of Atrocities) Act between 1997 and 1999. There were 808 cases registered in 1997 and 1,041 in 1999.

Overall, members of *dalit* and *adivasi* communities are less well educated than their non-*dalit* counterparts. Within *dalit* communities in Uttar Pradesh and Rajasthan, literacy levels amongst *dalit* women are amongst the lowest in the country. In Rajasthan an average of 8.3% (dropping to 4.73% in rural areas) of scheduled caste women are literate as opposed to 42.38% of the scheduled caste male population. In Uttar Pradesh an average of 10.96% of scheduled caste women are literate as opposed to 40.79% of the scheduled caste male population. The national average for female and male scheduled caste literacy is 27% and 49.91% respectively. The national average for non-scheduled caste literacy is reported by the UN Development Program to be 38% and 66% respectively.

While poverty is not directly responsible for violence — when Amnesty International delegates asked victims whether they felt they had been targets of violence because they were a *dalit*, they often felt that it was impossible to distinguish between their caste and their economic position of poverty, i.e. that exploitation was the root cause — the dependency of these groups on more powerful groups in the community encourages exploitation which is often accompanied by violent acts. While this situation affects both men and women from these groups, given that women embody the concept of honour, violence against women becomes a symbolic gesture of exploitation and discrimination within communities. During the hearing of India's initial report under the Women's Convention in January 2000, the Government of India representatives acknowledged that women bore the brunt of caste-based atrocities.

Dalits living in Munni Khera village in Hassanganj, an area in Unnao district of Uttar Pradesh, live in an area separated from the rest of the village. Thirty-five per cent of the village are upper castes, 25% are "backward castes", 12% are Muslim and the rest are *dalit*. Ram Chandra, a *dalit* from the village was married to Ramvathi and they owned a piece of land on which they had a house. Upper caste villagers were trying to take the land from them and Ram Chandra and Ramvathi had objected to this. In September 1998, Ramvathi was gang-raped by five men. Higher caste villagers are believed to have raped her as a means of isolating her and her husband within the village and the *dalit* community because of the stigma attached to rape and to punish them for refusing to give up their land.

After the rape, Ram Chandra went to Hassanganj police station to lodge a complaint. However, police refused to lodge a First Information Report (FIR).

There are allegations that police took money from one of the accused. The couple were constantly threatened by influential people in the village and their house was attacked. Ram Chandra finally made an application to the Superintendent of Police of Unnao district concerning the rape and the failure of the police to lodge an FIR. However, despite the Superintendent of Police ordering that the incident should be investigated (no action was taken against police for refusing to lodge an FIR) local police again managed to ensure that the incident was not investigated. Finally under severe pressure, the couple moved to Ramvathi's parent's village some distance away.

They returned to the village on 30 January 1999, reportedly determined to reclaim their property. They were met by three men armed with sticks and axes who were soon joined by others. Ram Chandra sent his wife to the house, fearing violence. He was then beaten by around 17 men with sticks. His left leg and left hand were broken. When he started screaming, Ramvathi and several other women came to find out what was happening. Ram Chandra described what happened next:

"They attacked my wife with stick, she fell down then and there. After that my wife came to me and laid over my body to save me, then they had beaten my wife with sticks and axes. She got deep injuries on the head and shoulder and her right hand and leg broken. [one of the attackers] put off all the clothes of my wife, raped her and inserted and pushed the stick in her private part".

The attackers left Ramvathi for dead and ran away. Ram Chandra and his wife were taken to the district hospital where Ramvathi died the next morning.

When the next day activists approached the Superintendent of Police about the incident which had been reported in the media, he reportedly denied that the incident had occurred and said that the media had exaggerated the facts. Activists went to the village to investigate but villagers were too scared to speak about it. They found Ramvathi's husband in the district hospital. He could only move his neck because he had been beaten so badly. He had not even been told that his wife had died.

After a series of demonstrations by activists, an FIR was filed against the accused under section 302 [murder] of the Indian Penal Code (IPC). They were arrested after some time. The court to which the case was sent is as of March 2001 hearing evidence although no evidence has yet been placed before it. Amnesty International delegates were told that the post mortem on Ram Vathi had not recorded all her injuries that there were fears that due to this and the reluctance of witnesses to come forward, there would not be sufficient evidence to convict the accused.

Eight months later activists heard that Ramvathi's husband had been prevented from entering the village as the accused and their relatives were continuing to threaten him. Activists tried to pursue the case with the National Human Rights Commission and the National Commission for Women but they reportedly took no further action.

As of December 2000, Ram Chandra was staying with his wife's parents in their home away from Hassanganj, continuing to fear for his life, and reluctant to pursue the case. He has received no compensation.

Placed within the context of both gender and caste discrimination, more often than not inhabiting rural areas of severe impoverishment, *dalit* women become an easy target for exploitation and violence. Male members of *dalit* families often leave to go to cities to find work leaving *dalit* women heading households. Sexual harassment by landowners, moneylenders and their hired thugs is common.

In June 1999 Amnesty International delegates interviewed Kali Bai [name changed for security], a Kol tribal (a community designated as scheduled caste in Uttar Pradesh — the same community is designated as scheduled tribe in neighbouring Madhya Pradesh) working for a contractor in Banda district of Uttar Pradesh. The area is largely inhabited by Kol tribals where many of them work as bonded labourers in stone quarries breaking large stones into chippings for construction work. Kali Bai and her husband had been working for ten years and were earning Rs.300 [$6] for every trolley of small stones filled — several days work. They were bonded to the contractor from whom they had borrowed Rs.3,500 [$75].

In August 1998 Kali Bai and her husband heard that another contractor in another village was offering Rs.600 [$13] for every trolley filled so they went to the contractor they were working for and asked him what they owed as they didn't want to work for him any more. The contractor along with three other men started beating them. He took Rs.9,000 [$193] from Kali Bai's husband and started pulling at her hair and clothes. Her whole sari was removed and she was left in a blouse and petticoat and her bangles were broken. She was dragged around the outside of her house. She ran away, embarrassed at her nakedness. She ran to her sister-in-law's house and borrowed a sari and went to the nearby town of Shankergah. She tried to file a complaint with police but they refused saying that her quarrel was with the contractor and not with them. A few days later the police came to Kali Bai's village in connection with another case. The Station House Officer reportedly advised her to leave the village.

An activist working against bonded labour also attempted to file an application to release Kali Bai and her husband from bondage. An application was filed with the Sub-Divisional Magistrate but no action was taken. When interviewed, Kali Bai expressed her helplessness: "they've stripped me. They can only now kill me". As a result of losing the Rs.9,000, she and her family were living a bare existence and continued working for upper castes who kept half of their earnings. Kali Bai has two children. A third child died of cholera when he was one-and-a-half years old. Kali Bai had approached the contractor who employs her for a loan to pay for medicines when he got sick but he had refused and the child had died.

Of serious crimes against scheduled castes including murder, rape, kidnapping and abduction, *dacoity* [banditry], robbery and arson, rape was the highest in the period 1996-1998 according to NCRB figures. The same was true of serious crimes against scheduled tribe women. While 516 cases of murder of scheduled castes were recorded in 1998, 923 cases of rape were recorded in the same year. Rajasthan officially recorded 136 cases of rape of scheduled caste women during 1999. This is certainly a severe underestimate. Well-known journalist P. Sainath, after researching the situation of *dalits* in Rajasthan, reported that on average a *dalit* woman is raped every sixty hours and that one *dalit* is murdered every nine days.

Dalit women also suffer violence within their own communities. Cases were documented by Amnesty International delegates of *dalit* women being raped by *dalit* men of the community. Despite the fact that they are forced by economic circumstance to leave their homes in order to work and thereby enjoy greater mobility and economic independence than many middle-class women, it is also clear that *dalit* women suffer domestic violence.

While it is undoubtedly the case that some economic development has benefited women, the pervasiveness of corruption and exploitation and disregard by economic actors of the livelihood of under-privileged groups has meant that women have often borne the brunt of economic "development" or economic empowerment of powerful groups. The fight against policies of economic development and corrupt economic practices which are perceived as benefiting only a privileged few such as the illegal liquor trade have often been led by women from marginalised communities who are adversely affected by these policies and practices through the break-up of the family or community unit, exploitation, the loss of income etc. In addition, economic empowerment of women has not been matched by equality of property rights. While many women in poor families are forced to contribute to the family income out of economic necessity, they do not have rights over property either in relation to their parents or within marriage so that in the event of the break-up of a marriage they are left destitute. In Rajasthan Amnesty International delegates heard of the widespread practice of *Natha* in which women are married several times. While a small percentage of these second or third marriages are reported to be through choice, the majority occur when women are pressurised into remarriage through desertion by their husbands and are forced by their families into a further marriage. In many of these cases women are literally sold by one man to another with her parents, former husband or relatives often acting as intermediary. In those circumstances where women do have rights over property — usually after becoming widows — they often become the target of violence by family or community members wishing to take the property from them. Property is thereby not only a context for violence but a reason for women being unable to escape violence.

Violence against women within the community is often characterised by attacks on the honour of women and by association their communities by one group against another. The stripping and parading of women who are seen to have broken the community's rules including the position of certain castes or to have called into question the community's honour in some way, is common in many states throughout India. It can also be accompanied by social ostracization. In some areas this extends to the killing of women as witches or *dayans*. Amnesty International delegates were unable to document this practice which is reported to be common in Bihar although it has also been reported in Rajasthan. It is widely believed that most women killed as *dayans* are in fact targeted as a result of property disputes — the majority are widows.

Atrocities on dalit women are an increasing trend. They are victims of landlord oppression, police excesses and goondaism. In all instances of caste tensions dalit women are victimised. Many of the women who have stood against the local landlords or supported inter-caste marriage are punished by being paraded naked. It was reported that on an average three dalit women get raped every day. [Report of discussions during a session on Dalit Women at the Sixth National Conference of Women's Movements held in Ranchi, Bihar, December 28-30 1997].

In May 1999 it was reported that a young widow named Chunni was tied to a tree and brutally beaten on the orders of the *panchayat* (which included seven women) for failing to prevent the deaths of livestock in Amara village of Banda district in Uttar Pradesh. She was reportedly hung upside down, her genitals stuffed with chilli powder and thrashed with lathis. She died of her injuries. Villagers told police she had committed suicide. All 13 *panchayat* members were arrested and charged with murder.

It also has to be recognised that the process of empowerment of women can lead itself to violence as male members of a family or community react in anger to challenges to the patriarchal social structure which benefits them. Of grave concern to Amnesty International in this context is the apparent punitive nature of much violence against *dalit* and other marginalised groups of women by other members of society including men from their own community, in response to attempts to assert their rights or fight against discrimination. This can be in relation to assertion of their economic rights regarding labour conditions, including attempting to extract themselves from situations of bonded labour as well as their political rights. While the advent of reservation for the participation of a certain number of women in the *panchayats* has had some positive impact, there have also been backlashes against women, particularly *dalit* women, who are elected to the *panchayat* and who attempt to assert their rights within that forum, especially when they challenge corrupt and illegal practices.

A study of the experiences of women *panchayat* members in four districts of Rajasthan found that many women had been subjected to abuse and violence within the *panchayat*. "In Pyari Devi Balai's *panchayat*, Mokhunda, the *Upsarpanch* [deputy village head], Gisulal Ganna, ran the affairs of the *panchayat* in the beginning. When some scandals involving embezzlement came to light, Pyari Devi took over the control of the *panchayat*. Since then he went against her. He would hurl casteist abuses at her and practice untouchability with her. He would say: 'A low caste woman cannot be the *Sarpanch* [village head]; ever have your grandfathers become *sarpanches*?'". In its conclusions, the study commented: "*The 1993 Amendments to the Constitution had raised hopes that the gender and caste ridden society would lose some of its strength with the support of the state. But our association with the work of Women in Panchayati Raj Institutions made us realise that the road to such change was not that simple. We realised that the state, while agreeing to share political power with women through enactment, was yet unwilling at the grassroots for such a change. The society had a major role in denying real flow of power to women*".

ACCESS TO JUSTICE: A CASE FOR NEGLIGENCE?

The area of accessing justice for women victims of violence in the community is one which brings into sharp focus continuing problems of discrimination at the grass-roots level in Indian society: where concepts of patriarchy, caste, community and honour have an immediate impact on victims and contribute directly to a situation of impunity for perpetrators. Given that the ability of women to access justice is part of the overall empowerment process essential to women's development and bearing in mind the priority being given to women's empowerment by the present government, Amnesty International believes that this crucial area must be addressed urgently by the state. In its first periodic report to CEDAW, India acknowledged that "*A large number of women have not been able to fully avail the benefits under the Constitution and other legal provisions. There are several deterrents in the way of women seeking legal redress. Insufficiency of legal aid, procedural lacunae and delays, lack of basic knowledge about the law and procedures and long drawn out trials continue to hamper women's access to legal redress."* Amnesty International agrees that these problems are real for women attempting to access justice. However, these problems are also apparent for many others in India and are characteristic of an overloaded criminal justice system which mitigates against a range of marginalised groups in society. Amnesty International believes that the problems faced by underprivileged and marginalised women in accessing justice go beyond those identified above by the government. Notably these involve gender, caste and class discrimination within society, organs of government and the criminal justice system.

Even today, as we approach the 21st century, violence against women is usually treated as a marginal issue by the law-enforcement machinery in our country, whether it be the police, the prosecutors or the medico-legal fraternity or often even the judiciary. It is essential to sensitize this entire machinery to gender issues, particularly violence against women. Often, the police and other personnel are unaware of the legal safeguards for women and the amendments to laws relating to such safeguards.

THE THEORY OF JUSTICE FOR WOMEN

The Law

The central government and state governments have taken several steps to protect woman through enactment of legislation and to prosecute those who perpetrate violence against them. The Indian Penal Code (IPC) has been amended several times in relation to crimes against women largely as a result of campaigns against violence led by the women's movement in the country.

Almost every campaign against gender based violence on women in the 1980s resulted in a new legislation providing protection to them. Each enactment resulted in making the punishment provisions more stringent, setting time limits for pending cases and extending compensation to the victims. Violence in its different dimensions has been sought to be tackled by legislative reforms, innovations in the structure and working of the police force, measures to sensitise the bureaucracy, media campaigns and new institutional structures

Section 375 of the IPC defines the offence of rape as sexual intercourse against the will or consent of a woman (punishable with between seven years and life imprisonment). Penetration is explained as "sufficient to constitute sexual intercourse". This has long been criticised for being too narrow a definition of rape. Section 354 of the IPC provides for punishment for "assault or criminal force to woman with intent to outrage her modesty", a wide-ranging provision which is commonly used in incidents of violence not amounting to rape (defined as penetration) but which invites a far lesser punishment of imprisonment of up to two years. The National Commission for Women and several women's organizations have been involved in attempts to establish a crime of "sexual assault" in its place — even drawing up a Sexual Assault Draft Bill, 1993 — but so far without success. In 1995 and 1996 numerous suggestions were made by lawyers and women's activists to strengthen legal safeguards regarding rape and other related issues in response to questionnaires on the criminal law distributed by the Law Commission of India. An Ad hoc Subcommittee of the National Commission for Women (NCW) conducted fairly widespread consultations about laws relating to rape culminating in a set of recommendations produced in September 1999. In March 2000, again after apparently widespread consultation, the Law Commission of India issued a Review of Rape Laws. The NCW also published a further study in August 2000, *Rape: A legal study*, again making recommendations for amendments to the law. In December 2000, Amnesty International delegates were told by officials of the Department of Women and Child Development of the Government of India that they were awaiting a final report on necessary amendments to the law from the NCW which would become part of the Empowerment Policy for 2001. It appears that the NCW had been asked by the government to consolidate its recommendations on laws regarding rape of women and children. However, it is not known what role the Law Ministry was to play in drawing up such legislation. Amnesty International is concerned that given the numerous discussions and studies that have taken place on this issue without a bill having been drawn up by government, draft legislation should be prepared and disseminated for discussion at the earliest opportunity with a time frame for its entry into parliament.

While the IPC provisions concerning rape are on paper available to women from all backgrounds in India, there are also special provisions in law which apply to sections of society, including women, who are deemed to be particularly vulnerable to abuses. Special protection exists in law for members of scheduled caste and scheduled tribe communities. The Scheduled Castes and Scheduled Tribes (Prevention of Atrocities) Act, 1989 was enacted in order *"to prevent the commission of offences of atrocities against the members of the Scheduled Castes and the Scheduled Tribes, to provide for special courts for the trial of such offences and for the relief and rehabilitation of the victims of such offences and for matters connected therewith or incidental thereto"*. Sub-sections of section

3(1) of the Act specifies "atrocities" against scheduled castes and scheduled tribes which are punishable with imprisonment of a minimum of six months and maximum of five years, and with a fine. While many of these atrocities are intended to protect men and women alike, some are specific to women (i.e. the assault or use of force against a women with intent to dishonour or outrage her modesty or using a position of dominance over a woman to exploit her sexually) or are atrocities to which women are particularly vulnerable — being stripped and paraded naked. Government officials have a central role to play in the implementation of the Act which contains a list of prescriptive measures, described as *"the duty of the government to ensure effective implementation of the Act"*. Listed in Section 21(2) are some of the measures which include the provision of legal aid, expenses for the witness and victims of atrocities, the provision of economic and social rehabilitation to the victims, the appointment of officers to supervise the action, periodic surveys, and special measures. The state government is instructed to designate one Sessions Court in each district to be a Special Court for trial of persons accused of offences under the Act.

The Scheduled Castes and Scheduled Tribes (Prevention of Atrocities) Rules, 1995 provide for reactive, preventive and promotional measures that can be taken in an effort to ensure that there is redress for the violations of the rights of scheduled castes and scheduled tribes and that such violations do not recur.

The Administration

Special administrative measures as a means of ensuring implementation of legislative protections for women were apparent in both Uttar Pradesh and Rajasthan. *Mahila thanas*— "all-women" police stations established to encourage women to bring their complaints to police by staffing them with women police officers — had been established in both states. Both also had Crime Against Women Cells in their police departments where cases of crimes against women are investigated and monitored.

In Rajasthan Amnesty International delegates heard from government officials and activists about *Zilla Mahila Sahayata Samitis* (ZMSS) [District Women's Support Committees]. These were established in Rajasthan on 6 August 1997 as a result of pressure from the women's movement in the state who were concerned about implementation of legal provisions designed to protect women and provide them with redress. The Committees were designed to establish a forum at the district level which women could approach and which would address complaints at that level and in a comprehensive manner, dealing with several aspects of a situation at once: the criminal aspect, the welfare aspect and potentially the civil law aspect, ensuring that throughout the process the woman was assured justice.

They are headed by the District Collector (the senior-most administrative official in a district) and consist of the district Superintendent of Police, a judge of the Family Court and representatives of non-governmental organizations from the district.

The Member Secretary of each committee is the Project Director of the district Women's Development Program who operate under the government's Women and Child Department looking after women and children's development programs. The committees are provided with and collect their own funds to distribute to women in the districts. Complainants can come to these committees and hearings are held *in camera*.

The committees review cases with officials from the local administration and police. However, Amnesty International is concerned that there appear to be no guidelines for the operation of these committees, or specialised training given to those involved. Women activists in Rajasthan claimed that the majority of the ZMSSs are "defunct". They also complained that those chosen to be representatives of non-governmental organizations on the committees were from amongst organizations such as rotary clubs rather than from grass-roots organizations who represented women and members of disadvantaged communities at the local level, thereby ensuring that they ceased to be a representative public platform. The State Women's Commission estimated that around 40% of districts in the state had functioning committees.

Amnesty International delegates were interested to learn during discussions with officials of the Department of Women and Child Development in Delhi subsequent to their visit to Rajasthan that the central government intends to replicate these committees throughout the country as part of its Women's Empowerment Policy.

INTERNATIONAL STANDARDS AND THE GOVERNMENT OF INDIA'S RESPONSIBILITIES AND COMMITMENTS

The responsibility of states for acts which impair the rights of women is sometimes mistakenly perceived as applying only when state agents or officials are the actual perpetrators of acts which violate human rights. The protection afforded by human rights law is far greater. There is a clear responsibility on states under international law which extends beyond violations by those acting on behalf of the state and its organs. Human rights treaties spell out the obligations of the State, including: to promote those rights; to secure those rights for all and translate them into policies and strategies; to prevent violations of the rights under the Conventions and to provide remedies to the victims should their rights be violated. The Declaration on the Elimination of Violence against Women, adopted by the UN General Assembly in 1993, affirms that states must "exercise due diligence to prevent, investigate and, in accordance with national legislation, punish acts of violence against women, whether those acts are perpetrated by the State or by private persons".

Applying international human rights law without understanding the responsibility of the state for abuses of women's rights by private actors — including employers, partners, husbands, family members or neighbours — simply robs women of protection and of remedies for the majority of abuses against them. Human rights law is not silent on these abuses. It clearly points to a positive responsibility on the part of the state.

As a party to the Convention on the Elimination of All Forms of Racial Discrimination since 1968 and the International Covenant on Civil and Political Rights since 1979, India has been committed for many years to ensuring civil and political rights to all its citizens without discrimination of any kind. This commitment was reinforced with its ratification of the Convention of the Elimination of All Forms of Discrimination against Women (Women's Convention) in July 1993. India's Constitution sets out fundamental rights made available to all its citizens which it explicitly states are to be realised without discrimination. The Constitution upholds the right to equality before the law (Article 14) and prohibits discrimination on the grounds of religion, race, caste, sex or place of birth. Various laws reinforce safeguards against discrimination and provide for positive discrimination for certain groups identified as vulnerable within society. These include scheduled castes and scheduled tribes and women.

As a vast democracy with many regional variations and a "developing" economy, India has an enormous amount to achieve and an enormous amount of commitments to fulfil to all its citizens, including women. Recognizing its international commitments towards the rights of women and urged on by a dynamic women's movement, successive governments have unveiled policies of empowerment for women which have sought to address the full range of women's human rights. As a result, there are many positive aspects of women's empowerment which have taken place in recent years in India. This includes political representation of women at the lowest levels of government, increases in life expectancy amongst women and education. There have been several government initiatives to empower women economically and politically, many of which are operational in Uttar Pradesh and Rajasthan. In Uttar Pradesh the government-backed *Mahila Samakya*development scheme has contributed to the increased empowerment of thousands of marginalised women through education and other programs. Amnesty International delegates were told by officials of the Government of Uttar Pradesh of schemes which provide financial support to widows who often find themselves ostracised socially and economically, pension schemes and self-help schemes running in 20% of the districts of the state for women to mobilise savings and run rural banks. In Rajasthan, the state-sponsored women's development programme posed a challenge to feudal patriarchal values by empowering women at the local level to question and oppose feudal practices such as child marriage. Amnesty International delegates were told of the establishment of self-help groups in rural areas in Rajasthan encouraging economic empowerment through thrift groups and how training programs presented opportunities for women to have their complaints heard by local officials.

Political representation of women has increased at the local level. The 73rd Constitutional Amendment Act, 1992 (Panchayati Raj), included a provision for statutory minimum reservation of 33% seats for women in Panchayati Raj Institutions (this Amendment came into force on 24 April 1993). This has allowed a number of women to participate in community decision-making processes, including those from marginalised communities given that there are also reservations for scheduled caste, scheduled tribe and backward caste categories. The involvement of women in *Panchayats*[village councils] was noted by Amnesty International delegates in both Uttar Pradesh and Rajasthan — there are reported to be around 3,000 women *Sarpanches*[village heads] and 33,000 elected women representatives on *Panchayats*in Rajasthan — although there are continuing problems associated with womens' participation. Political reservation for women at the central level has however proved more problematic and successive parliamentary sessions have failed to reach a consensus on the Constitutional (85th Amendment) Bill 1999 which would provide 33% reservation for women in the national parliament and state legislatures.

Following the Fourth UN World Conference on Women in Beijing in 1995, the Government of India promised several measures to ensure the advancement of women's rights in India. The Department of Women and Child Development began work on a National Policy on Women which would seek to bridge the gap between the equal de-jure status and unequal de-facto position of women in the country. In January 2000, while hearing India's first periodic report, the Committee on the Elimination of Discrimination Against Women (CEDAW) recommended that a national plan of action be developed to address in a holistic manner the issue of gender-based violence, in line with the Committee's general recommendation 19. In January 2001 the Prime Minister of India announced that 2001 would be the year of Women's Empowerment and that a National Policy on Women's Empowerment would soon be unveiled. The policy (Amnesty International has so far been unable to obtain a copy) reportedly included a plan to ensure that all laws deemed discriminatory to women be reviewed and suitably amended by 2003. It also included plans to establish an effective machinery to monitor the delivery of justice to women in a context of rising crimes against women and suggested requesting State Governments to set up District Committees to monitor and expedite disposal of cases of atrocities against women. On 22 March 2001 it was announced that the Cabinet had cleared the policy.

Amnesty International delegates were interested to see the Rajasthan government's Women's Policy which was launched in March 2000 and to obtain a copy of the Uttar Pradesh government's draft Women's Policy. Both refer in part to measures to ensure justice to women victims of violence although the majority of these policies relate to economic empowerment of women.

Amnesty International welcomes these indications that the Government of India and state governments wish to address continuing problems of violence against women throughout the country. However, it is concerned that these policies should be more than just further rhetoric and should firmly address ongoing problems of non-implementation and/or discriminatory implementation of safeguards and impunity for perpetrators of violence against women. By highlighting some of the problems it identified in the course of its research in two states in India and by suggesting remedies, Amnesty International hopes to contribute to discussions about how to change this situation.

The reality of the situation on the ground for women and members of vulnerable groups continues to be extremely harsh despite the Constitutional, legislative and administrative framework in place in India. The failure to implement protective provisions and continuing gender, caste and class biases within society ensures that Constitutional and legal safeguards are rendered meaningless to many. In January 2000, CEDAW, hearing India's first periodic report made a series of recommendations on the basis of a broad range of concerns about implementation of the Women's Convention. These included the establishment of a comprehensive and compulsory system of registration of births and marriages and implementation of laws. The Committee expressed concern at the failure of the Government of India to provide adequate information relating to the general issue of violence against women.

Amnesty International acknowledges that at the highest levels of government the directives are clear that the fundamental rights set out in the Constitution should be granted without discrimination. It also acknowledges that numerous policies for the empowerment of women are in place around the country. However, Amnesty International is concerned that its research in Uttar Pradesh and Rajasthan indicates that despite this, at the level of implementation there is sufficient discrimination and inaction in bestowing rights to argue that the Government of India is failing to exercise due diligence in preventing abuses.

Amnesty International is well aware of the Government of India's argument that changing discriminatory attitudes and practices which are so deeply ingrained within society is something which cannot be done overnight, and that they are making progress in particular in bestowing economic and political rights on women throughout the country regardless of caste, religion or other identity. The organization recognizes the challenges presented to the state given the size and complexity of the country, and the continuing need for women to be provided with state help to access the most basic amenities such as food and water. Amnesty International is publishing this report to highlight the continuing problems of violence against marginalised women in Uttar Pradesh and Rajasthan which occur in the context of many other abuses of women's rights — many of them social and economic — because it believes that women cannot enjoy the full range of rights while being repressed through violence and while sections of the administration and the criminal justice system reflect and perpetuate discriminatory practices prevalent in society. Violence against women does not only have a physical impact but also an impact on their ability to enjoy the full range of rights including social, economic and political: the right of women to enjoy the full range of rights is indivisible.

THE CONTEXT OF VIOLENCE AGAINST WOMEN IN INDIA

Despite the many positive developments in securing womens human rights, patriarchy continues to be embedded in the social system in many parts of India including Uttar Pradesh and Rajasthan, denying the majority of women the choice to decide how they live. The over-riding importance of "community" in a patriarchal sense ensures that women rarely have an independent say in community issues. The way in which the concept of "honour" is used is also a severe barrier to the realisation of women's rights. Practices persist which led one member of the UN Human Rights Committee to observe in 1997 that "women are expendable in India". Female foeticide continues to be common. Impoverished families have little interest in educating girl-children and will often engage them in marriage as children as a means of ensuring that they are provided for economically from an early age.

As in many parts of India, levels of violent crime against women in Uttar Pradesh and Rajasthan are extremely high (alarm at these high levels have led to recent calls for the imposition of the death penalty for crimes of rape). According to National Crime Records Bureau (NCRB) figures for 1998 issued by the Ministry of Home Affairs, Uttar Pradesh ranked first and Rajasthan ranked fourth in the ratings of recorded crimes against women. These include rape, kidnapping, dowry death, mental and physical "torture", molestation, sexual harassment and trafficking. According to Rajasthan government statistics, crimes against women in the year 1999 reported an increase of 6.7% over the year 1998. In particular "torture" (which they categorise as crimes under section 498A of the Indian Penal Code (IPC)) registered an increase of 9.66% and "molestation" (crimes of sexual violence not amounting to rape) an increase of 6.91% although rape registered a decrease of 5.37%. The draft Policy on Women of the Uttar Pradesh government claims that every year more that 1,500 cases of rape, nearly 2,500 cases of indecent behaviour and nearly 200 kidnappings are recorded in the state.

Violence within the home is also widespread in both Uttar Pradesh and Rajasthan and affects women throughout society — in wealthy urban households as much as the poorest rural households, across all religious, class and caste boundaries. It includes beating, slapping, kicking and rape. Methods of killing women in the home include soaking them with kerosene and setting light to them and poisoning, either claiming that the death was accidental or that the woman committed suicide. Violence within marriage in India is often associated with the practice of "dowry" although it is by no means the only cause of violence. The practice of dowry has been prohibited in law since 1961 when it was recognised that it was contributing to high levels of violence against women as husbands and their families harassed wives for increased dowry. However, the practice continues. According to the Annual Report for 1999 of the Rajasthan Police, dowry deaths over the period 1997-1999 increased by 24.43%.

Women activists in India have played a crucial role in highlighting the problems faced by women. Amnesty International delegates saw clear evidence of this in Rajasthan and Uttar Pradesh where alliances of women's organizations come together regularly in protest against incidents of violence and put pressure on the authorities to take action against the perpetrators. Without such pressure, many victims would be left alone and without any means of obtaining justice. Many of the positive initiatives of the state have been taken as a result of the forceful arguments of the women's movement in the country. However, for women in Uttar Pradesh and Rajasthan as in many other parts of India, the challenge in defending human rights is compounded by gender discrimination inherent within traditional societies as well as within state structures. Women are often condemned by their own families as well as their community for speaking out against discrimination and abuse. When they seek help from the state to enable them to carry out their legitimate activities they are often confronted with further discrimination from the criminal justice system and from the state machinery which pushes them to conform to a gender stereotype which decrees that women should not question the *status quo*and thereby undermine family and community.

THE NATIONAL AND STATE COMMISSIONS FOR WOMEN

The National Commission for Women was established in January 1992 under the 1990 National Commission for Women Act. A statutory body, its aim was to check incidents of violence against women and to promote social, legal and economic equality of women. In addition to the NCW, several states of India have established State Women's Commissions (there is no formal relationship between the state and national bodies). As of March 2001, there were reported to be State Women's Commissions in 17 states.

The Rajasthan State Women's Commission was established in May 1999 under the Rajasthan State Commission for Women Act, 1999. The Chair, appointed by the state government, is to be an "eminent woman committed to the cause of women with sufficient knowledge and experience in dealing with problems of women". Its function is to inquire into "unfair practice" (the definition includes "mental or physical torture" of a woman), address inadequacies in laws, monitor enforcement of laws, inspect prisons, police stations, lock-ups, refuges for women victims of violence or other places of custody where women are held as prisoners or shelters and make recommendations for prosecution in individual cases. Between 1 April and 30 September 2000 the Commission received a total of 354 complaints, 154 of which were reported as "resolved".

Uttar Pradesh has no State Women's Commission. When Amnesty International delegates asked Home Ministry officials in Lucknow, they were not able to say when one might be established. In January 2001 it was reported that the National Commission for Women had directed the Uttar Pradesh government to establish a women's commission, alarmed at the number of complaints relating to atrocities on women received from Uttar Pradesh (the largest number from any state). The Policy on Women drafted by the Uttar Pradesh government states its intention to establish a Commission which will "work towards women's rights, relief against exploitation and also keep an eye on the implementation of the Policy". The Policy envisages task forces under the Commission in every district "to make available to the Commission, regular district level information on women's exploitation, domestic violence, misbehaviour towards women and also cases of non-compliance to laws". It will also have the function of reviewing laws. Uttar Pradesh has no State Human Rights Commission either. As an apparent alternative it has a human rights wing of the police department headed by an Additional Director General of Police to which all complaints against police are directed. However, when interviewed by Amnesty International delegates he appeared to be unaware of how special provisions for women victims of violence were operating in the state.

While the good intentions of the staff and members of the NCW and the State Women's Commissions are not doubted, they have suffered greatly from inadequate powers and resources. The Commissions have no powers to enforce or to exert pressure for the enforcement of their recommendations. In Rajasthan, recommendations are made on the basis of hearings, individual investigations or simply on the basis of the complaint. Many cases are simply "monitored". In many cases the Commission asks police to investigate and make recommendations on the basis of police reports. Amnesty International delegates were told that in only 168 out of the total number of the almost 1,000 complaints received by the Commission so far had hearings been held at the Commission itself. In January 2001 it became apparent that as part of the Women's Empowerment Year, amendments would be made to the National Commission for Women Act 1990. In January 2000 CEDAW had recommended that the NCW's powers should be as wide as those of the National Human Rights Commission (NHRC) and include a complaints procedure. Media reports in January implied that the Commissions powers would indeed be enhanced along the lines of the NHRC allowing it to recommend initiation of prosecution proceedings against individual perpetrators following inquiry. Reports also indicated that a new Section 10(1)(e) of the NCW Act would empower the Commission to "take up cases of violation of the provisions of the Constitution, and of other laws relating to women, with appropriate authorities and recommend measures for the effective implementation of those provisions". No draft of the amendment Bill was available at the time of writing.

THE PRACTICE OF JUSTICE FOR MARGINALISED WOMEN

Attempts by women to seek justice through the criminal justice system are regularly forestalled. Although legislation exists, measures to ensure its full implementation — including communicating provisions to the public, training officials responsible for administering the legislation, providing legal support services to enable beneficiaries to invoke legislation, monitoring implementation and ensuring further development of legislation in response to the reality on the ground — have not been sufficient. Unless supported by male relatives or a strong social group, women victims of crime are at a severe disadvantage within the criminal justice system. Threats and harassment by perpetrators and their communities and social pressures which exist within families and communities force them towards compromise or withdrawal rather than pursuing justice. Gender biases which exist within institutions of redress are often exacerbated by ingrained caste and other biases against members of disadvantaged communities.

Not many of these cases reach the courts for trial, partly in view of the shame and honour involved and partly due to the existing difficult and complicated procedural laws. It was also noticed that the police are generally apathetic to the registration of complaints involving rape. Even in those cases which come up to courts for trial after going through all the investigations and medical examinations; our courts had not been sensitive to the trauma undergone by the rape victims, both during the actual commission of the offence and during trial in the courts. The courts are also oblivious of the social stigma and ostracism a victim of rape has to face throughout her life and all rapists to be acquitted on wholly irrelevant and flimsy grounds of age, religion, caste, status and other considerations. [National Commission for Women Annual Report for 1995-96]

Registering a Complaint

Non-registration of crimes is a general problem in India. Political influence over the police and caste, class, religious and gender biases mean that it is extremely difficult for members of disadvantaged groups to file complaints, particularly against powerful individuals. A case cannot continue and a victim cannot receive justice if a First Information Report (FIR) is not completed and registered by police on the basis of a person's complaint.

A lawyer in Uttar Pradesh estimated that a maximum of 20% of cases of rape are registered and reach the courts. An activist working with *dalit* women estimated that only 5% of cases of violence against *dalit* women are registered. The under-reporting of cases was also acknowledged by officials with whom Amnesty International delegates spoke in both states.

It is clear that many women victims of violence in India do not approach police with a complaint because they know that they will be dismissed or further abused. Amnesty International delegates visiting Uttar Pradesh and Rajasthan in December 2000 were repeatedly told by activists working with women that the majority of cases were not reported to police for fear of dishonour or reprisals. Most women will only visit a police station with a male relative or will think twice about making a complaint without the support of a male relative. During a training program carried out by the United Nations Development Program in India in 1999, several police officials including one woman police officer, were sent in plain clothes to a police station to file a complaint. Out of 14 visits to file complaints in only two cases did the officials manage to file complaints after waiting 6-7 hours despite the fact that police are legally obliged to take down in writing a complaint of a cognizable offence. The woman police officer who tried to file a complaint of molestation was verbally abused by the Station House Officer, who refused to file her complaint.

In a study of women's participation in *Panchayats* carried out by the *Mahila Jan Adhikar Samiti* in Ajmer in 1999, it was found that "Of all the respondents who had to deal with the police in their four years of term 17.5% women said they experienced uncooperative attitude. But in the case of many *sarpanches* wherever there was sexist, casteist or other type of abuse or violence the women desisted from reporting to the police because they felt they would take the side of the powerful of the village. Ninety percent of the cases registered in connection with abuse/violence against women *sarpanches* were found to have been closed by the police. Most cases were claimed to have been closed because the investigation felt they were registered by the women for political rivalry."

As mentioned above, as a means of encouraging women to bring their complaints to police, many states have established *mahila thanas* (women's police stations). However, the majority of these are in large cities, thereby denying access to the most marginalised women in rural areas and there are few of them even in large cities. Rajasthan currently has nine *mahila thanas* and as of December 2000 was planning to establish a further three. This to cover a population of well over 44 million in the state. Uttar Pradesh's draft Women's Policy stated its intention of establishing *mahila thanas* in every district of the state. The *mahila thana* in Ajmer, Rajasthan was said to have been headed by a male Station House Officer until recently and there is no evidence that women police officers dealt significantly more sensitively with women victims or recorded a higher number of FIRs than men, given that they were provided with no specialist training. Women police officers working in *mahila thanas* have reported that investigations into complaints of rape are always carried out by male police officers although sometimes accompanied by women. Amnesty International knows of no systematic evaluation of the role of *mahila thanas* having been carried out by police or the administration as a means of assessing whether they are an effective means of providing an accessible and safe avenue of redress for women. Several women's orgnanizations, notably in Mumbai, have argued that *mahila thanas* marginalise women's issues and studies carried out by the Ford Foundation at the Tata Institute of Social Studies have reportedly identified several problems with them.

Crimes against Women Cells have also been criticised for not responding appropriately or effectively to cases of violence against women although the majority of crimes referred to these cells relate to violence within the family.

Police are reluctant to file FIRs citing offences under the Scheduled Castes and Scheduled Tribes (Prevention of Atrocities) Act, 1989, because the perpetrators — often powerful individuals within the community or even caste group to which police officers themselves belong — receive such stringent punishments. Amnesty International delegates were told that *dalits* and others are so reliant economically on upper castes that they are afraid to even think of filing a case under the Act because of the possible consequences. Several days prior to Amnesty International's visit to Lucknow in Uttar Pradesh, a *dalit* woman had reportedly been gang-raped by a group of men at gunpoint. Rather than registering an FIR the woman simply disappeared for fear of further consequences. Many *dalits* are not aware of provisions of the Act and their rights under it and it is rare for police to voluntarily inform them of those rights.

Many of the cases documented in this report demonstrate the refusal of police officers at the local level to file complaints brought by disadvantaged groups and particularly women and the problems members of these groups face in even approaching police. Well-known journalist P. Sainath during a visit to Rajasthan was told that there is an entry fee into police stations in Bharatpur district (Rs.225 [$5]) and more for filing a complaint. When Amnesty International delegates raised the problem of non-registration of FIRs by police, officials in Uttar Pradesh admitted that this was a general problem but maintained that they were dealing with it by issuing executive and departmental instructions to police to respond according to the law to complaints made by women and other sections of the community. However, they gave no indication that they followed up such orders with mechanisms for monitoring adherence.

In September 1999 the Ad hoc Subcommittee of the NCW recommended an amendment to the IPC to provide for punishment of a police officer who refuses to record a complaint relating to the commission of a cognisable offence. This proposed amendment — and the many others which accompanied it — has never been pursued.

The Scheduled Castes and Scheduled Tribes (Prevention of Atrocities) Rules strengthen the procedures in the Code of Criminal Procedure (CrPC) for the recording of an offence by the police, and specify that the officer-in-charge of a police station should record any offence under the Act, whether given verbally or in writing and give a copy to the informant, free of charge. Recognising the difficulties that a person may have in registering an offence under the Act, rule 5(3) states: *"Any person aggrieved by a refusal on the part of an officer in-charge of a police station to record the information... may send the substance of such information, in writing and by post, to the Superintendent of Police concerned who after investigation either by himself or by a police officer not below the rank of Deputy Superintendent of Police, shall make an order in writing to the officer in-charge of the concerned police station to enter the substance of that information to be entered in the book to be maintained in that police station."* While many of the victims interviewed by Amnesty International delegates had pursued their complaints with higher authorities having been refused at their local police station, in many cases the directions of higher authorities continued to be ignored by police officials locally. Amnesty International did not come across a single case in which action had been taken against a police official who had failed to register an FIR or otherwise neglected his duties under the Act despite the fact that Section 6 of the Act provides for up to one year imprisonment for public servants wilfully neglecting their duty.

During Amnesty International's visits to Uttar Pradesh and Rajasthan, repeated concern was expressed about the failure of police to file proper FIRs in cases of rape and other forms of violence against women. Biassed handling of the original complaint by police can have disastrous effects on a case. Police were alleged to often record cases under section 354 IPC (*assault or criminal force to woman with intent to outrage her modesty*) which is bailable or section 376 read with section 511 (*attempt to rape*) both of which invite lesser penalties than section 376 (*rape*) which is also non-bailable, despite the fact that the victim clearly indicated that she was raped.

Lack of legal or even basic literacy on the part of complainants means that it is rare for them to detect that an inaccurate provision has been used until it is too late. Attempting to amend FIRs can also have serious consequences as complainants can be accused of changing their story for malicious motives.

Problems of Evidence

Police are also accused of withholding and destroying evidence in many cases, often at the behest of the alleged perpetrators who might have caste or other community links with the police officers. Police also have the ability to delay the recording of medical evidence. It is not a legal requirement for police to send women who allege that they have been raped for an immediate medical examination. Much medical evidence is lost because this simple procedure is not followed. In one case that Amnesty International documented in Rajasthan when the victim asked about a medical examination she was told by police that she didn't need to have one until several days later by which time valuable medical evidence was lost.

Poor access to medical facilities necessary to document violence, including rape, is also a problem. Health centres are often scarce in rural areas leading to delays which mean that valuable evidence is lost. Obtaining sufficient evidence to prove rape — as strictly defined in Indian law and by the courts as penetration by the penis — can be very difficult. However, while prompt medical examination can provide strong, and in some cases irrefutable evidence, a victim's testimony also constitutes vital evidence. Contrary to the apparent view of many judicial officers in India, lack of medical evidence of sexual penetration should not refute an allegation of sexual abuse. According to the Istanbul Protocol, "even on examination of the female genitalia immediately after rape there is identifiable damage in less than 50% of cases [and lesions] in less than 30% of cases [of anal rape]". This underlines the importance of victim testimony as well as careful expert medical interview, examination, with the informed consent of the victim, and laboratory testing of specimens.

In the case of Narbada, when the medical examination did take place, police officers were present throughout and spoke to the medical officer carrying out the examination. This is in clear violation of the Principles on the Effective Investigation and Documentation of Torture and Other Cruel, Inhuman or Degrading Treatment or Punishment (Istanbul Principles — see above) which have been endorsed by the UN Special Rapporteur on Torture, article 6a of which states that "the examination must conform to established standards of medical practice. In particular, examinations shall be conducted in private under the control of the medical expert and outside the presence of security agents and other government officials".

In September 1999, the Ad hoc Subcommittee of the NCW recommended making the refusal or failure of a medical practitioner to conduct a medical examination of an alleged victim of sexual assault punishable with imprisonment of up to one year.

It also recommended inserting specific procedural guidelines in the Code of Criminal Procedure for medical examination of victims of sexual assault. Neither of these recommendations have yet been taken up by the government and there are reports that many victims of rape are given cursory examinations by doctors with no attempt to document the testimony of the victim.

Reliance on the evidence of witnesses is also extremely problematic. It is common for witnesses in cases of violence against women to withdraw their testimony, often having arranged a financial deal with the accused. A lawyer in Uttar Pradesh estimated that around 25% of witnesses withdraw their testimony because of pressure placed on them by the accused or members of their community and noted that in cases regarding women this percentage would only increase because of the patriarchal pressures which exist in these contexts. It is also reported that in many cases witnesses give contradictory statements in court because they have been planted by police or defence lawyers.

Time and Money

The length of time it takes to pursue a case of torture through the courts encourages victims to make compromises under pressure from perpetrators and often their own community or family. All lawyers and activists interviewed by Amnesty International spoke of the reluctance of victims to file cases because of the time and money involved. There are often significant distances between the village where a victim lives and the block [administrative unit within a district] court where a case is being heard. Money is lost in attending hearings not just on travel expenses but lost working hours for those women in employment and their male relatives who accompany them to the hearings.

The average time period taken for a case of rape to find its way from the Sessions Court to the Supreme Court was between 10-15 years [Gender and Judges: A judicial point of view, A preliminary Report based on research findings by a non-governmental organization Sakshi, June 1996]

The Scheduled Castes and Scheduled Tribes (Prevention of Atrocities) Rules provide for transport and other expenses for victims to enable them to attend hearings and in the case of women for an attendant to accompany them and covering of wages lost during days attending hearings. However, MARG's study, "Efficacy of the Enforcement System in Delivering Justice to Raped Scheduled Caste Women" found that many sections of the Rules had not been implemented in any of the fifty rape cases that were studied in Meerut and Banda districts of Uttar Pradesh, including provision for travelling and maintenance expenses. Often women simply do not have the money to pursue a case and having no economic independence, if their family do not support them in pursuing the case they drop it.

Amnesty International is interested to note statements in the draft women's policy drawn up by the Uttar Pradesh government which reads "The government will ask the High Court to undertake periodic review of crimes against women in the state and to set a time limit for settlement of cases relating to serious criminal offenses against women". It also talks of reaching decisions in rape cases with efficiency and promptness. "Officials found guilty of laxity in such cases will be punished and successful officials rewarded". In its Third Report covering the period 1994-95 & 1995-96, the National Commission for Scheduled Castes and Scheduled Tribes recommended that "Police should take timely and effective action in investigating the cases and submitting the chargesheet in the Court which would greatly help in curbing crimes. It is necessary that investigation on complaints are initiated soon after the FIR is lodged. It is also necessary to have regular monitoring and examination of cases which are closed without *challanning* [charges being filed in court], so that genuine cases are not closed".

Extract from a report on a series of attacks on women in Kanpur district of Uttar Pradesh by a *Sarpanch* (also the local landlord) including the rape of a *dalit* woman, Ram Rathi, in 1985. The extract is describing the perception of villagers concerning redress for the victims. The case against the perpetrator, which was pursued by Ram Rathi has been closed as he is reported to have killed the main witness. Above all, to get justice the judicial process is no less than the suffering of rape itself. Criminals will blame her as a characterless woman. She will have to prove that she was raped and the criminal has to prove that he has not raped. Questions and answers during arguments are no less than rape.

If it would be decided to tolerate this and fight till the end, even then the judgement is not made up of only the courage of a woman. A lot of money is required to have good advocate, to pay bribes to clerks, peons, servants, even to bribe the judge as it is said. Anybody needs a lot of money too for travelling from Pali to Kanpur court, Allahabad High Court and Supreme Court. Getting justice is a game of money. Krishna Pratap Singh [the accused] has sufficient money and means to escape from the punishment. Ram Rathi's husband is a labourer in a factory. Providing meals to his family is enough for him. Ram Rathi can get justice only from god.

It is clear that time and money involved in pursuing cases leads to a large number of women deciding not to file complaints or to withdraw complaints once filed. The long time periods allow victims to feel the effects of social ostracisation, harassment and intimidation and for witnesses to withdraw their testimony under similar pressures.

Legal Support and Aid System in India

The legal aid system in India is entirely inadequate to deal with the number of people who require legal aid. This is particularly the case for women victims of crime. In three years of sitting on the district legal aid board, one lawyer that Amnesty International spoke to in Uttar Pradesh said that she was aware of legal aid being given in only two cases of violence against women. Under the Legal Services Authorities Act 1987, a wide range of groups including members of scheduled castes or scheduled tribes, women and children are all entitled to legal services. It is common knowledge that legal aid cases are given the worst lawyers and even if not taking legal aid, poor victims are at the mercy of unscrupulous lawyers who exploit their lack of knowledge of the legal system.

Constitutionally women have equal access to legal services but because of low levels of education, limited exposure to laws and legal procedures, social taboos and limited financial means, women cannot always utilize legal services... government has sought to remedy this condition by providing legal aid, legal literacy and promulgating the Family Courts Act.

MARG's study in Uttar Pradesh again found that in not a single of the 50 cases of women victims of rape studied had legal aid been provided to the victims as envisaged under section 21(2)(i) of the Act. Victims were merely given monetary relief of a few thousand rupees. The study concluded: "...we have seen that though on paper there are provisions for legal aid in the form of fees of lawyers, in reality the victims get no such aid. It seems either the Legal Aid Committee is not functioning at all or, people are not aware of its existence and procedures involved or, corruption amongst the lawyers has rendered it ineffective".

The draft women's policy of the Uttar Pradesh government states: "Women will be made aware of the various legal provisions affecting them, in their local language. For this, the government will set up camps at the village level, with the help of voluntary organizations and *Panchayats*... No fees will be charged from women for cases related to violence, property, divorce and maintenance. Women will be given free legal assistance on cases relating to violence and sexual exploitation". However, this policy is a draft policy and such provisions are far from being incorporated into law.

Discrimination within the Criminal Justice System

As argued earlier, state institutions continue to reflect discrimination within society and Amnesty International believes that insufficient steps — both preventive and punitive — have been taken to address this. The effects of discrimination can range from direct connivance of police with perpetrators to inaction by police or members of the legal profession, to cursory treatment of trials by members of the judiciary.

WOMEN DEMONSTRATING AGAINST POLICE ABUSES

Police officers have their own caste and gender biases and often behave towards *dalits* and *adivasis* in a discriminatory way— acting within the norms of their social surroundings. The presence of caste biases within the police force was confirmed repeatedly to Amnesty International delegates by activists, government officials and police alike. Officials in Rajasthan also acknowledged that gender sensitivity is not institutionalised within the police force. Amnesty International delegates were told that a new syllabus was being developed with a topic on women for Constables, Sub-Inspectors and Deputy Superintendents of Police.

The state must train police and other state officials to separate their caste, gender and other prejudices from their duty to protect citizens if legislative and administrative policies are to have any meaning. The state cannot afford to overlook this problem any longer otherwise all its sincere efforts will be wasted. In its recommendations for the prevention of torture submitted to the Government of India in December 2000, Amnesty International referred at length to the need for reform of the police — emphasising amongst other things the continuing problem of political influence over the police which invites discriminatory behaviour. In its brief response to these recommendations, Amnesty International was disappointed to note that no indication was given by the Government of India that it would be taking action in this regard.

Reference has been made above to the problems within the police force in relation to registration and investigation of offences. Amnesty International is concerned that discrimination and abuse within the police demonstrated by individual incidents of connivance, extends to the administration of policing and the manner in which crimes against women are viewed. Amnesty International delegates visiting Rajasthan were extremely concerned to hear of a large number of cases of violence against women which after the filing of an FIR were subsequently logged as found "false" after investigation. The labelling of these cases as "false" is itself a concern as it implies that women have falsely or maliciously filed the cases and plays into the hands of those who argue that women misuse legal provisions to wrongfully accuse men as a means of punishment. In fact, government and police officials explained in Rajasthan that it usually meant that the victim had reached a compromise with the perpetrator of violence, witnesses had turned hostile or there were other reasons for withdrawing the complaint. In these cases "Final Reports" were filed, indicating that a complainant had formally withdrawn a complaint. The Rajasthan government indicated that 30% of all cases of crimes against women in the state had been found to be "false" after investigation. As noted earlier, information was not provided by the government of Uttar Pradesh.

The case of Narbada, an *adivasi*, documented by Amnesty International delegates in Rajasthan clearly demonstrates the problems of discrimination faced by marginalised women throughout the process of trying to access justice through all stages of the criminal justice system. In Narbada's village in Udaipur district of Rajasthan — Samdhora — Rajputs (upper caste landowning caste) dominate, owning more than 50 acres. They practice untouchability in relation to the *adivasis* who are not permitted to take food or water from upper castes. Most of the *adivasi* villagers work for Rajputs as sweepers or agricultural workers and no-one dares speak out against them. However, Narbada and her uncle, when interviewed by Amnesty International delegates in December 2000, said that there were no previous incidents of rape of women by Rajputs in the village.

Narbada's family owns three *bighas* [2.5 *bighas*is the equivalent of one acre] of land. They do not work for the Rajputs. Narbada was married in 1999 and normally lives with her husband's family around 12 kilometres from Samdhora village. However, at the time of the incident she was staying with her mother for a holiday.

18-year-old Narbada testified that she was raped by a Rajput landlord on the afternoon of 10 March 2000. The incident took place about one and a half kilometres from her house when she went to buy a chicken in the upper caste area of the village. She was kneeling by a river and the Rajput threw her into the river and then raped her. Her attacker's mother reportedly heard Narbada's screams but did nothing to stop her son and when Narbada ran crying back to her section of the village his mother caught hold of her, beat her and told her not to go to the police.

Narbada told her mother and brother what had happened and they called her uncle. When they tried to go to the police station around 50 Rajputs stopped them. However, they went to the police station in Jhallara district on 12 March. An FIR was lodged but Narbada's uncle was not given a copy. He questioned the fact that they had filed the FIR under section 354 of the IPC [*Assault or criminal force to woman with intent to outrage her modesty*] rather than section 376 [*rape*]. One of the constables reportedly threw her uncle out of the police station saying: "who do you think you are". Police told her uncle that if he wanted a "true" FIR he would have to give them Rs.500 [$11] which he refused to do. Narbada and her uncle asked police for a medical examination but were told by police that this would be done only after an initial investigation. The two constables recorded a fresh FIR once the uncle was out of the police station. He was given a copy of the FIR the next day, 13 March. No case had been filed under the Scheduled Castes and Scheduled Tribes (Prevention of Atrocities) Act. The police constables were themselves Rajputs and are reported to be close to the accused who sells illegal alcohol in a shop which is a regular haunt of police.

On 15 March Narbada and her uncle went to Udaipur, the district headquarters, to see the Superintendent of Police (SP). Udaipur is 90 kilometres and a three and a half hour journey from Samdhora. They told the SP about the rape and their subsequent treatment at the police station. The SP recorded their complaint and ordered an investigation to be carried out into the allegation of rape. No action was taken against police officials who had originally refused to file the FIR and abused Narbada and her uncle. On 26 April the Deputy Superintendent of Police went to Samdhora to begin an investigation.

A medical examination was not carried out until 8 April at Bhopal District Hospital. Police constables who had earlier abused Narbada and her uncle went with them to the hospital. Narbada told Amnesty International delegates that the police officers were present when she was undergoing medical tests and x-rays and that her uncle was not allowed to stay with her. She said that the police spoke constantly to the doctors but she could not make out what they were saying. Narbada and her uncle were told that no medical evidence of rape was found during the examination but they were not given copies of the medical records.

After strong protests from local human rights organizations, the case was challaned in the special court for crimes against scheduled castes and scheduled tribes in Udaipur under section 376 IPC and sections 3(i) and 3(ii)v of the Scheduled Castes and Scheduled Tribes (Prevention of Atrocities) Act, 1989. On 20 May Narbada was told to come to the court at 10am to record her statement. The Public Prosecutor made her and members of her family who were present as witnesses wait for two hours after which he reportedly urged them to make a compromise with the accused and withdraw the complaint. He reportedly told Narbada and her family that if she pursued the case she would just do the rounds of the court and not obtain justice. Narbada and her family refused to withdraw the complaint. They waited until 4pm when the statements of Narbada's aunt and mother were recorded. However, there was no presiding officer or public prosecutor in the court when their statements were recorded by the clerk. Only the lawyer for the accused was present.

The accused, his mother and members of the Rajput community continued to put pressure on Narbada and her family to compromise. Her relatives were also reportedly threatened with detention by police as a means of putting pressure on her to compromise. On 11 October at midnight two police constables (including one of those who had originally refused to file the FIR) came to her parent's house and threatened her. They were drunk. They knocked on the door and asked her to come out. When she refused they went to her uncle's house insisting that she be sent to the Police Station. He refused and eventually the police went away.

On 6 October 2000 Narbada and her uncle gave their statements to the Additional Superintendent of Police, Udaipur, who is heading the investigation. However, no further progress has been made in the case. Narbada has not been provided with legal aid or received any immediate financial relief as required under the Scheduled Castes and Scheduled Tribes (Prevention of Atrocities) Act, but has been helped by a local union with legal fees.

Narbada's husband was initially supportive of her following the incident but has now indicated that he will not take her back. Although Narbada described villagers as supportive, she said that they had encouraged her to compromise with the Rajputs.

Section 15 of the Scheduled Castes and Scheduled Tribes (Prevention of Atrocities) Act provides for the state government to specify a public prosecutor or appoint an advocate. Amnesty International delegates were told that public prosecutors regard cases of poor women as easy money.

There is little communication with the victims and it is common for prosecutors to take money from the accused's side in return for putting pressure on the victim to compromise or withdraw the complaint. The judiciary is also blamed for failing to take sufficient care in cross-questioning witnesses and investigating officers during hearings. The draft women's policy of the Uttar Pradesh government says that "The government will make required changes in laws to ensure that court cases related to sexual exploitation of women are presided over by women judges only" and that "Persons associated with the legal processes to increase sensitivity towards girls/women will be provided training from time to time". A further problem appears to be the failure of prosecuting authorities to oppose bail (see also under Threats and Harassment below) which is routinely sought by the accused who often have the means to pay significant amounts of security in order to obtain bail.

Judicial decisions have also shown clear bias against women. In a now famous verdict given in November 1995, a lower court in Rajasthan commented that an incident of alleged rape could not have taken place because upper caste men would not rape a woman of a lower caste and acquitted the alleged perpetrators.

Bhanwari Devi, a *saathin* (village development worker) working to eradicate child marriage with the state-sponsored Women's Development Programme, was raped on 22 September 1992 in Bhateri village, Rajasthan, by five men of a higher Gujjar caste. The rape was widely seen as punishment for her actions in challenging accepted social and cultural norms including a particular child marriage which occurred in the village. Police had come to the village and attempted to stop the marriage, which had already secretly taken place, and the Gujjars held Bhanwari Devi responsible for the police intervention.

The police initially refused to record Bhanwari Devi's statement. She was also initially prevented from undergoing a medical examination. After much protest, the government ordered an inquiry to be carried out by the Central Bureau of Investigation. It finished its investigation in September 1993 but was reported to have subjected Bhanwari Devi to unnecessarily excessive questioning about the incident. It found Bhanwari Devi's allegations to be true and chargesheets were filed against five men. The trial began in a lower court only in October 1994. In a verdict given in November 1995, the Court found that the delay in filing her complaint with police and in obtaining a medical examination indicated that she had made the story up. Shockingly, it commented that the incident could not have taken place because upper caste men, including a Brahmin, would not rape a woman of a lower caste. The men were acquitted of the charge of gang rape but convicted of minor crimes.

Bhanwari Devi has been ostracised from the village community since the incident in 1992. Throughout, constant pressure was put on her to withdraw the case by members of the local community as well politicians.

Central and state government officials with whom Amnesty International delegates talked, all acknowledged that sensitisation of the judiciary was lacking, a central government official commenting that it had not been "mainstreamed". Officials of the Department of Women and Child Development in New Delhi told Amnesty International delegates that the government had set up a national centre for gender training and sensitisation at the Indian Administrative Service Academy in Mussoorie. However, they indicated that the centre had not yet started functioning having been approved a year previously. It was explained that this Academy would be the apex agency for mainstreaming gender in all government departments.

The law itself includes provisions which facilitate discrimination against women. Section 155(4) of the Indian Evidence Act provides that "when a man is prosecuted for rape or an attempt to ravish, it may be shown that the prosecutrix was of generally immoral character". This is in clear violation of Article 2(g) of the Women's Convention which requires state parties to repeal all national penal provisions which constitute discrimination against women. While successive Supreme Court judgements have ruled that the antecedents of victims are not relevant, lower courts continue to refer to these legal provisions in making their judgements and section 155(4) has never been repealed.

Threats and Harassment

This report focuses on violence against marginalised groups, much of it perpetrated by those in powerful social, economic or political positions and able to exert enormous influence over victims and their communities as well as state institutions if threatened by criminal action.

Despite this, there is no protection program for victims or witnesses in India leading generally to a very high number of acquittals in criminal cases due to victims or witnesses withdrawing testimony and the resulting lack of evidence. In the case of women victims from marginalised communities, the odds are stacked against them and without some form of protection or removing them from the context in which they might be receiving threats it is not surprisingly rare for women to pursue complaints through the courts. In numerous cases documented by Amnesty International, victims received direct or indirect threats from perpetrators but received no protection from the state despite complaining to the authorities — ensuring that perpetrators could continue to harass them and in several cases commit further acts of violence.

Interestingly, in 1995 the Supreme Court upheld the validity of the Scheduled Castes and Scheduled Tribes (Prevention of Atrocities) Act in its entirety in the face of a challenge to Section 18 of the Act which denies anticipatory bail (provided for in section 438 of the CrPC) to those charged under the Act. The Supreme Court argued that Section 18 "has to be viewed in the context of the prevailing social conditions which give rise to such offences, and the apprehension that perpetrators of such atrocities are likely to threaten and intimidate their victims and prevent or obstruct them in the prosecution of these offenders, if the offenders are allowed to avail of anticipatory bail". Amnesty International is concerned that the same fears about threats and intimidation have not been addressed by establishing victim and witness protection programs, recognizing that perpetrators of violence against such women exercise enormous influence over the victim, their community and sections of the administration, even from inside jail, and by extending these safeguards to all vulnerable members of the community who may not be covered by the Scheduled Castes and Scheduled Tribes (Prevention of Atrocities) Act.

Gangawati, a 25-year-old "Backward Caste" woman, was allegedly raped by an upper-caste Thakur [higher caste] on the evening of 31 May 1999 in her home in Lalua Nagla village in Badaun district of Uttar Pradesh. The village is dominated by the Thakur caste and Gangawati's house is surrounded by houses belonging to Thakur families. Her attacker [N] entered her house with a gun while her husband was away. Her nine-year-old daughter was present and witnessed the rape. After her husband returned and she told him about the incident they visited the Khader Chowk Police Station the next day to file a complaint. On their way to the police station, [N] reportedly threatened them with a gun saying he would kill them. The Station House Office (SHO) of Khader Chowk Police Station refused to file an FIR. A Police Inspector reportedly told the Circle Officer [police official] not to register a case against [N] as he was one of their caste — a Thakur — and useful to the police. The

Circle Officer reportedly advised the family not to pursue the case and also told them that too many days had elapsed so that there would be no medical evidence.

Gangawati then went to the Senior Superintendent of Police of Badaun and requested him to order the registration of a complaint. An order was sent to the Khader Chowk Police Station but no complaint was registered by police at the police station.

On 4 July the SHO of Khader Chowk police station visited Gangawati's house after first visiting [N's] house and asked Gangawati to go with him to have a medical examination conducted. Fearing some trick and in light of the fact that he refused even to take her statement, Gangawati refused.

On 3 June 1999, Gangawati had gone to Lucknow (325km from Gangawati's village) and presented a complaint to the Chief Minister. She had also sent petitions to the National Human Rights Commission. Apparently as a result of these petitions, the Superintendent of Police (SP) of Badaun District was ordered to conduct an inquiry. An FIR (No.259 of 1999) was finally filed on 15 October 1999 accusing [N] under sections 376 (*rape*), 452 (*house-trespass*) and 506 (*criminal intimidation*) of the IPC. However, an initial inquiry carried out by local police dismissed Gangawati's claims and the case was closed for lack of evidence: no medical reports were produced and no statement was taken from Gangawati. The NHRC also closed the case on the basis of this police report.

However, in February 2000, Gangawati made a statement before the court of the Chief Judicial Magistrate, Badaun and the court reopened the case. Amnesty International understands that examination of Gangawati's clothes have now substantiated her claims of rape.

[N] was arrested on 13 April 2000. Immediately after his arrest his brother and several of his supporters threatened to kill Gangawati and her husband and other of their relatives. A complaint to this effect was sent to the SP, Badaun on 15 April 2000. The SP reportedly ordered the SHO to ensure the safety of Gangawati. However, on 29 April [N] was released on bail and threats against Gangawati and her husband continued to be received from [N] and also from the SHO. The prosecution reportedly raised no objection to the granting of bail.

On 12 May 2000 the National Commission for Women wrote to the Uttar Pradesh police asking them to protect Gangawati and her family and to transfer the SHO and other police officers accused of connivance from the area. No action was taken.

On 10 October 2000, Gangawati's husband, Suresh Chand, went to Khader Chowk Police Station to make a complaint about further threats. In a statement, Suresh Chand has given the following account of his encounter: "I told him [the SHO] that I was working as the district correspondent for Dalit Hitaishi, a national monthly newspaper published in Delhi and asked him to help me. [The SHO] stood up from his chair and said, "swine you recorded a case under 376 against [N] and you have got three policemen from amongst my staff into trouble, today, swine, I will kill you and dispose of you". Then [the SHO] searched my pockets. He removed seven hundred rupees I had in my pocket and removed my Dalit Hitaishi press card from my pocket, tore it up and threw it away. He also tore up my statement and threw it away and gave me a severe beating. He locked me in the cell and pointed a revolver at me and said, "swine, either settle with [N] or else I will call [N's] wife and have her register a case under 376 against you. And I will charge you with 3-4 cases and let you rot in prison". Then [the SHO] summoned [N] from the village in a jeep and said to him "look I have your enemy in my hand today. Do what you want".

Suresh Chand was beaten with a stick on the back and buttocks and threatened at gunpoint to withdraw the case of rape against [N]. His detention was subsequently recorded under section 151 of the Code of Criminal Procedure. Following this incident Suresh Chand went to Lucknow to appeal to a local Minister with influence in the area to intervene in the matter. The Minister reportedly told him that if he continued to pursue the case against [N] he would be sent to jail.

On 18 November 2000, a criminal case of theft was filed against Suresh Chand. He was arrested but released on bail pending investigation of the case by police which is ongoing. Amnesty International has learnt that non-bailable warrants for the arrest of Suresh Chand have subsequently been issued — reportedly at the instigation of [N] — and that he is now in hiding. Gangawati also continues to receive threats from police officials and from [N]. Amnesty International was informed in March 2001 that further threats had been made to Gangawati and her daughter. They are reported to have left the village to live with relatives.

The National Human Rights Commission and the National Commission for Women are reported to have taken up their cases and requested information from the state government. However, as of mid-March 2001, both Commissions were said to be still awaiting a final report from the Uttar Pradesh authorities. Amnesty International delegates provided information about Gangawati and Suresh Chand's case to officials with whom they met in Uttar Pradesh in

December 2000 and requested a response to the concerns raised. However, to date, no response has been received.

Relief and Rehabilitation

The Scheduled Castes and Scheduled Tribes (Prevention of Atrocities) Rules, 1989 provide for compensation to be paid to members of those communities who have suffered abuses including Rs.50,000 [$1.073] to a woman who has had her "modesty" "outraged" or been sexually exploited and Rs 2 lakh to a woman who has been raped. However, MARG's study found that many sections of the Rules had not been implemented in any of the fifty rape cases that were studied in Meerut and Banda districts of Uttar Pradesh: there was no economic or social rehabilitation for the victims and there were serious delays in the sanction of monetary relief for victims.

A lawyer involved in numerous cases of violence against *dalits* and *adivasis* in Rajasthan told Amnesty International delegates that he had not come across a single case in which a woman was given immediate compensation and travel and maintenance expenses as set out in the Act. He did however refer to financial relief provided by the Chief Minister of Rajasthan from his discretionary fund or by statutory bodies such as the National Commission for Women. Amnesty International delegates learnt that the Rajasthan government had set up a rehabilitation scheme for victims of rape which provides them with Rs.10,000 [$215] in immediate relief if they need financial assistance. The Rajasthan government's welfare measures for scheduled castes and scheduled tribes include payment of Rs.100,000 [$2,147] for victims of rape from those communities. However, the Scheduled Castes and Scheduled Tribes (Prevention of Atrocities) Rules indicate that in cases of murder, death, massacre, rape, mass rape and gang rape at least Rs.200,000 [$4,294] should be given in compensation. Rajasthan government officials with whom Amnesty International delegates spoke in December 2000 recognised the need for a cohesive rehabilitation policy for victims of rape and other forms of violence.

Many women victims of violence are in desperate need of relief and rehabilitation. Many need to be at least temporarily and sometimes permanently placed outside the community where the offence took place. This rarely happens. There are no efforts towards social rehabilitation of women victims of violence. They are left entirely on their own or subject to the mercy of their families and the social pressures inherent in that situation. Professional counselling of women victims is virtually unheard of.

Outside the formal criminal justice system, women in India can turn to other bodies for support and redress. There are a large number of active non-governmental and voluntary organizations which provide legal support and temporary shelter and economic support to women. However, given their localised nature, the lack of resources available and the vulnerability of such initiatives to pressure from families, police, community or state, these initiatives cannot wholly address the scale of the problem in a country the size of India. There is clearly room for discussion on ways in which the state can address the needs of abused women through supporting the work of voluntary sector organizations.

Justice or Impunity?

One of the main factors in assessing whether governments have shown due diligence in addressing violence by non-state actors is whether those responsible for such violence are brought to justice. As can be seen above, a very high percentage of crimes against women go unpunished because cases are not filed, end in compromise and/or complaints are withdrawn. This is clearly so in cases where the victims are from marginalised communities and particularly vulnerable to discrimination, threats and pressure.

Figures produced by the National Crime Records Bureau (NCRB) under the Ministry of Home Affairs indicate a relatively high percentage of cases of crimes against women investigated by police in comparison to very low percentages for the number of cases processed through the courts. These percentages hide the fact that many incidents of violence against women do not reach the stage of registration because of the role of compromises, threats and harassment as well as direct refusal by police to register such cases.

According to the NCRB figures, in cases of rape overall, the number of trials completed within a year is extremely low. Of 58,655 cases of rape pending trial at the start of 1998, 48,685 remained pending trial by the end of the year. Only 16% of those cases went to trial during 1998 and only 4.4% of the 58,655 cases resulted in conviction. 83% remained pending trial. The percentages are similar for molestation (under section 354 IPC).

In its research undertaken in Uttar Pradesh and Rajasthan, Amnesty International found evidence of complicity of the police in covering up the crime in several cases of violence against women. While in several cases action has subsequently been taken to arrest the perpetrators, those state officials guilty of complicity invariably went unpunished. Transfer of officials was the only form of punishment which Amnesty International delegates heard of. Transfer is often temporary and delegates learnt that a common "punishment" is to be transferred to "police lines" for a period. This in effect means that police are removed from a community policing situation and placed within police accommodation and training areas, the primary punishment being that they are no longer able to exert power and influence including by obtaining bribes from members of the public as a means of supplementing their income.

Mohini Devi and her husband Laxman Singh are *dalits* who live in Guthakar village in Bharatpur district of Rajasthan. Mohini Devi recounted to Amnesty International delegates how she was raped in the early morning of 10 April 1999 by three of her neighbours while her husband was away. When her husband returned they attempted to file a complaint at the Wire police station nearby but they were stopped by the perpetrators who reportedly threatened to kill them. Laxman Singh took Mohini Devi to Sawai Mansingh hospital in Jaipur on 12 April 1999 for treatment for injuries sustained during the rape. As a result of the medico-legal report compiled by medical staff at the hospital, an FIR was filed (No.46 of 1999) alleging rape (under section 376 IPC) of Mohini Devi.

The investigating police officer is reported to have immediately put pressure on Mohini Devi, her husband and several witnesses (who saw the rapists running away) to withdraw their statements. On 24 April 1999 the perpetrators and several of their supporters from the village reportedly went to the home of Mohini Devi and Laxman Singh and forced Laxman Singh to sign a piece of paper withdrawing the complaint of rape. Attempts to complain to police about their being forced to withdraw the complaint were ignored by police. Human rights activists tried to put pressure on the authorities to order an independent investigation into the incident but no action was taken.

Mohini Devi was subsequently accused by police of Wire police station of making a false statement against the perpetrators at the instigation of one of the witnesses — Bhagwan Singh — who is also a *dalit* and member of the Bharatpur *Zilla Parishad* [District Council]. Mohini Devi did not pursue the case and no action was taken against police officials who appear to have been complicit in the cover-up of this crime. Shockingly, this complicity was repeated more recently when Laxman Singh and his brother were repeatedly attacked by upper caste members of the village — Gujjars. On the last occasion in October 2000, Laxman Singh's legs were beaten with iron rods and after developing gangrene, both of his legs were amputated. Local police from Wire police station consistently ignored complaints of threats and attacks filed by Laxman Singh and his brother and abused them for daring to file complaints against the Gujjars. No protection was offered to the *dalits* and the police reportedly told the Gujjars that if they killed Laxman Singh they would be protected. Although some of those responsible for beating Laxman Singh were arrested, they continued to harass Laxman Singh and his family members as well as Bhagwan Singh who gave his support to the family; they were released on bail in January 2001. In March 2001 police registered a case of rape against Laxman Singh's brother and Bhagwan Singh. Human rights activists allege that police and Gujjar villagers have falsely filed the complaint of rape as a means of pressurising Laxman Singh to withdraw the case and to harass Bhagwan Singh who has consistently supported the family. At no stage has action been taken to investigate the involvement of police in this series of incidents or to initiate action against them for unlawful activities.

The Role of the Community

Members of the victim's caste community or their family members can place enormous pressure on women victims of violence to either compromise or not pursue justice at all through formal justice systems. Dominated by men, caste groups often consider that women victims of violence should suffer their ordeal in silence. In many cases, women who insist on pursuing justice are punished in some way — often by social ostracisation, but also by being abandoned by their husbands and his family — for what is seen as bringing further dishonour to the community. MARG's study referred to earlier found that "In almost all the cases we find that the victim has got no support from the village in fighting for justice. This as it is leads to psychological stress on both the victim and her family. People in the village do not forget such incidents especially when the official summons keep coming to the victim, and so the ostracization continues, increasing the psychological trauma."

Maya Devi, a 22-year-old domestic worker and member of a "backward caste" was raped by two backward caste and one *dalit* man in the late afternoon on 18 April 1999 in Bhadasa village, Kanpur district in Uttar Pradesh. The rest of her household were in the fields cutting wheat. Her children were playing outside the house. The men were constructing a wedding tent behind her house and attacked her when she was returning from fetching water from the well some way from the house. One of the men hit Maya and she fell down. They closed the door tied her hands behind her back and then all three raped her. She described to Amnesty International delegates how they kept arguing with each other as to who would have a go first.

"All three of them tore off my blouse and stuffed it into my mouth. They then took off all my clothes, tied my hands behind my back and proceeded to rape me. After raping me they tied me up with more strings and then poured the bucket of water over me and started beating me. Then they pulled off my gold bangles, took out about 11,000 rupees from my husband's money box and ran away."

When her husband, Chotelal Sahu, returned he found her in the dark house, unconscious and naked. Seeing that money had been stolen he immediately filed an FIR concerning the theft. He did not immediately report the rape but when Maya Devi regained consciousness the next morning and told her husband of the rape he took her to a nearby hospital — Ursula Kanpur Convent hospital — and filed a fresh FIR with police under section 376 IPC (*rape*). A woman police officer went to the hospital and looked through Maya's medical records. Maya subsequently recorded her statement in front of the local magistrate.

Following protests by women's organizations the accused were arrested ten days after the incident. However, they are currently on bail and are continuing to threaten Maya and her relatives. Maya has complained to police about the threats but no action has been taken. Maya and her family received very little help from villagers. Those who did sympathise are too scared to help. Maya's family have been told that they should compromise or they will be killed. When Amnesty International delegates interviewed Maya and her husband, he clearly wished to drop the case but she was keen to pursue it. One of the accused had previously been in jail for the murder of the local *sarpanch*.

In the face of a hostile and discriminatory criminal justice system, many communities look within to provide "solutions" to violence against women. During their visit to Uttar Pradesh and Rajasthan, Amnesty International delegates heard of several cases in which caste *panchayats* (councils made up of representatives of particular castes from a particular area) had sat in judgement over cases of violence against women. These *panchayats* are dominated by men and gender biases mean that even within the same caste women are often punished for bringing dishonour or forced to come to a compromise with the perpetrator. An activist in Rajasthan has commented: "Our experience in Rajasthan of combatting cases of violence against women in the last few years has shown that most institutions of justice at the village and community level have been used against women, the poor and *dalits*... On the other hand, the performance of the state institutions of justice like the courts and police has been as dismal." Reports of the judgements of these caste *panchayats* include women being forced to marry the man who has raped them as a means of "solving" the problem of lost honour and future economic dependence (due to lack of marriage offers) that confronts many victims of rape.

2

Indian Dalit

The origin of the Dalit community, and of the caste system itself, is unclear. Adherents of the Aryan migration hypothesis theorize that the caste system was a product of the invasion, with the Aryans reserving the higher castes for themselves and relegating the darker-skinned, native inhabitants that they conquered to lower castes and untouchable status. An alternative theory accepts this general outline, but holds that Dalit existed before the Aryan migration as an oppressed class among the native Dravidian peoples of South Asia. In this latter theory, the Dalit status was simply preserved and expanded by the Aryans as part of the integration of Aryan and Dravidian societies.

In the context of traditional Hindu beliefs, Dalit status has often been historically associated with occupations regarded as ritually impure: any occupation involving killing or handling dead bodies, or anything involving disposing of refuse or human waste. Engaging in these activities was considered to be polluting to the individual who performed them, and this pollution was considered to be 'contagious'. As a result, Dalits were commonly banned from fully participating in Hindu religious life (they could not enter the premises of a temple), and elaborate precautions were sometimes observed to prevent incidental contact between Dalits and higher-caste Hindus. Historically, there may not have been clear demarcation between Dalit castes and the lowest Shudra castes. Before the freezing of lands and territories during the British colonial period, it may have been possible for Dalits to move up the ladder as Shudras or higher castes. In the same way, some people from the lowest Shudra communities may have been reduced in status to that of the Dalits. Culturally there appears to be continuity across the caste spectrum. In modern India the word 'Dalit' has been applied to all people who do not belong to any of the four castes of Hinduism. Defined in this way, 'Dalit' includes not only low-caste or outcaste Hindus, but also aboriginal followers of animist religions, and possibly may have included immigrant communities that subscribed to beliefs that were seen as incompatible with orthodox brahman 1st and Hindu traditions.

Dalits are not a single identifiable race or caste. Instead, they are divided into various subcastes known as or ' jatis', the lowest ranking of which is generally considered to be the Bhangis. Most genetic studies have found no significant evidence that members of 'untouchable' groups are substantially different from other groups in similar locations. Castes within a region are probably less genetically different than people of the same caste across different regions. While at least one studyfound a correlation between caste status and genetic markers seeming to indicate a more European lineage, no clear biological basis for caste distinctions has been conclusively revealed.

The absence of strong genetic differentiation between Dalits and non-Dalits is often regarded as evidence that the caste barrier was historically more permeable than commonly perceived. Intermarriage (which is again growing in popularity in Indian society), or sexual infidelity (the prevalence of which is difficult to assess) across caste lines may be more common than was previously thought. Additionally, Dalit diversity may be due to newly outcaste individuals or communities over the years. It is noteworthy that certain regional tribes that are considered Dalits are sometimes seen by Indians as racially distinct-they are often regarded as more closely related to Burmese, Thais, and other Southeast and East Asians. Many Dalits who have converted to other religions in the past few centuries continue to retain their Dalit identity. In the 1991 census, Dalits constituted more than 16% of India's population, with the greatest numbers living in Uttar Pradesh, West Bengal, and Bihar. They are also found in Nepal. In Pakistan, more than 60% of all Hindus are Dalits, keeping in mind that Pakistan is predominantly Muslim.

Dalits and Indian Politics

M.K. Gandhi made it part of the Indian National Congress's mission to eradicate untouchability. For this reason, untouchability has been officially abolished in India, although social practice has lagged behind, particularly in rural villages. In a few of these extremely traditional villages, Dalits are still not allowed to let their shadows fall upon Brahmins for fear of ritually contaminating them; and they are still required to sweep the ground where they walk to remove the 'contamination' of their footfalls. In some of these villages, rural Dalits are forbidden to worship in temples or draw water from the same wells as caste Hindus, and they usually live in segregated neighbourhoods outside the main village. In urban areas and most villages the old concepts of a rigid caste system and untouchability usually no longer exist, though most Indians still voluntarily hold on to their caste origins. Some seats in the National and State Parliments are reserved for Scheduled Caste and Tribe candidates, a measure sought by B.R. Ambedkar and other Dalit activists in order to ensure that Dalits would obtain a proportionate political voice.

Dalits and Religion

One of the tougher questions in modern Indian society is whether the Dalits are really Hindus. Traditionally, Dalits have been barred from many activities that were seen as central to Vedic religion and Hindu practices. The wide variety of practices and beliefs observed in Hinduism makes any clear assessment difficult. Defined narrowly as the practice of rituals associated with the Vedic teachings and Brahmin-centered orthodox religious complex, then many Dalits would be classified as non-Hindus. But if ' Hinduism ' is viewed in wider terms as simply a convenient label for the full range of Indian religious practices, then most Indians-including Dalits-would fit into that category. Many Dalits continue to debate whether they are 'Hindu' or 'non-Hindu'. Some have succesfully integrated into urban Indian society, where caste origins are less obvious and less important in public life. In rural India, caste origins are more readily apparent, and Dalits remain excluded from local religious life. Because many Dalits feel they must have a formal religion, they have been drawn to other religions to improve their social and economic standing by removing them from a religious environment where they are excluded and denigrated. Dalit politician and activist B.R. Ambedkar was influential in encouraging many Dalits to convert to Buddhism in order to escape the inequities of the caste system. Ambedkar himself converted to Buddhism shortly before his death. The interpretation of Buddhism popularized by Ambedkar and his followers borrowed heavily from the Theravada tradition and emphasized the Buddha's teachings on social equality, particularly his rejection of castes for Sangha members, and the Buddhist teaching that the 'true Brahman' is one who engages in ethical behaviour, regardless of birth. This movement is sometimes called Neo-Buddhism.

In recent years, the use of mass conversionas a Dalit political tactic (often to Christianity or Buddhism) has become controversial—some politicians called for bans on mass conversion ceremonies.

Dalits and Social Policy

The central government and many state governments reserve places for Dalits in all educational courses and government jobs, but many poor Dalits remain poorly educated. Most Dalits, like other poor Indians, cannot afford private schools and tutoring. The improvement of public education remains a priority for many Dalit activists, who believe that the poor quality of public primary schools prevents Dalits from taking advantage of the educational opportunities supposedly provided for them by quotas and preferred admission to institutions of higher learning. Education of rural Dalits remains particularly problematic. Additionally, a recent Supreme Court decision removed the quota system from private and unaided professional colleges, limiting preferred admissions criteria for Dalit students to government-run and funded educational institutions. Some Dalits believe that the jobs traditionally reserved for Dalits are no longer lucrative, and should be supplimented by reserved jobs in the private sector. Recently, some Dalit politicians attempted to secure action from international business groups and the World Bank that would provide reserved jobs for Dalits in foreign funded development projects, and foreign business investments.

Rural Dalits face many of the problems as other poor, rural Indians. Dalits in poor communities may be the target of the frustration and fear of non-Dalits. These individuals, often desperately poor themselves, may target Dalits who are seen as living 'above their station'-either through economic prosperity, or by acting without regard for traditional caste restrictions on behaviour and relationships.

CONCEPT OF DALIT : ORIGIN AND DEFINITION

The concept is believed to be originated in the 1930s in journalistic writings according to Michael, and as a Hindi and Marathi translation of 'Depressed Castes', the term the British used according to Webster. The term, however, was chosen, according to Zelliot, by the group itself and is used proudly. In her view, 'Dalits' implies those who have been broken, ground down by those above them in a deliberate and active way. There is in the word itself an inherent denial of pollution, karma and justified caste hierarchy. However, according to Massey, 'dalit' more as a concept and in its present use has its seed in the writings of two great Indian personalities, Phule and Ambedkar. He believes that Phule in his writings used the title Shudra-Ati-Shudra for Dalits and he knew it was a Brahmin conspiracy against Shudra-Ati-Shudra (both being Indigenous people) to divide them into two castes or classes in order to make them their slaves. Similarly, he says that for the 'Dalit', Ambedkar used the title 'untouchable' (achuta) in his writings. Guru also explains that the category dalit was first used by Ambedkar himself in his fortnightly Bahishkruit Bharat. He (Ambedkar) defined it comprehensively: Dalithood is a kind of life condition which characterises the exploitation, suppression and marginalisation of dalits by the social, economic, cultural and political domination of the upper caste brahminical order. But Massey makes one point clear that is many Dalits today prefer to be called Dalits (name self-given) as it is not merely a name or title but has become an expression of hope for them in recovering their past self-identity. Shah however argues that with the change in market structure in the post-independence and the rise in education among small sections of Harijans, small entrepreneurs and a white-collar middle class have emerged among the Scheduled Castes. These have become militant and call the Scheduled Castes the 'Dalits' that is a poor and exploited class.

Oommen, on the other hand, argues that the Dalits suffer from cumulative domination (socio-cultural, economic and political) and multiple deprivation. He has however excluded the section of the 'Harijan bourgeoisie' among the SCs from this category since they are economically well-off and politically privileged (even though not entirely emancipated from socio-cultural oppression). Thus, in his view, only those Scheduled Castes who have low ritual status, appalling poverty and powerlessness fit into the definition of Dalits.

Contradiction, Multiple Terms and Heterogeneity

According to Guru, the term 'dalit' is not accepted by all those who belong to this category. It has faced criticism, particularly by the urban, educated middle class dalits, as socially regressive, derogatory and hence undesirable. Thus, they look at the term with disdain. Guru also states that a small section of neo-Buddhists rejects the concept of dalit which includes all the oppressed classes and prefers to be called Buddhists and tries to restrict it to those who suffer from untouchability and other social handicaps. Some even prefer to confine the term Dalit only to Ambedkarite Buddhists, but for many others, Dalit is not necessarily only Buddhist but also all socially oppressed persons in general and untouchables in particular.

There is also a section of the community, according to Guru, who prefer bahujan over both the Buddhist as well as dalit categories. However, the problem with such a formulation is that it neglects the dialectical relationship between 'dalit' and 'bahujan' which has a bearing on the formation of the dalit category and its marriage with bahujan. Similarly, speaking on the notion of harijan vis-à-vis dalit, Guru argues that the category harijan is artificially imposed on the untouchables and is an ascribed one as it does not flow from the untouchables' own experiences. Given its divine association, it is inadequate for capturing the specific realities since it also replaces the need for internal critique. On the other hand, the category dalit derives its epistemic and political strength from the material social experience of the community which renders it authentic and dynamic rather than passive and rigid. Ambedkar also said that even though Gandhiji wanted assimilation of the untouchables with the mainstream, he made it impossible by his euphemism, Harijan. In his own words, '... such assimilation was not possible from the new name, Harijan given to the untouchables... his new name counteracted assimilation and made it impossible'. However, in Sharma's view, historically dalits imply not a structure, but a processual phenomenon emanating from a politico-legal entity known as 'Scheduled Castes' and the latter being an outcome of the preceding moral-political entity which Gandhiji referred as Harijan. What I believe is that the concept of 'Harijan' has to be seen in its proper historical context.

In the context of various dehumanizing terms such as Achhuta, Dhedh, Chandal being used for the Dalits, Gandhiji's euphemism did provide some respectability even though only in name. What is important to understand is the evolutionary framework and the specific context and time in which 'Harijan' appeared. Today almost all conscious and educated Dalits are scornful of this notion and reject it out rightly. So, now it is imperative to discard this notion in the context of contemporary discussion on dalit issues though it will be unavoidable in the context of a historical account of such issues. However, Dalits in general do not have any problem with the constitutional concept of SCs. They are relatively comfortable with it even though the notion, they believe, reminds themselves and others about who they really are and where their social space is.

However, it must be borne in mind that the category 'Dalit' is not a homogeneous category. It involves a number of castes. According to Shah, they have internal hierarchy. Neo-Buddhist Mahars look down upon with contempt on the other Scheduled Castes who have not converted to Buddhism. There is also conflict between the Mahars and the Mangs. In this connection, Michael Moffatt argues that the cultural system of Indian untouchables does not distinctively question or revalue the dominant social order. Rather it continuously recreates among untouchables a microcosm of the larger system. Even Ambedkar realized that 'graded inequality' within the untouchables was a hurdle in their emancipation from their controls of the caste Hindus. Similarly Shah argues that there are middle class Dalits and the poor Dalits whose problems and interests are of different kinds. While for the former, the problem of identity and reservation is important, the latter is grappled with the problem of poverty and exploitation.

Webster's Critical Analysis

Webster's critical analysis of two of the prevailing ways to define 'Dalits'-class analysis and communal analysis-holds much significance here to simplify the understanding of the concept. Those using a class analysis of Indian society subsume Dalits within such class or occupational categories as peasants, agricultural labour, factory workers, students and the like. This can be seen in most Marxist historical writings, the sub-altern studies volumes and to a lesser degree, in the Dalit Panther Manifesto. In fact, the concept was made popular by the Dalit Panthers in the 1970s. This class analysis is fraught with serious problems, according to Webster, since it not only fails to take account of the basic contradiction and oppression of the Dalits but also hides these by using categories which diverts attention away from them. By their own admission, Webster argues, Ambedkar as well as Jagjivan Ram indicated the existence of such contradictions.

Similarly, those using a communal analysis of caste tend to view only those untouchables as Dalits who remain Hindus by religion. If they convert to another religion, then they cease to be Dalits. Webster argues that this view is at serious odds with the realities uncovered by studies of castes among Christians and Muslims. Thus, he says that at least for Dalits, the stigma of untouchability and its accompanying disabilities based on caste are an Indian rather than Hindu phenomenon. And '... these were and still are the defining characteristics of a Dalit even if a Dalit moves up in a social class or changes religion.

CONCLUDING STATEMENT

It becomes clear that despite various interpretations, there is agreement that the 'Scheduled Castes' is an important component in the construction of the dalit category. And as is the common knowledge, other caste people or categories also face certain disabilities in the society but they have never experienced the totality of disabilities, more prominently caste disability like the Scheduled Castes. There is also dialectical relationship between the Dalits and other castes. All achievements: economic, political, educational howsoever gargantuan will stand dwarfed in the face of caste disabilities. A Dalit who is educationally qualified, economically well-off and politically privileged may get a better treatment than his caste brethren who have not got any secular achievements (Education, Wealth, Power etc.) like him but he is not completely free from socio-cultural indignities which Oommen has also admitted. So, though Oommen has excluded the 'Harijan bourgeoisie' among the Scheduled Castes from the dalit category, I am however inclined to view the category 'Dalits' as an inclusive one comprising all the caste people who suffer from caste ignominies irrespective of the fact that some of them are upward in secular fields. What I try to impress here is that caste disability is central to the construction of the notion of 'Dalits'; other factors do play a role but they are not central.

The communal view of defining 'Dalit' as a Hindu phenomenon has been critiqued by Webster. Though it is true that the Dalits even after conversion suffer from the same caste disabilities but theoretically religions like Islam or Christianity are egalitarian and there is no room for caste discrimination even though in practice, revealed from many studies, it is found to be there. Would the religions like Christianity or Islam admit to the existence and practice of caste-based disability in their religions? They could not as it would normatively negate the egalitarian character of these religions. So, on the one hand, there is absence of a formal acknowledgement of such an evil practice, on the other hand, there is indeed such a practice prevailing in reality. The contradiction notwithstanding, the Constitution also confines caste disability to being a Hindu phenomenon. Reservation is also given on this basis. So, for the purpose of the present discussion, we can restrict the notion of Dalit in its scope to include all those who are scheduled in the Constitution and are eligible for reservation even though Dalit Sociology is the perfect sub-field to generate a thorough discussion and debate on this issue. There is indeed a necessity for this as even though the caste system with institutionalized iniquitous social structure is a product of Hindu society (most sociologists believe so), over the years, it has been able to penetrate many other religions in India. Ambedkar had also admitted this. Recently, even the Supreme Court – the custodian and the interpreter of the Constitution – has admitted a petition relating to the issue of Dalit Christians being considered for reservation benefit. So this issue being a complex issue, I believe, it is in the fitness of things that a meaningful debate takes place.

EVOLVING NECESSITY OF INDIAN SOCIETY

Having made an effort (of course, not exhaustive) to demystify the notion of Dalit, it is, however, necessary to talk about Dalit Sociology now. We have already sub-fields like Political Sociology, Industrial Sociology, Rural Sociology,

Urban Sociology, Sociology of Education, Sociology of Knowledge, Sociology of Agriculture, Sociology of Development, Sociology of Science, Sociology of Religion, Historical Sociology, Medical Sociology, Gender Sociology etc. to name a few. So another new accretion to the already existing sub-fields should not be a problem at all. In the course of evolution and growth of Sociology, many new sub-fields have come up keeping pace with the changing time and evolving necessity of a period and society. Dalit Sociology is the evolving necessity of today's Indian society. A distinct and wholly dedicated full-fledged sub-field can do justice to the myriad issues related to Dalits. It can also convey a substantive and symbolic meaning to the otherwise marginalized sections of the Indian society that Dalits and dalit issues are not only being tolerated but also being accepted. Substantive because issues of substance, concern, importance and meaning to the Dalits can be deliberated, debated, and disseminated. Symbolic because it will make Dalits aware of the fact (a sense of acceptance) that their issues are being represented as relevant issues.

Upper Caste Bias of (Higher) Education

Now the question that arises is why there is suddenly a necessity for Dalit Sociology. Interestingly, the necessity was always there, it is only being articulated in recent times. Sociology in Indian context has studied many issues including dalit issues, but, as many dalit intellectuals believe, the legitimate/due representation has always been lacking. It is because there were very less number of Dalits coming to higher education leave alone the issue of showing any interest in dalit issues. Except a few, non-dalit intellectuals did not have much fascination for such issues. So, besides a minor representation here or there, dalit issues have never been the dominant themes in sociological discourse. In fact, as Dalits complain, the values and ideals imparted in school, college and university curricula only represent upper caste values and have squarely ignored the dalit cultures and values. Thus, education in general and higher education in particular, instead of respecting the history and culture of different communities, has, in their considered opinion, become the promoter of higher caste values alone. As Ambrose Pinto argues, most stories, anecdotes and examples in our textbooks and syllabus are from the dominant culture... There is no place for dalit history, geography, medicine, anthropology and culture in the curriculum. Making similar observation Illaiah argues that the Dalit-bahujans find that their culture, life-style, production-based skill etc. are not part of the history. It is as if they never had a history. The literary texts are full of condemnation of their culture and are brazenly silent about caste inhumanity. They were never told that Phule, Ambedkar were as competent as Gandhi and Nehru were. They were always told only about Gandhi, Nehru, Subhash Bose and so on, people they could never relate to, people whose upbringing had nothing to do with their upbringing. Similarly, the nationalist movement was presented as a Brahmin-Bania fight against colonial power and the role played by the Dalit-bahujans was never mentioned, according to Illaiah.

A Historical Fact and Emerging Changes

It is, however, not surprising that dalit issues have not been given the due they deserve. It has always happened in history that who wields power dictates terms. Dalits were always made to live in a condition of subjugation, marginalization and dehumanization in the society. They were not allowed education, dignity and self-respect. So, powerless as they were, they could not possibly have strived for the propagation of dalit values and ideals. Even today, to a great extent, the condition of Dalits has not significantly changed. Many continue to experience ignominies, indignities and inhumanities, but things are not exactly the same today. Education has penetrated and awareness has built up. A few have come up economically, politically and educationally whom we can say middle-class Dalits. Dalit intellectuals are an important component of middle-class Dalits. It is these sections who are really spearheading the movement for a legitimate place for dalit issues in the academic discourse. The presence of Dalits both as students and teachers in the academic field has necessitated a re-look at the contents of knowledge being imparted. No wonder, there is, therefore, a clamour for correcting imbalances in the projection/non-projection of reality, especially with regard to dalit issues.

Dalit intellectuals themselves are engaged in extensive research into exploring their own past, unravelling their own history, genealogies etc. Since 'Dalits' is not a homogeneous category, different sections within it must have different genealogies and histories. They can contribute rich ethnographic data for sociological understanding.

Apart from the history of exploitation, discrimination and humiliation, they can also explore the saga of resistance, triumph, entrepreneurial trait and ability, other achievements and successes. There are quite a number of educated Dalits who are bringing out autobiographies and biographies which are also a source of rich sociological contents. Dalit Sahitya (literature) is another development which provides an opportunity for generating consciousness through writings, poems and poetries. Non-dalit scholars have also shown flexibility and shunned intellectual apartheid to take up dalit issue related researches. So, now nobody can say that there is dearth of literature on dalit issues to impact upon academic discourse, even though, there is still the need for a relentless effort to undertake more of such researches in an expeditious manner.

So, today, at the attitude level as well as at the literature level, the educational arenas/centres of learning are better suited to take up a study of dalit issues in its entirety along with the clamouring for the same by the dalit intellectuals. Dalits being an integral part of Indian society, their issues need to be an integral part of educational discourse. So, the need for Dalit Sociology can not be overemphasized.

Developing a Perspective from Below

Many dalit scholars have strived to make people look at the society and the world from an otherwise neglected/different/other/counter perspective, which has been variously called the perspective from below/the sub-altern perspective. Dalit Sociology can help shape and sharpen such a perspective by giving enough scope for it to find a place in academic discourse where dissemination can lead to debate and debate can lead to the development of sensitivity and refinement of attitude, outlook and perspective. It can prepare the ground for understanding the history of suffering of marginalized groups and from this standpoint, critique the dominant viewpoint. In fact, Ambedkarism is such a perspective, which inspires Dalits in their struggle for self-respect and assertion, and, at the same time, talks about a society where social justice is the main goal, and where everybody can live with his/her head held high. It can be a very important ideology in Dalit Sociology. Apart form this, there are other important ideologues like Phule, Periyar whose ideas inform a dalit's mind and inspire him/her in the struggle for emancipation.

Incorporation of 'Diversity' in Curriculum

Dalit Sociology can bring to the fore that Dalits are such individuals in society who always have to adjust. This is, in fact, not only true of Dalits, tribals etc. in India but also true of all underprivileged or disadvantaged anywhere in the world. They are the ones who have always to adjust/'fit-in', the institutions (educational) or others (people) do not adjust to them. The cultural difference: one at home/their own community, the other in society in general/educational centres in particular, very often results in the development of inferiority complex in them contributing sometimes to their underperformance, which is construed as student deficit.

This may not be true always because the potential is constrained at the outset by the prevailing social structure in society in general and educational centres in particular that do not leave any scope for it to unfold. Dalit students can recount many such experiences of subjugation or marginalization, which can help see things in perspective and this can enrich Dalit Sociology. It is important to mention that education and more particularly higher education must orientate towards the 'diversity project', which can include changes necessary to truly educate a diverse population of students for the society in which we live, and the changes may be incorporated in various aspects, most notably, in the curriculum and pedagogy, and teaching styles. The incorporation of diversity in the curriculum through Dalit Sociology can affect students' attitudes, knowledge and outlook and, at the same time, can demonstrate to students of so-called lower castes that the educational institution is working on change.

This, however, can help in unlearning and relearning much of what has been known. According to Morgan etal, a revealing work by Lopez using Michigan data in a longitudinal study of the impact of inter-group contact and coursework dealing with racial/ethnic changes in student attitudes, found that coursework had the most significant positive impact on attitudes toward educational equity. This finding is consistent with other evidence that coursework influences not only attitudes but knowledge, skills and cognitive development.

Astin, for example, in one of the studies found that 'students responded positively to diverse faculty, as well as to what they taught (multicultural courses or courses with multicultural issues imbedded in them). Students also noted positive cognitive and affective development if they participated in diversity activities: (1) taking a women's studies or ethnic studies course; (2) taking a world cultures course; (3) participating in racial and cultural awareness workshops; (4) discussing racial or ethnic issues; or (5) socializing with someone from another ethnic group'. In addition to the above, according to Astin, students also reported increased commitment to promoting racial understanding.

Astin sums it up this way: "[T]here are many developmental benefits that accrue to students when institutions support an emphasis on multiculturalism and cultural diversity". In fact, it is important that institutions committed to educating all students for a complex multicultural society should create curriculum that recognizes and engages diversity.

Through the contents of Dalit Sociology, the difference between 'the equality of opportunity of access' and 'the equality of opportunity of success' can also be highlighted as it is important that the two should not be confused. While the emphasis should be initially on the former, the latter should always be the final goal. So, the effort should be to create more equality in society. And Dalit Sociology has an important role to play in this.

Process of De-peripheralisation

We know that books by Dalits are rarely discussed. It is not that they are not discussed at all. But they are very rarely discussed. Dalit Sociology can provide a meaningful platform for surfacing of de-centered knowledges or to use Foucault's terminology, 'an insurrection of subjugated knowledges'. Through this, the process of de-peripheralisation can be said to, at least, begin. It is important that the excluded and silenced get an opportunity to make their points of view heard as, according to Anne Seller, the excluded and the silenced have a privileged vision, because they can tell that the silencing is working. This can help build an inclusive knowledge as the perspective from the below is incorporated in the knowledge pool. In fact, this is also compatible with the pluralistic stand of postmodernism. According to Seller, as Harvey expresses it: 'The idea that all groups have a right to speak for themselves and have that voice accepted as authentic and legitimate is essential to the pluralistic stand of postmodernism'. Postmodernism is, in fact, concerned with the validity and dignity of 'the other' and it has a commitment to the oppressed, says Seller. It must be mentioned here that Dalit Sociology is not an endeavour to produce value-free knowledge. In fact, as Seller argues, 'there is no such thing as a value-free education, we cannot produce and disseminate value-free knowledge'. As the knowledge of a particular group, it issues from a particular perspective, says Seller.

Women's Studies and Inclusive Education

According to Robert Engvall, questions have arisen more frequently in recent years over the treatment of diverse human experiences in the curricula of our institutions of higher education. He further says in the context of women's studies that cultural pluralism and increased awareness of the value of human diversity have heightened curricula response to the needs and wants of those seeking greater inclusion within the higher education sphere. The concept behind the invention of women's studies was the perceived need to overcome some of that bias and to bring to light previously omitted histories, literature, and ideas. He also holds that increased democratization has allowed former outsiders to openly question the role that bias has played in higher education and more fully explore the intersection of gender and race with other identities. What he says of women's studies and race holds true in case of Dalits in India. Indian society is characterized by cultural pluralism and there is also increased democratization in the society. This has resulted in the demand for inclusion of diverse human/cultural experiences in the curriculum. In fact, inclusive education (in the sense of including dalit issues) is integral to a democratic society. Explaining the meaning of inclusive education, Barton says: 'Inclusive education is not merely about providing access into mainstream school for pupils who have previously been excluded. It is not about closing down an unacceptable system of segregated provision and dumping those pupils in an unchanged mainstream system. Existing school systems in terms of physical factors, curriculum aspects, teaching expectations and styles, leadership roles, will have to change. This is because inclusive education is about the participation of all children and young people and the removal of all forms of exclusionary practice'.

Afro-American Studies: A Precedent

In the context of making a case for Dalit Sociology, it is worth mentioning Nellie Y. McKay here who says how Blacks struggled in the 1960s and 1970s to include their life/cultural experiences in the American educational system. According to McKay, 'In launching efforts to integrate the white mainstream academy in the 1960s and 1970s, black students and faculty, as "others," were violently opposed to the system that denied their human and intellectual worth. They determined to change the demography of the institution with their presence and to alter the premises of previously perceived knowledge to take cognizance of their racial and cultural experiences. Predictably, the system responded by resisting changes to its long-held authority. But the outsiders fought well, and when the dust settled, around the middle of the 1970s, Afro-American Studies, as a field of inquiry, had taken firm hold in white colleges and universities across the country.... They became the vanguard, and their successes paved the way for Women's Studies and other Ethnic Studies Programs that followed in the closing years of the 1970s. By then, too, the first group of black students and faculty on the front lines of the action, and the whites who had supported them in their struggle, had absorbed the worst of the system's resistance to change. It was time to look toward building a unified intellectual structure that was not a closed system of knowledge controlled by a privileged group of knowers'. From the above, it is clear how the Blacks had to struggle to include their cultural/racial experiences in the academic milieu, and how their struggle paved the way for other marginalized sections to press for the inclusion of their cultural/

racial/gender experiences in the curricula. Similarly, the Dalits in India had to struggle hard to get self-respect, which was historically denied to them. And the struggle is still on. Society is yet to fully become sensitive to dalit rights, but it is, undoubtedly, in the process of purging itself of its traditional/ discriminatory character. In such a context, I believe, unlike black issues, it may not be that difficult for dalit issues to be incorporated in the teaching-learning process in India. But, there is the necessity for continued pressure: intellectual, social and political. Dalit issues are indeed relevant social issues for sociological understanding. They can be legitimately seen as forms of knowledge because they have their own way of conceptualizing and making sense of reality, approaching a problem, and ascertaining truth. In fact, dalit issues can broaden epistemological base. And this fact cannot be lost sight of for a long period.

Moral and Sensitive Society

While 'knowledge is power', true knowledge is wisdom. And it should be everyone's effort to build a wise, moral and sensitive society. It may not be untenable to say that Dalit Sociology can help build a more wise, moral and sensitive society. While society will be immensely assisted in its effort to be able to groom sensitive, wise, responsible, moral individuals, Sociology is also likely to gain immensely because Dalit Sociology will be an important contribution to the pool of knowledge. It is important, however, that more and more non-dalit scholars should come forward to work on dalit issues. It is equally important that Dalits extend whole-hearted cooperation to such scholars without being obsessed with the idea of suspecting their intentions. True, it may sometimes happen that some non-dalit scholars may be selective in their portrayal of the dalit situation, but to criticize and discourage only on the basis of selectivity will be antithetical to the final goal of generating an attitudinal change and sustaining it over time. The debate regarding an insider's subjectivity and an outsider's selectivity is quite old. The change needs to be welcomed without, of course, sacrificing the motivation for constructive criticisms, since they are the necessary ingredients for the growth of knowledge. Another thing which needs to be emphasized is that Dalits themselves and scholars sensitive to dalit issues must find a place in different academic bodies which decide curricula and syllabi in order for dalit issues to find their due place. It is important to mention that Dalit Sociology becomes a compulsory rather than an optional subject in Sociology as a part of higher education programme. It is equally important that other social sciences also have dalit studies as part of their course structure.

IMPACT OF THE REFORMS ON DALITS

The social disadvantage suffered by dalits in India was taken note of in the Constitution of India which was drafted under the chairmanship of Dr. Ambedkar-a person who had spearheaded the most momentous anti-caste movement of the depressed classes. It provided dalits with many safeguards, viz., 1. social, educational, cultural and religious safeguards, 2. economic safeguards, 3. political safeguards and 4. safeguards for employment. The free market ethos of the Reforms, conceptually can neither confirm to the democratic spirit of the Indian Constitution of 'one vote, one value', nor can it coexist with the system of positive discrimination embodied in these safeguards. For, the market grants moneyed person more value, and overtly believes in the jungle law of 'might is right'. To a large extent, the primary motivation behind these Constitutional provisions was liberal democratic aspirations that characterised the freedom movement. However, these aspirations and the initial ideological zeal of the founding fathers withered away in no time and what survived was its utilitarian dimension for the electoral politics. The sorry state of the executive compliance with these Constitutional provisions amply bears out the fangs of the Indian society. The Reforms will bring a kind of legitimacy to this attitudinal resistance. These safeguards will stand eroded as the Reforms gain in momentum. Influence of the Reforms is bound to be all pervasive. However, only a few issues of importance to the dalit masses have been picked up for discussion here.

Financial Assistance in Education Institutions

Reservation in the educational institutions and the financial assistance in the form of scholarships and freeships constitutes perhaps the most important factor in the development scheme for dalits. For, it is primarily responsible to make the basic input of education available to them. Without education, all the constitutional safeguards including the reservation in services would be infructuous. Under this scheme the dalit students whose parental income is below a specified level, get freeship, reservation in admissions to all the colleges getting grants-in-aid from the government, and scholarships. Without this assistance, even today, it would be difficult for dalits to send their children to school. The Reforms have already resulted in freezing the grants to many institutions and in stagnating, if not lowering, the expenditure on education.

The free market ethos has entered the educational sphere in a big way. Commercialisation of education is no more a mere rhetoric, it is now the established fact. Commercial institutions offering specialised education signifying the essential input from utilitarian view point, have come up in a big way from cities to small towns. Their product-prices are not only based on the demand-supply consideration in their market segment but also are manipulated by their promotional strategies. In a true spirit of globalisation, many foreign universities, are invading the educational spheres through hitherto unfamiliar strategic alliances with non-descript commercial agencies, of course at a hefty dollar equivalent prices. Many elite institutions like IIMs, IITs, suddenly facing fund crunch had to raise their fee structure and other prices many fold. They were already beyond the reach of dalits. When they eventually turn self-financing, their prices would be benchmarked against their international counterparts, which any way would be affordable to the same top market segment that constitutes the focus of all the Reform-talk. As the job markets become acutely competitive, owing to a sharp decline in job opportunities, the polarisation between the elite and commoner would also sharpen. Various kinds of price barriers would be erected to thwart the entry of downtrodden. Even the sphere of primary education the coverage of which has been so miserably inadequate as to leave out multitude of children in villages as illiterate, could not remain unaffected, notwithstanding its already existing divide between the vernacular and English schools.

Corporatisation has entered this arena, transforming the education into an enterprise for profits. The quality of input these expensive schools will provide will benchmark the products in the contracting job markets. Even today, because of preponderance of the English language in business circles, the divide between village and towns is almost complete in the field of education. It is so difficult for a village student, educated in vernacular medium to compete with his convent educated (now an understatement!) counterpart in cities and towns. If this is the situation of general village population, the plight of dalits who besides being the poorest of the village population carry additional Bretton Wood of social discrimination, is indeed a worrisome matter. Despite several kinds of State assistance, dalits are plagued with alarming rate of school drop-outs. This may be explained out as much by the need for dalit children to supplement their meagre family incomes for meeting the two ends as also the erosion of their faith that education could be the instrument to change the pathetic course of their lives. This sense of alienation is going to grow with the progress of the Reforms.

Reservations in Services

Whatever may be the other costs, the government policy of reservations in employment sphere has undoubtedly played an important role for dalits.

The policy broadly envisages representation of dalits in proportion to their population in all the public services which includes the government, public sector, autonomous bodies and institutions receiving grant-in-aid from the government. A cursory glance at the figures of this representation is enough to get a pathetic state of implementation. Howsoever, unsatisfactory the results of the implementation may be, the importance of reservations from the dalit viewpoint cannot be overemphasised.

As could be evidenced by the organised private sector, where it would be difficult to find a dalit employee (save of course in scavenging and lowliest jobs), without reservations dalits would have been totally doomed. The importance of reservations thus could only be assessed in relation to situations where they do not exist. Whatever be their defects and deficiencies, they have given certain economic means of livelihood and some social prestige to the sons and daughters of over 1.5 million landless labourers. Whether they get real power or not, over 50,000 dalits could enter the sphere of bureaucratic authority with the help of reservations. Besides these tangible benefits promised by the policy, it has instilled a hope in dalit community. This hope predominantly manifests in the form of spread of education among them. Their emotional bond with the nation and its Constitution despite heaps of injustice and ignominy they bear every moment of their life may also be significantly attributable to the Reservation Policy. The winds of privatisation under the Economic Reforms have already shaken the very foundations of the Reservations.

The Reforms clearly envisage the minimalist government. Wherever the Reforms patterned on the Structural Adjustment Programme of the World Bank were carried out, denationalisation of the public sector and privatisation have come in a big way. Being the late starter, India has not reached the scales achieved by others, say, the Latin American countries. However, the start has not been any unimpressive. Almost all sectors of economy stand opened up for private investment. The disinvestment in existing public sector companies has already been allowed upto 49 per cent by the policy. The public stake being more than 50 per cent, the public sector as such is not yet dismantled in policy. It continues to be the State, as before, and hence attracts application of the reservation policy. However, the Reform package has already endangered, if not abolished, the reservations through back doors. In the name of preparing the PSUs for global free market regime, the PSUs are being allowed/encouraged to have strategic alliances with private companies from India and abroad.

As such, over the last five years, many profit making PSUs have formed the joint venture companies (JVC). These JVCs are strategically structured as not to fall in the ambit of the PSU-framework. The typical equity stake for the PSU and private could be 49:51. There appears to be a great deal of receptivity for this scheme in the government circles. There are no policy barriers on the business to be pursued by these JVCs. Theoretically, an existing PSU can hive off its business divisions into private JVCs and transform itself into a financial holding company with a skeleton staff. Even if technically it remains a PSU, and assuming that it followed the reservation policy sincerely, it would have little scope to absorb dalits in its staff. Whatever may be the strategic considerations, the fall out of this process practically amounted to shutting the doors of these new age companies to dalits and to potential neutralisation of the reservation policy. The policy of limited disinvestment of PSUs not being in conformity with the spirit of the Reforms, is bound to be relaxed in favour of privatisation any time.

But still, all the PSUs may not get privatised at once. The better ones would be gobbled up by the bigger sharks. The worst ones may be closed down or distress-sold. And the middle ones may for quite some time, continue to be the relic of their past. Whatever the scenario, the residual structures of the 'reformed' PSUs are never going to be the same, as far as dalits are concerned. The ethos of privatisation and the excuse of competition, superimposed on the traditional caste prejudice, will never allow reservations to happen, any more. Other public services are also bound to slip out of the reservation policy. Most of the sectors, which were the traditional domain of the government investment, have already been released for the private investment.

Atrocities and Socio-Cultural Suppression

The caste atrocities are an integral feature of dalit life. The government machinery keeps on collecting their statistics year after year and issues it in a report of its Commissioner for SCs and STs (now the National Commission for SCs and STs). There are at least three Articles (15,17 and 23) in the Constitution of India which seek to mitigate the evil. To give effect to these Constitutional provisions the following acts also have been in operation:

1. The Untouchability (Offences) Act, 1955, later amended and re-titled as the Protection of Civil Rights Act, 1955
2. The Scheduled Castes and Scheduled Tribes (Prevention of Atrocities Act) 1989 and The Bonded Labour System (Abolition) Act, 1976

Despite this, the statistics of the registered atrocities read like a balance sheet of a blue chip company with consistent rise every successive year. It is pertinent to remember that owing to the dependency relationship of dalits with the perpetrators of atrocities, not every occurrence of the atrocity gets registered. Rather, it can be safely assumed that behind each registered atrocity over ten atrocity cases go unreported. As per the latest statistics, every day nearly 50 cases of atrocities are registered all over the country. Over three dalit women are raped and six are disabled on each day round the year. The National Commission analysed the causes of each of the atrocities in a sample of 45 cases. The analysis shows that out of 45 cases 13 are clearly attributable to the economic reasons. The balance can also be explained out by some kind of weakness of dalits. Coupled with the weakness of dalits, their growing assertiveness and refusal to submit to the casteist dictates of the village lords, rebellion ethos assimilated through the Ambedkarian struggle and process of general awareness, also cause atrocities to increase.

The atrocities occur where the dependency relationships are more pronounced and bear economic implications. Villages, where dalits as landless labourers depend upon landlords or rich farmers for their livelihood and where the traditional caste equations have a potential to yield economic surplus to the latter, provide ideal setting for atrocities. What impact would the new regime have on the socio-economic setting of Indian villages? In face of it, the unbridled capitalism inherent in the Reforms is not compatible with any feudal structure. But this thumb rule does not seem to be entirely validated by the developmental experience in India. The capitalism in India did not have to sprout through the bedrock of contradictions of feudalism as in Europe. It was planted in the fertile soil of Indian feudalism. It has grown here on its nutrients. Thus it would be too mechanical to have a theoremic expectation about the demise of feudalism and thence the end of the caste through the growth of capitalism. The caste institution moreover, has defied the classical mould of feudalism by possessing many unique features. The most important being its resilience and adaptability. What we experience in the mysterious growth of casteist politics today in India is precisely this ability of caste to adapt to changing times. The annihilation of caste is only possible through economic empowerment of dalit masses and waging an uncompromising and concerted struggle against its non--economic manifestations.

Can the new regime afford these economic empowerment of dalits? Can it, for instance, grant them land? Does it have the wherewithal or motivation to catalyse their struggles against the caste system? The answer to all these questions will be in negative. Instead of talking of land reforms, the new regime will promote depeasantisation of Indian agriculture and consolidation of their holdings to start corporate farming. Barring perhaps the example of

East Asian countries, the Bretton Wood institutions sponsored reforms have always aggravated the economic inequality everywhere. The experience of other countries where similar Reforms were brought in, bears testimony to the fact that with increasing inequality the social tensions also increased as a result of the Reforms.

The capital influx in the rural areas will have natural ally in the rich farmers who have hegemonic hold over their areas. These sections, will be the main beneficiaries of the improved terms of trade and capitalist development in the rural areas. All the dalits would be thrown into the job market along with many non-dalit marginal to middle farmers. The vast army of unemployed thus created by this developmental dynamics will need appropriate instruments for being controlled. The history bears ample testimony to the fact that whenever the people tended to come together with a common identity, the ruling classes have deftly used the time-tested weapon of castes to divide them. Unlike elsewhere, the Reforms thus are likely to enliven and rejuvenate the archaic value system.

The economic reforms in the mould of macro-economic stabilisation and structural adjustment programme of IMF and World Bank have essentially a pro-rich bias. Wherever they were implemented, they have worsened the situation of the masses of poor people in absolute as well as relative terms. Some contrary data to this general observation (say, of the east Asian countries) are rather attributed to the departures from the standard blueprint given by the Bretton Wood institutions. The dalits in India, being the poorest of the poor have been hit the hardest. Their social disabilities, largely reinforced by and sustained on the economic deprivations, are bound to get accentuated with these policies. The Indian reforms were essentially 'crisis driven' and not 'strategy driven' when they were adopted. There have since been changes in the formation and key persona. The new government for instance has imparted them a form of 'strategy' through their Common Minimum Programme. However, there has not yet been any evidence of this strategy being any different from the course followed by the previous government. The complete discourse of Reforms appears to be either grossly off the mark of Indian reality or to assume out its momentous features. The broad Indian reality is that India has too many poor. As per the Human Development Report, 1996, there are 229 million income poor but more than twice as many, 554 million are capability poor. In terms of capability poverty, its 61.5 % population is poor. Its rank according to descending poverty among the 174 countries of the world, is 135. Even today India is predominantly an agrarian economy, with over 70 per cent of its population living in villages. No statistics moreover can adequately capture the heinous socio-cultural inequality that is an abiding part of Indian reality. It has acute inequalities not only in economic terms but in the socio-cultural terms.

The free market oriented reforms ought to take this grave Indian reality into consideration. Unless there is a wide spread purchasing power in the economy the market can never be free and sustainable. The reform strategy thus should embody sustainable economic empowerment of rural masses; investments to enhance their capability and effective measures for accelerated development of the disadvantaged sections like dalits. The pre-requisite to reforms therefore could be the radical land reforms, massive investments in rural areas into agriculture-related infrastructural projects, universalisation of primary education, primary health care system and reinforcement of positive discrimination in favour of dalits. The devil of casteism could be tamed only by freeing general masses of people from the anxieties and uncertainties about basic survival. The general condition of deprivation has rendered them vulnerable to be the preys to the frequent machinations of the vested interests that make them see the enemy within their own class. The relative equality thus can be the bedrock for launching the socio-cultural offensive in the form of mass-education programmes. But this all may still not be enough. The policy of positive discrimination in favour of dalits will have to be reinforced much more vigorously in all the sectors of economy, than ever before. They need to be reframed and simplified for effective implementation. Unlike the current provisions, this may be stopped once their representation comes on par with the general population. The specific reform package can be formulated in terms of the conditions existing then.

There arises a question of capital. Where will the capital for the investment in basic reforms come from? Not an easy question to answer, indeed. But some pointers may not be impertinent. It is acknowledged since number of years that India has a parallel economy in black money. The recent spate of scams is a mere corroboration of this hypothesis. The Reforms appear to have given them a boost. Whatever little that has surfaced can be likened to a tip of iceberg. Some five years ago, an unofficial estimate by the World Bank had put the unaccounted money of Indians kept in various tax havens at $ 100 billion. As per *Finance India,* (an article in the September 1995 issue) the range of capital outflows was from $ 1065 million to $ 370 million just in one single year-1993. Much of the $ 10 billion money in the non-resident account is said to be belonging to the resident Indians. The evidence of this kind abounds. As against this vast sum of our own money, what the government aims at out of the Reforms is the paltry sum of some four to five billion dollars of foreign direct investment a year to come in the country! The size of the money indicated above, that rightfully belongs to the people of the country, may be good enough for the task. But to unearth this treasure certainly requires a political will. India does not need capital as much as it does the political will to better its destiny.

THE SITUATION OF DALITS IN INDIA

Historically, the caste system classified people by their occupation and status. 'Each caste had a specific place in the hierarchy of social status'. Although in 'scriptural terms' social and economic status were supposed to be separate, the economic and social status of the various castes tended to coincide (Shah, 2006). However, since the 19th century, the link between caste and occupation has become less rigid as it became easier for people to change occupations. This change has accelerated with the economic boom which has taken place in India since the early 1990s. There has not, however, been a corresponding fluidity in caste, as intermarriage is very rare. Privileged sections of society tend to be from 'upper castes' while the disadvantaged sections come from the so-called 'lower castes'. Caste 'can be seen as the institution that has been structuring and maintaining for centuries relations of power among different communities, and seeks to legitimize these power relations through systematically dispensing mixes of economic and cultural assets/ opportunities and deprivations to different communities.'

Many have commented on the robustness of the caste system, 'which has survived in the South Asian societies in one form or the other, despite the fundamental ideological and structural changes that have occurred through the spread of religions like Islam and Christianity as well as of model secular and egalitarian ideologues, all opposed to the very idea of hierarchy based on inherited statuses.'

For Dalits (the term meaning down-trodden or oppressed), at the bottom of this hierarchical system, it is their status as 'untouchables' which puts them at the heart of an insidious form of discrimination. This particular phenomenon results in the social unacceptability amongst people of other castes to touch the same food and utensils, draw water from the same source, or enter the same temples.

The specific structure and hierarchy related to castes is specific to various states and regions in India, with only the highest caste, the Brahmins, consistently faring better throughout the country. Not only are there differences in the names of the various castes, but the hierarchy between them may also be different between regions. However, castes who traditionally suffered discrimination based on untouchability, which was an element of the caste system throughout India, have been identified, enumerated and incorporated in the 'schedule' of the Constitution. 'The implicit criterion for inclusion in the Schedule Caste list is the social and religious disability suffered by a caste on account of untouchability, i.e. being at the pollution end of the social hierarchy.' In defining who would be included in the Schedules, the government originally used the 1931 census report, and to a large extent duplicated a list created in 1936.

Currently, the National Commissions for Scheduled Caste (SC) and Scheduled Tribe (ST) are vested with the responsibility of considering castes for inclusion or exclusion from the Schedule, which then needs to be ratified in Parliament.

The discriminated communities are then officially designated as Scheduled Castes (SCs). Included in the SC category are communities from three different religions, Hinduism, Sikhism and Buddhism, all having within them communities traditionally suffering from untouchability. The term Dalit is the generally accepted term for the 'ex-untouchables', which corresponds to Scheduled Castes, which as mentioned above denotes the legal status as coined in the Constitution.

Mehrotra (2006) recognized that there has been political and social mobilization of SCs in India, particularly in certain poor states such as Uttar Pradesh (UP), which is one of the poorest states in India. However, this mobilization has failed to translate into positive change in the social sector for this excluded population. As Mehrotra wrote, 'while UP's mobilizers of the Dalits (SCs) have focused exclusively on capturing power, the gains to the lowest castes have been entirely of a symbolic nature.'

The Situation of Dalits in Nepal

As in India, the term Dalit is a politically coined word meaning 'the poor and the oppressed' and is less sensitive than the meaning of 'Harijan' or 'Acchhoot' or so-called 'untouchable'. The Nepal Legal Code of 1854, the Muluki Ain, formulated on the basis on Hindu Orthodoxy included five hierarchical categories. They are: i) Tagadhari (wearers of holy thread); ii) Non-enslavable alcohol drinkers (Namsinya matyali), iii) Enslavable alcohol drinkers; iv) Impure but touchable (Pane nachalnya, chhoi chittto hlnu naparani); and v) Untouchable castes (pani nachalnya, choi chhito halnu parniya – caste from whom water is not acceptable and whose touch requires sprinkling of holy water).

It is believed that this caste hierarchy was influenced by political considerations and it was endorsed by state counsellors who were mostly from high castes. It is also accepted that the political ideology of Nepal as a Hindu state (which changed as of 2007 – Nepal has now been designated as a secular state) has remained highly exclusionary. Despite the legal provisions, caste-based discrimination continues to be practised.

Indeed, the Dalits themselves practise discrimination among their own group. Thus there are two kinds of 'untouchabilities': i) between upper caste and Dalits; and ii) within the Dalits. Dalit women and men suffer equally from the practice, but terai Dalits face more discrimination than those living in the hills.

Unlike in India, Nepal has no single defined schedule of castes. Different Dalit organizations such as the Dalit Vikas Sammtte formed in 1997 and the National Dalit Commission have identified different groups as belonging to the Dalit caste. As the list fluctuates, the numbers of the Dalit population also vary according to different sources. Estimates range from 12% to over 20%.

Lack of national consensus on the Dalit population is one of the factors hindering a better understanding of the magnitude of disparity and discrimination faced by the Dalit community.

The Dalit community in Nepal is also not homogenous. Dalits can be examined in three broad regional groups: i) dalits in the hill areas; ii) Dalits in the Newari community; and iii) Dalits in the terai areas. The practice of untouchability is more severe among the Madeshi community in the terai and in the hills of the Mid Western Region and Far Western Development regions of Nepal. Some Dalit groups fare better than others. For example, the literacy rate among the gaine (singers) is 49% and is higher than the national average. The lowest literacy rate is found among the Mushar community, who live in the terai. On most socio-economic indicators, Terai Dalits fare worse than hill Dalits.

The Phenomenon of Untouchability

In order to address the situation of Dalits, it is important to understand the phenomenon of 'untouchability'. The Hindu version of untouchability also has a racial basis as the impure status is based on birth and religion. Bhattachan *et al.* (2002) listed a total of 205 existing practices of caste based discrimination which can be grouped into nine categories. They are: i) denial of entry into houses, restaurants, temples; ii) inability to perform important religious service because wearing a sacred thread is not permitted, etc.; iii) access to common resources such as using water from tap or pond used by upper caste is denied; iv) denial of participation in public activities or entry into public places such as religious functions, government functions; v) forced labour or discriminatory practice of labour; vi) dominant behaviour towards Dalits such as Jadau system (practice of obeisance); vii) atrocities such as more rape cases among Dalit women than others; viii) social boycott – if a 'high caste hindu' member marries with a Dalit of either sex, he or she is banned from the society; ix) Attitudinal untouchability such as if one sees a kami (blacksmith) early in the morning it is considered inauspicious, or if there is a Dalit teacher then children of high caste groups will not attend the school.

Multiple, Overlapping Disparities and Discrimination

These affect Dalits in various spheres of life, including in education. Poverty In *Nepal,* Dalits are poorer than most other social groups. While the proportion of the population below the national poverty line is 31% nationally, 47% of Dalits live below the national poverty line.

Eighty-six per cent of Dalit households have an income lower than the national average. Multiple regression analysis of Nepal Living Standards Survey (NLSS) II data also found: a) per capita consumption of Dalit households is about 46% lower than that of the Brahmin and Chettri (the highest Hindu caste groups); and b) the 'social penalty' for being a Dalit translates to Rs. 4,853 (or US$ 67) less per capita consumption.

Poorer families have less to spend on their children's education. Families in the poorest quintile spend NRs 416 per family on education compared with NRs 8,691 for the richest quintile. Most schools in Nepal rely on families to provide stationery, uniforms and many schools charge exam or registration fees.

Child labour is prevalent among poor families, although employment of children under 14 years as labourers is prohibited by the Child Act 1991. NLSS II found that the proportion of children aged 5–14 who are working and not attending school is highest among the poor (21% in the poorest quintile) and decreases for the richer quintiles.

The opportunity costs of schooling for poor families is significant. Many Dalit families also make a precarious livelihood, earning their income in the informal sector, through daily wage labour, often involving seasonal migration. This insecurity deters families from making longer term investments by educating their children. In *India,* scheduled caste (SC) children remain disadvantaged across many social indicators. Estimates from the 2000 National

Sample Survey suggest that SC 'constituted 20 per cent of the rural population, but 38 per cent of the poor.'

Conflict

The internal conflict in *Nepal,* which expanded in scope and intensity from 1996, affected education and children in many ways, including accelerating the trend of migration (due either to security concerns or difficulties in maintaining livelihood). Family migration to urban centres may disrupt or end children's schooling for financial reasons, because of difficulties in finding places in crowded urban schools, particularly in the middle of a school year, or children not being able to keep up with the classes as the quality of teaching is poorer in rural areas.

Lack of official documents, such as transfer or birth registration documents, can also present an obstacle when transferring to a new school. Migration of male family members may increase the work burden of the remaining members, particularly women, resulting in children being pulled out of school to take on their share of the burden. Children may also be sent away for fear of being arrested, tortured, abducted or recruited by the army, police or Maoist forces. The precise impact of the conflict on Dalit children and their schooling is unknown, but it would be safe to assume that they are more affected due to their lower socio-economic position in society.

For example, a study by the Central Child Welfare Board and Save the Children Alliance found that one third of the 17,583 children found to be leaving Nepal for India during a three month period (July–October 2004) were Dalits.

They were the largest group, followed by Chhetris and Brahmins, who together only constitute 33 per cent of the total population. Despite the progress towards peace in Nepal, issues still exist. Demonstrations by new groups continue to result in closure of schools, and previous dynamics at district level have not yet ceased entirely.

Gender

Since the Dalit society is also systematically integrated in the patriarchal mode of the Hindu caste system, in *Nepal,* the social and economic status of women is much lower than that of men. This is manifested in the lower health and nutritional status of Dalit women, as well as in the political representation of Dalit women, which is negligible. However, as compared with the high caste women, Dalit women have greater mobility. This is due to the economic need to go out and seek for employment and income for their families. Data on literacy rates show the gender disparity among Dalits. Whereas 44% of Dalit men are literate, only 24% of Dalit women reported they could read and write a simple sentence.

Terai Dalits have lower literacy rates than hill Dalits. Poverty affects schooling for girls more than for boys. The gender gap in enrolment is bigger in poorer households than in richer households.

In *India,* the literacy rates of women, SC and ST continue to be below average. The percentage of the ever-married women by caste who are illiterate in India, and in two selected states: Uttar Pradesh, which is one of the most disadvantaged; and Tamil Nadu, which is among the most advantaged states in India.

One can see that there is a significant difference in the level of illiteracy in the two states among all the castes, therefore confirming the significance of disparities between regions in India. However, SC ever-married women were disadvantaged in both states, with 85% of SC women illiterate compared with 57.2% of other higher castes in Uttar Pradesh, and 64.1% of SC women in Tamil Nadu compared with 5.0% of higher castes. Dalit women have to face three pronged discrimination – they are women, they are Dalits and then they are Dalit women.

3

Women's and Dalit Movement

The history of both women's and Dalit movements are five decades old. So far women belonging to the dominant caste-Bahun-Chhetris and the newars dominate women's movement. Most of the leaders of women's right movement do not like an idea of social, cultural and religious pluralism among women. Unfortunately, they wrongly believe that it is divisive and communal. Dalit women and women belonging to other minority groups hardly get any opportunity to hold key positions in such movements.

Therefore, we see negligible presence of Dalit women in the activities and programs organized by the organizations leading women's movement. Dalit movement is also gaining momentum. Although most of the leaders of the Dalit movement are Dalit men, nevertheless Dalit women leaders are also coming up. Dalit women are organized under the feminist Dalit Organization and Dalit NGO Federation with more than fifty affiliated Dalit NGOs is led by many Dalit women. There is no doubt whatsoever that Dalit women can contribute significantly to both women's and Dalit movement in eliminating gender-based and caste-based discrimination respectively. Similarly, Dalit movement also needs strong support of the women's movement. Unfortunately, both movements are heading in two opposite directions concerning mutual help and cooperation.

Victimization by Development Industry and NGOs

In Nepal donors open their wallets for women's empowerment (or gender issues) and poverty alleviation or reduction. Both development industry and NGOs claim to work for women and poor but in reality they sustain status quo. They indeed never reach out to the poorest of the poor, that is Dalit women.

Whether it is the government or non-government, in both sectors high caste men and women reap the harvest. The development industry run by both the government and non-government is more project-oriented than movement-oriented. Democracy is the system that is of the people, to the people and by the people but in Nepal there are organizations which work to the or for the Dalit but they never give opportunity to the Dalit to work by themselves. Some smart Dalit women and men are co-opted by these " main-stream" governmental and non-governmental organizations killing the movement.

Feminization of Poverty and Dalitization

It is indeed true that there has been a feminization of poverty in Nepal. It is also true that there has been dalitization of poverty in Nepal. Combined together Dalit women are at the bottom of poverty and socio-economic discrimination. Clearly they are the double victims of poverty, one as the women and the other as the Dalit. CARE-Nepal (1996:4) has indetified the disadvantaged groups as those groups who are at the lowest social and economic positions, including illiteracy or low literacy. According to this definition, Dalits and indigenous people belong to the disadvantaged groups. If we add another criterion, that is women, in CARE-Nepal's definition of disadvantaged group, Dalit women remain at the bottom.

If we look at the economic and social indicators of Dalits provided by Dr. Shiva Sharma, it becomes clear that there is Dalitization of poverty within the Dalit community the gender proportion of economically active population is 85:101.

Economic Condition

The overall economic condition of most of the Dalits is miserable. It is unfortunate that the Dalits who have traditional skills in sustaining agrarian economy live in poverty.

Lack of Access to and Control Over Resources

Due to dominance of patriarchy originating from Hindu religious norms and values, most of the Nepalese women are deprived from access to and control over economic and other resources. Dalit women have access neither in private sphere nor in public sphere due to continuing practices of patriarchy and untouchability. Few Dalit women, as exceptions, may have some access to resources but they may not have any control over them. Displacement from traditional occupation and lack of employment in both agriculture and non-agriculture sectors are common problems of Dalit women and men. Dr. Haribansha Jha (1999), an economist, has estimated that about 68 percent total

Nepalese population who live below the absolute poverty line most of them are Dalits. In a country where Dalit men are suffering from the problem of unemployment it is difficult to imagine about employment of Dalit women.

There is no doubt whatsoever those Dalit women and men are rich in skills related to their traditional occupations. The processes of modernization or Westernization, urbanization, globalization and liberalization that have been unfolding in the last five decades have further marginalized knowledge, skills and products based on the Dalits' traditional occupations. Dr. Haribansha Jha (1999:4) has noted that the Hill Dalits, such as Tatma, Khatbe, Mushar and Dom have lost market of their traditional skills and products. Such processes of marginalization have pushed them to rely on agriculture or non-agriculture sector but there too they have no place for employment. In such a situation women become the hardest hit victims of poverty. In Nepal, ownership of land means a lot in terms of wealth, power and prestige.

For the middle and low class people, ownership of land means self-employment and non-ownership means unemployment. Data of Dalits' land owners 23 percent are landless, 48.7 percent own less than 5 ropanies, 15.6 percent own 6 to 10 ropanies, and 9.6 percent own 10 to 20 ropanies and 3.1 own more than 21 ropanies of land. If we mix up data of the Dalits and some selected indigenous peoples as done by Shiva Sharma (1999:11), about 60 percent and if we analyze the data of the Dalits only then about 88 percent families are unable to make a living from their land. Thus they are forced to find employment in agriculture or non-agriculture sectors but employment in these sectors are simply not available. Lack of land ownership and denial of purchasing milk produced by Dalits by the diary industries have made it impossible for the Dalits to engage in animal husbandry.

Activities Required for the Socio-Economic Upliftment of Dalit Women

To uplift the socio-economic condition of the Dalit women, His Majesty's Government of Nepal (HMG-Nepal), donors, women's rights activists and Dalits should do the following activities:

1. While preparing long-term and short-term plans and budgets Dalits should also be allowed to participate in the decision making process. In the case of plan and programs for Dalit women, Dalit women also should be allowed to make decisions while preparing such plans and programs. The continuing practices of for or to the Dalit women and men should be abandoned.
2. HMG-N should identify the Dalits and list in the Nepal Gazette.

3. All government documents should include issues and problems of and policies, strategies, and programs for the Dalits in general and Dalit women in particular.
4. Both HMG-N and all international donors, including multi-lateral, bio-lateral and INGOs should make sure that Dalits participate in the decision making process concerning planning, designing and implementing programs or projects. If Dalit organizations need capacity building, such programs should also be implemented.
5. HMG-N should formulate and implement positive discrimination of affirmative action for the Dalits in general and Dalit women in particular. Also, Dalit Women's department and Dalit Women's Cell should be established in the Ministry of Women, including ministries of education, health, agriculture and forest.
6. Both HMG-N and the donors should accept the fact that the battle against poverty, illiteracy and socio-cultural discrimination can not be fought if the plans and programs are not Dalit-centred. It must be realized that the development of Dalit women and men means the development of Nepal as well. Without their development, particularly of the Dalit women, development of Nepal would be a mirage.
7. Dalit women should claim and find their due space in the "main stream" women's movement. Also, Dalit women should be organized in such a way that they themselves should be able to launch a strong movement even at the streets. The "main stream" women's movement also thinks seriously to give due space to Dalit women without whose support women's movement would never achieve its mission and goals.
8. Each Dalit caste should get organized at the national level and all such castes should be federated into a Dalit Federation. All Dalit caste organizations should work together for the common causes and issues to fight against the continuing Brahmanism. Each Dalit caste should form its own women's organization.
9. Dalit women (and also men) should form and alliance with other victims of Brahmanism (Bahunbad) and seek their help and support for their liberation. The most natural allies of the Dalits are indigenous people. In any case, Dalit movement should be intensified (Bhattachan 2056).
10. The human rights organizations and human rights activists of Nepal should take up the issue of untouchability and plight of the Dalits very seriously. Effective implementation of the convention on All Forms of

Discrimination Against Women (CEDAW) and the Convention Against All Forms Racism and racial Discrimination are important for the upliftment of Dalit women.

DALIT FISHING WOMEN, STRUGGLING WOMEN

We met some 150 of the Dalit women from this village, in a community visit organized by Tamil Nadu Women's Movement. We were welcomed with so much energy and excitement-lots of drum playing, flowers and warm embraces. Heavy garlands were put around our necks; tikka, tumeric powder made into paste, was put on our forehead; and misri which were sugar crystals were placed on our tongue. While we were all standing there, with amazement and anticipation, two women came in front of us-one holding a brass bowl, the other a coconut husk, each with flames inside.

Both women raised the bowl and husk, and moved them in circular motion around us-to welcome us, and to drive away evil spirits. And that was how we started our gathering-with a lot of good will, sisterhood, and laughter in our hearts. Throughout the sharing, one would see that it is with the same level of energy, and more, and with strong spirit that they confront and fight against those who come and threaten their survival as a community. The Chinnu Aqua Farm Private Limited which was established in Chennai and started operating three years ago would definitely know how it is to be on the other side of this-how the Dalit women can make someone feel oh so unwelcome.

Umapathy

She is part of the sixth generation who has lived in Kolathur, and has been living and working on lands which were never put in their names. Umapathy and her husband would work on these farms owned by the upper caste men. She would grow and take care of the fruit trees surrounding her house, but were never allowed to touch any of the mangoes, jack fruits and coconut from these trees without the permission of the owners. The other families in her community would be working on agricultural lands of the upper caste men where they would cultivate paddy, ragi and groundnuts.

Umapathy, along with the other Dalit women in the village, used to spend hours in the backwater to gather prawns and fish with her hands. After selling them, she would earn 100Rps/150 Rps at the end of the day. This would be enough for food for her family. Today, she could not spend that long in the water, which meant lesser catch, and lesser food for her family. On the other hand, the agricultural lands were sold by the upper caste men to Chinnu Aqua Farm. This meant no more paddy, ragi and groundnuts to grow on. Umapathy of course has no input whatsoever in the decision of the upper caste men. She and the other members of the Dalit community were simply workers on these lands.

Kalpana

Just 25 years old, one would think Kalpana had lived her life three times over, for how else would she gain so much courage and determination to fight the aqua farm, the uppercaste men supporting it, and the Indian bureaucracy who make it almost impossible for the Dalit community to legally and peacefully challenge its operations. Perhaps it's giving birth on top of a hill after running away from the tsunami waves. Or simply being a Dalit mother who knows that fighting is the only way to survive. Kalpana tells us about the public distribution system in Tamil Nadu. It is a fairpriced shop of basic products-rice, oil, soap, sugar. There used to be a 3 Rp subsidy from the government for all products, then was reduced to 2 Rp subsidy. However, she could not avail of these subsidized products as much as she needs to. As a Dalit woman, she could not stand in line to cue along with non-Dalit, upper caste people. Thus, she had to wait when she could fall in line. By that time, all the basic products she needed would be all gone.

Most of the time, she would go after fishing, and by that time, the shop is already closed. Fishing in the backwaters now takes longer, as the prawns, crabs and other fish are harder to find. They are dying, and disappearing. "Where can we go for food? Where can we go to fish?" asked Kalpana. "The shrimp farm has taken over." Kalpana is one of the more active Dalit women who organizes community actions for their voices to be heard, and to campaign against the aqua farm.

Shanti

"I used to catch enough prawns to earn decent living for my 4 children," Shanti said. "Then came Chinnu Aqua Farm." The prawns and other living organisms in the backwater were found dying, in the increasingly polluted backwaters. Now, they can catch worth 30-40 Rp a day, less than a US dollar. Then the tsunami came in 2004.

Their area is part of the badly hit area in the Indian coast. Though not as bad as the other villages in Indonesia, Sri Lanka and Thailand, for Shanti and her family, the impact was bad enough to make their lives more difficult. Their house was heavily damaged, and lost most of whatever they had.

However, they received no compensation from the government as they were not considered affected, being on the side of the backwaters. The relief packages never reached their villages, as these were handled by upper caste people. "Life as Dalit is hard enough. The Chinnu Aqua Farm is making our lives even more so."

Rajam

Rajam was supposed to be one of our resource persons in a workshop on tsunami and women's rights that APWLD organized last year in Aceh. But she wasn't able to process the necessary documents for her to travel abroad. She has a police record. She was one of the 33 Dalit women who were beaten up and arrested by the police men two years ago.

Rajam and some 2,000 other villagers blocked the road to the shrimp farm, as one of their acts of resistance. Rajam is one of the more vocal and active in resisting the shrimp farm, making her more vulnerable to harassment and violence. One of the women stood up while Rajam was telling her story. She said that when police came, the men ran away and left the women.

This drew laughter among the women who were all in agreement with the remark; even among the few men who were standing nearby. But while that lightened the mood a bit, the intensity of the anger and frustration was determined to be felt.

Rajam went on to talk about the different ways and actions the communities are taking to reclaim their source of livelihood and their way of living-peaceful protest actions, dialogues with the officials, asking the help of the media people to expose what's happening in their villages. There was one attempt by some unknown people to poison the aqua farm. As a consequence, the security in the premises was tightened; ferocious dogs are now milling around the farm. There was one incident when one of the dogs bit one of the farmers who was passing through. When we were there, a fact-finding mission has just been conducted; and a legal suit was filed against the aqua farm.

Kaliyammal

She came to me after we all had our lunch. We sat away from the big group as she wanted to show me something. She showed me her arms, where her skin was intensely dry. She lifted her sari to show her skin below her breasts, in her midrib, inner thighs, legs-scaly whitish skin. These were Kaliyammal's body parts which were regularly immersed in the backwaters, as she would go fishing.

Wading through the waters until chest level, Kaliyammal and other Dalit women would stay there and catch prawns, crabs, lobsters with their bare hands for hours. She has been doing this since her younger years. But lately, the itchiness on her arms and everywhere else has become unbearable. She stopped fishing. Her other companions had similar health problems, and more-some are suffering with white discharge and urinary infection. Kaliyammal had to rely now on her children who are working in salt marsh for support. The other Dalit women are now relying on the produce of their fishing husbands. The fisher men who use boats and large nets, go further and deeper for fishing, for bigger catch.

Chinnu Aqua Tech Private Limited

When the Chinnu Aqua Tech fenced off the shrimp farm and started their operations, other major changes started to happen. As the barbed wire fences were to prevent the villagers to come inside the shrimp farm and cause problems, these fences were not enough to contain the problems within it. The effects of the shrimp farm go well beyond double its size; and profit from this for one corporation, outweighs the number of lives it has destroyed. But the company flatly denied they were causing these problems. When faced with the protests and criticisms, they would simply brandish the permit they have acquired from the pollution board. Indeed, they have a permit.

So what does the permit cover? Basically, the permit issued by the pollution board meant that the company has met the anti-pollution standards and that therefore, the Chinnu Aqua Tech can operate. What does this exactly allow the company to do? The permit practically allows the Chinnu Aqua Tech to suck large amount of water from the backwater and fresh groundwater to recreate the environment that shrimps thrive in. To keep the shrimp pond clean, water has to be changed daily. The shrimp ponds are stocked with shrimp larvae, usually not of the endemic specie of the local area. To prevent then the shrimp population from getting sick as it is not adjusted to the local environment, the ponds are pumped with pesticides and antibiotics. So when they clean the pond, the water flushed out from these ponds is filled with chemicals. And this goes to the river, or sea. In Kolathur's case, the polluted water goes to the backwaters, where Kaliyammal and the other Dalit women fish. This permit then, is a permit to cause health problems to fisherwomen such as skin, eye and cervical infections. The permit, further, allows the Chinnu Aqua Tech to poison, and so, eliminate the shrimps, lobsters, crabs, mussels that the Kolathur fisherwomen have been living on for generations. The permit, basically, is a permit to eliminate the Kolathur villagers.

Resistance

The songs, dances and drum beating which followed the story-telling were equally passionate. If only these would be enough to lure the shrimp farm businessmen into the circle of the Dalit women and realize that this spirit is what the shrimps in their ponds are destroying. But that would be too naive of me to think. The lure of profit is too strong. Profit has destroyed nations, and peoples. For them, what is one poor village to dispense with. Laughter, they say, is the best medicine-too bad laughter is not enough to cure the skin peeling off, nor the cervical infections; the mirth in our conversations which enthralled me and my companions who came all the way from Kyrgyzstan, the hills of Chittagong and Nepal, from the plains of Philippines, Burma, Thailand, and the shores of Sri Lanka, will not be enough to bring back the shrimps and crabs into the backwaters of Kolathur to once again bring livelihood to its women. But is the courage and determination of the Dalit women to fight their ground, and their waters, which will bring changes in the Bay of Bengal. It is with the solidarity of women across seas and mountains which will ensure that the voices of Kaliyammal and Umapathy will be heard, and the struggle of Shanti and Rajam will be duplicated, inspiring other women to resist and defend their songs, their laughter, their lives.

HISTORY OF ANTI-CASTE MOVEMENTS

But reservations for the OBCs have come to stay. Unlike the superficial portrayal which depicts V.P. Singh as the villain who has suddenly opened the Pandora's box of reservation for the OBCs, the social and political implications of the aspirations of those downtrodden in Indian society, has been with us before independence and during the past four decades. These facts of history are deliberately suppressed by the likes of Arun Shourie who have railed against reservations. He is only being consistent in his Hindu upper-casteist outlook. Advocating the "shifting" of Babri Masjid from its site in Ayodhya and pouring scorn over the aspirations of the lower castes, are both of one piece.

An aspect of the prolonged struggle against upper-caste domination was the non-Brahmin movements in the south and in Maharashtra for well over a century. In the north, the anti-caste social reform movements had a belated start. Bihar saw this phenomenon earlier than in other north-Indian States. In the pre-independence period, these anti-caste movements spearheaded the fight against the upper caste domination. Their main weakness lay in their alienation from the anti-imperialist movement a feature due also to the approach of the Congress party. It sought to fight caste-domination not by advocating a thorough-going agrarian revolution which could have altered the relations of production in agriculture, but by an upper-caste approach of reformism which was exemplified by Gandhism, both before and after independence, with its reliance on preaching against untouchability by inter-caste dining, inter-caste marriages, and of course reservations.

Need of Agrarian Revolution

The Marxist analysis of contemporary reality holds that the anti-caste movement, if it is to be successful in eliminating caste domination, requires linking the anti-caste movements with the movement for agrarian revolution, for building the unity of the working people, and advancing the democratic movement. Where this task remain unaccomplished, or where this impulse is weak, the consciousness of the oppressed mass within the lower caste considers reservations as the only safeguard for their advancement. The working class party, therefore, while supporting reservations, seeks to strengthen its links with the rural mass which will be a main force of the agrarian revolution.

At the same time, it also considers the building of unity of the toiling people of all castes to be the crucial question. Unfortunately, some sections of the intelligentsia with democratic inclinations are opposing reservations for the OBCs on the plea that it perpetuates casteism and fragments society. This is to ignore the fact that it is the casteism of the upper-castes attendant with the monopoly of the means of production, which has perpetuated backwardness. If with capitalist development, class and caste alignments are getting redefined and divergent, the end to casteism and building class-based movements requires a dual approach.

The CPI(M) recognises that a big section of the working people come from castes and communities who, though not belonging to the SCs or OBCs, are economically exploited and suffer from social deprivation. They constitute an important and advanced section of the democratic movement. The modern working class and the organised movement of the working people can advance only the basis of the unity of both sections of the working people — the advanced sections of the urban working people and rural mass who suffer from both caste and economic oppression. Those who advocate reservations without any restrain and recklessly compete to hike up quotas for the backward classes and scheduled castes are not mindful of the vital need for unity. Their stand mirrors the approach of those upper caste sections who seek to oppose any increase in reservations as a threat to their interests. Both the proreservationist and the anti-reservationist leaders work within the bourgeois mould and foster the illusion that the distribution of the limited number of jobs at stake is a life and death question for the advancement of their communities. Both these approaches have to be countered and the working people of both sections mobilised on a common platform. Let it be emphasised that reservations alone cannot solve any of the basic problems facing the socially and economically oppressed.

Protect Unity

The CPI(M) attitude to OBC reservation stems from its class standpoint. It seeks the unity of the toiling people, of all castes, both urban and rural, against the main exploiters who perpetuate a social system which is retrogressive. This unity is necessary to fight monopoly capital and concentration of wealth which should unite both the forwards and backwards who comprise the working class. It is necessary to fight landlordism, for which the entire rural poor has to be mobilised breaking caste oppression and divisions. The democratic sections amongst the toilers not covered by reservations, both working class and peasantry, have to accept the necessity for reservations, so that overall unity can be cemented.

Call of the 13th Party Congress

Unlike the past, the CPI(M) cannot see the anti-caste struggles as only a sphere for social reform. The Left has to channelise this anti-feudal current into its agrarian movement. The Thirteenth Congress of the CPI(M), in its Political Resolution, addressed itself to the situation of the masses belonging to these downtrodden castes and state: "Large sections from these masses often stand alienated from the democratic and working class movement, and are swayed by sectional leadership which diverts their discontent and anger into narrow channels. The period since our last Congress has witnessed a new militant awakening among these sections — the adivasis, harijans and backward classes. It is necessary to make all efforts to draw this new awakening to the common struggle developing a correct attitude and tactics towards their organisation".

The resolution proceeds to point out that the successive Congress Governments have attempted to rally these sections, tempting them with the promise of reservation of jobs in Government service. "This was also a device to bypass the question of land reforms and redistribution of land". Since reservations cater only to a small minority amongst them, "the growing misery of the uneducated mass is bursting forth in militant protest and action.

These protests against social discrimination, caste tyranny, police repression, are at present carried out under the leadership of their caste leaders. They represent the anti-feudal, anti-landlord discontent of these agrarian masses."

The resolution exhorts: "The Party, the democratic movement and class organisations should led support to their struggle against caste tyranny and repression, and enable them and their organisations to join the common struggle." This applies to the SC and ST, toiling sections as well to the oppressed in the OBCs.

BJP's, Cong(I)'s Double Standards

The RSS has come out openly against the declared reservations for the OBCs. Denouncing V.P. Singh, the Organiser stated: "He wants to undo the great task of uniting Hindu society from the days of Vivekananda, Dayanand Saraswati, Mahatma Gandhi and Dr Hedgewar." The RSS view, not surprisingly, is governed by its Hindu chauvinist upper-caste bias. Notwithstanding the official position of the BJP leadership, that reservation should be there with an economic criterion, its ranks are active in the student agitation.

One of its M.P.s, Dr. J.K. Jain, went on a hunger strike against the announcement. Both the BJP and Congress(I) activists are actively competing to lead the anti-reservation agitation. Their representatives in the executive of the Delhi University Teachers Association have ganged up to try and pass a resolution condemning the implementation of the OBC reservations. From these activities it seems that for these parties, (unlike the CPI(M), the demand for an economic criterion is not meant to improve the scheme of reservations, it is a ploy to try and scuttle its implementation.

Responsibility of Democratic Forces

One has to condemn the manoeuvrings of bourgeois political leaders who seek to make reservation a device for consolidating their influence and thereby fan caste divisions and divide the people. This is a cynical manipulation of the aspirations of the most oppressed sections in the downtrodden castes. At the same time, the advanced democratic movement, the fighting organisations of the different sections of the people have a heavy responsibility before them:

1. To oppose movements against reservations.
2. At the same time, explain to the democratic sections not entitled to reservations, the necessity to accept this limited concession to those deprived of the capacity for equal competition due to historical-social conditions.

3. Counter caste-exclusive movements which stress only reservations and seek to keep the SC or reserved categories of employees and workers away from the common movement. This requires championing their special demands and problems.

Strengthen the United Fight

All efforts must be made to see that people do not get divided on the reservation question. For this, it is essential that the struggle to change the present direction of policies is stepped up. The National Front Government has promised the right to work in the Constitution; it is yet to be implemented. The struggle to expand employment and ensure the right to work can be the basis of the broadest unity encompassing the crores of the unemployed. In the sphere of land reforms, the fight to distribute land already identified as surplus (63 million acres) but not taken over the distributed by the Government (58.5 million acres), provides the basis for uniting the rural poor. The right to education and expansion of education facilities to make them accessible to all is vital in view of the continuing trend to restrict higher education and neglect the primary school sector. If increased reservations in educational institutions are there, it must go hand in hand with compensatory increases in seats in higher education, so that no one deserving is deprived of higher education.

The National Front Government has been unable to make a radical break with the old economic policies of the Congress. It has no plan to revive the over two lakh sick units which are closed in the industrial sector; its industrial policy pronouncements with a bias to foreign capital and privatisation will restrict the scope of employment. It has not withdrawn the ban on recruitment in Government services and public sector undertakings. Many State Governments do not want to proceed of land reforms on the specious plea that its implementation is completed. All these policies have to be reversed, and this requires the broadest unity of all sections of the people.

The stand taken by the CPI(M) Politbureau and Central Committee on the OBC reservations, in practice, is the way the unity of the people, the toiling sections can be maintained and strengthened to see that the main struggle against the bourgeois-landlord system further advances.

SITUATION OF DALIT WOMEN

The ignorance to the Dalit women by the Government is the common case. On top of that, the political parties and the international aid agencies have ignored them. They are similarly neglected by Nepalese women's movement. Women activists in Nepal never tried to merge Dalit women in their movement. They hardly pay attention towards Dalit women. They advocate for the women in general in their manifestoes and constitutions. But, while the question on Dalit woman is raised, they stay with folding hands. Voiceless Dalit women, therefore, are deprived of their rightful place in the governance process. It is an irony that even the Dalit activists raise the issue of Dalit males and largely overlook the case of Dalit women. It is a fact that no political parties have supported Dalit women by way of associating them at different levels. In the Nepalese context, gender, caste and ethnicity are the three interlocking institutions or critical fault lines defining social identity.

The constitution has enshrined for equality and equal opportunity before the law. But these three groups and communities are subject to exploitation, discrimination and unfair treatment. One Human development and welfare indicators states: Nepali women are almost invisible in the civil service making up only 8% of overall staff and 4% of officers. There is hardly any representation of Dalit women in public services. Dalit women's literacy rate account for 9% compared to 42.9% on national average (CBS, 2001). Their life expectancy remains the lowest among Nepalese women: 42 years (Mushar women) while national average stands for 59.8 years. High rate of infant mortality, child mortality and maternal death amongst the Dalit women are serious problems. A small tribe namely the Badi women are still forced to continue the traditional prostitution. They suffer from trafficking and prostitution due to their poverty and ignorance. Similarly, the Dalits are highly disadvantaged groups. Dalit females have one of the lowest levels of literacy of all groups in Nepal. Their low level of literacy is due to three interrelated factors:

- Continued monopolization of so-called high caste women and men,
- The stronger influence of casteism in rural areas on Dalit females, and
- The control of Dalit males over Dalit women and girls.

As a consequence, Dalit females' access to even basic literacy education is limited. As mentioned above, Dalit women's literacy rate accounts for 9% compared to 42.9% on national average (CBS, 2001). Close to 95% of Dalit women are rural; most are landless or marginal farmers who live in subject of poverty with grinding labour. Many work as day-to-day manual workers. Wage of the women is less than that of men. Their economic situation has worsened due to the overall deteriorating rural economic conditions over the centuries. In all cases of caste conflict, the Dalit women are first victims.

They are raped, gang raped and even made pregnant showing the temptation of marriage and finally left. Even though these incidences of violence against women are extreme, nevertheless, some of these caste biases exist in schools among Hindu teachers. In addition, Dalit females are invisible in school curriculums and textbooks.

There are still various words and sentences hostile to the dignity of Dalit and women. Malnutrition among Dalit women is high. Controls by men over women starts as a girl child where infant mortality due to neglect and malnutrition is very high.

Many Dalit girls and women are used and abused by drunken male relatives. The sexual division of labour, child marriage and restricted mobility also limit Dalit females' access to education. Most importantly, it must address issues important to Dalit women and be accompanied by other social and economic reforms such as the following; sanitation, health, childcare, credit and loans, land reform, conservation, reservation and scholarship for Dalit women.

EXISTING POSITIVE ACTIONS FOR WOMEN AND DALITS AND IMPACT UPON DALIT WOMEN

There are about 150 existing positive legal provisions and policies for the substantial change of women at large Though, in general, these provisions were made intentionally to upgrade the status of women, only few from so called high caste and class women have benefited to a larger extent only. No impact on the Dalit women is seen so far.

Actions for Women

- Reservation of Women in National Assembly: There is also a provision in the constitution for three seats in the National Assembly of the Parliament. Only the women from so called high caste have got the advantage by this provision. There is not any instance of the Dalit woman as beneficiary of this provision.
- 5% candidacy from women for House of Representatives is mandatory to all political parties. But the practice has shown that only elite women have succeeded and benefited by this provision. Since personal identity of a candidate rather than of political parties is the attraction, the political parties fear to put candidature from Dalit community.
- Reservation in Local bodies: In the Local Self-governance Act, there is a provision of the reservation to women for at least one seat in ward Committee. But no Dalit woman benefited by this provision. Similarly there is a provision for the participation of women in the Development

Council. Nominal Dalit women have got chance to participate in the Local Councils at the Municipal, Village Development Committee and District levels.

- Free Education: The education act obliged all state schools for free education to women. However, Dalit women are not able to have such access due to early marriage and low economic status.
- Mandatory Provision for Inclusion of Women: For the compulsory participation of women in all committees, this provision has been made in various laws i.e. consumer law, local motion pictures, central children welfare, steering committee of local development, breast feeding protection and promotion committee.
- Scholarship: The scholarship rule has mandated for 20% reservation in scholarship. But none from among the Dalit girls could benefit from this arrangement. Every seat is provided to the so-called higher castes girls and the girls of high economic profile.
- Women's Bodies to be searched by Women Police: If the body of woman has to be searched in connection with investigation of a crime, the search has to be conducted by women police without insulting her. Under the existing arrangement, the body of a Badi woman is searched by male police even without prior notice, which is not only objectionable but an insult to the pride of the women folk.
- Relaxation in Age for Civil Service: The civil service rule (amendment) has relaxed the age limitation for the enrolment for public services to women. Maximum age limit for women to join civil service is 40 years, whereas it is only 35 in case of men. But, there lacks the record of the beneficiary from Dalit women by this provision. Major beneficiaries of this provision of reservation are women from the forward castes.
- National Commission for Women: The Commission is established with a view to protecting and promoting the women's rights. But, the composition of this Commission lacks any representation form Dalit women. As such, the Dalit women have not got any positive feeling towards this institution.

Actions for Dalits

- Deprived, Depressed and Dalit Community: His Majesty's Government has established this community with a view to planning and executing the welfare policies for Dalit, but there is no any woman's representation in the composition. The males dominate the committee. This situation is self-defeating as the women from Dalit community have no control over the policy and programmes executed through this body.

- Committee for Formulating Reservation Policy: The Government has formulated a main committee under the chairmanship of Finance Minister and several sub-committees with a view to formulating the model of reservation policy to women, Dalit and Janajati. But apparently, there lacks representation of Dalit women in any committees.
- National Dalit Commission: A single Dalit woman was appointed in the commission out of ten members from the Dalit community. There were several claims that there existed potential candidates from the Dalit women for this august body.

Though the government has taken several positive actions for the gender justice Dalit women are considered neither at the time of planning nor in the executing of the policies.

AFFIRMATIVE ACTION ELSEWHERE

With the transformation of the nature of state structure, it becomes the liability of all state to initiate the welfare programs for the marginalized communities. The motto of democracy itself advocates for the rule of law and wide participation. Wide participation and rule of law will not be meaningful, without giving due respect to the empowerment of all backward and marginalized communities. Various states have included the reservation policy for women, backwards and handicapped. Few examples are: In South Africa, an Employment Equity Act was promulgated with a view to empowering the blacks. This Act has come for promoting equal opportunity, implementing affirmative action measures to redress disadvantaged in employment experienced by designated groups to ensure their equitable representation in all occupational categories. The Act goes also to elaborate measures that constitute affirmative actions.

These measures are to be taken by employers to ensure that members of designated groups are adequately represented in the workforce and equal opportunity to compete for and advance in jobs. In India serious efforts are being made towards the enhancement of their participation as well as imparting training to the elected women representatives. The members of women elected to the rural and urban bodies in Karnataka exceed the mandatory reserved for them. Districts are selected as the population of Dalit women in the constituency. Under the 1983 Karnataka Act, 25% seats were reserved for women. The reservation for the SC and ST was in the proportion to their population. The new law of 1993 reserves one-third seats for women (from all caste categories) and one-third for backward classes. The amended 1995

Act provides for reservation of seats for the SCs and STs and the OBCs and women on rotation basis. There is a provision for not less than one third of the total no. of seats to be reserved for women, which includes not less than one third of the seats reserved for SCs and STs belonging to these respective categories.

DEMAND FOR PRO DALIT WOMEN MEASURES

Time has come to execute the affirmative action policies and implementation as well. Realizing the need of the reservation for bringing the disadvantaged community into the mainstream of the governance process, the government has called for formulation of the reservation policy to the marginalized communities namely; women, Janajati and Dalit. Affirmative policy is generally perceived as steps taken to correct historical disadvantages a n d unfair discrimination by enabling access to full opportunities and benefits.

Therefore, the Dalit women should be given specific focus. There should be 10% reservation in Dalit reservation and 10% in reservation for Dalit women. Otherwise only the creamy layer or the forward women will be benefited and rest of the real oppressed women will not be benefited which is not real objective of the reservation policy. Within the women and Dalits, there should specific provision for Dalit women and ensure their participation in policy formulation positions as well.

Other Program oriented activities to be focused are:

- Revise the civil service curriculums and make it Dalit women friendly,
- Create one contact officer in all ministries,
- Family friendly provision should be made for public services like day care, husband and wife in same district, increased maternity mourning leave and paternity protection,
- Gender audit specific reference with Dalit women,
- Dalit women should be given information about the positive policies and provisions and their impact,
- Programs should be framed for the voters' education and for their encouragement in the contest of election.

Following measures are recommended in the plan on reservation:

- Specific land reform and allocation programs should be implemented where the population of Dalit women is high. Allocation of state resources for the advancement of women's equality is essential for the fulfilment of the state parties obligations under the ratified international human rights instruments also,

- Skill providing program should be launched and provide them the job as per their skill for their economic survival.
- Specific programs should be planned for exemption of loans to Dalit women.
- There should be provision for compulsory and free education. Mere free education is not enough. The school-going children, particularly from the Dalit communities, should be provided necessary books, bags and school materials as per their needs free-of-cost.
- For the participation in civil service, the curriculum for examination should be made Dalit women friendly. These women should be provided travel cost, relaxation in fees and extra costs. Provision should be made for preferences to Dalit women in coaching classes. Separate merit list system should be made for encouraging them to be participated in public services.
- Seats should be separated for Dalit women in gazetted class.
- Participation in political and public life has traditionally been regarded as a male dominated sector in Nepal. However, women have been active in various political movements and benefited. But Dalit women are not included within the ambit of political beneficiaries. The factors behind this are their illiteracy, lack of resources and support for their mobility. So, for their political participation, there should be specific provision in the constitution and other laws for the reservation for women. In them Dalit women also should be given special preferences.
- Dalit women are in a disadvantaged position in every sphere of political life. Therefore, 10% seats in constitutional bodies, commissions, committees and mission should be separated from the quotas visualized for women in general.

SOCIAL AND POLITICAL BACKGROUND OF THE DALIT MOVEMENT

Jotirao Phule's first activities were completely based on education of the lower class masses. He was for sure aware of the reason of the backwardness of his people, which have been held away from any form of education for thousands of years. Modern teaching was first established in the Mesopotamian area 4 millenniums before Christ. But the lower castes of Hindu society were intentionally kept illiterate with the help of peoples' religious beliefs.

- The change was to come through education. In the beginning, as told earlier, Mahars tried to push their children into the public schools run by the government or by the missions. When they realised that this was not enough, they started establishing their own schools.

Being aware of this fact Jotirao Phule knew that to overcome the millenniums long Brahman superiority the only way was to create a literate society and also Dalit intellectuals.

- Phule had begun his social service activity with schools for Untouchables and women; had founded the Satyashodhak Samaj with backing from the well-to-do non-Brahmans, primarily contractors and a few professionals; and had moved fairly quickly to establish a peasant base."

When it is considered that the low castes had always been the majority of the over populated India (Shudras 58%, untouchables 24% apprx.) , we have to assume that those movements were a drop in the ocean. Because of the completely ignorance of the low castes against any intellectual human ideology whether coming from West or India, the organizational and institutional besides cultural development of the low caste society was too slow, when compared to the literate Brahman society. Following the struggle put forward by Phule, there were still only two or three newspapers were being published by the Dalit society. This is an indication of the poor environment for the ideas to flourish and the low number of people who were really capable of intellectual communication. But for the Brahmans the situation was different. Phule mentions this situation in his famous book "Slavery: (Under the Cloak of Brahmanism)".

- All the editors of the Marathi papers in Poona are Brahmins and they naturally do not want to write anything against their own caste-men. The Chairman of the Municipality was an Englishman and he would not allow the trickery of the Bhat. All the Bhats then raised a chorus of criticism (a hue and cry) against him to the effect that his policies were harmful to the interests of the riots, which were totally untrue; they ganged up against him and troubled him a lot. Finally he was so disgusted with the shabby situation that he resigned his chairmanship in sheer exasperation and washed his hands of the Municipal Committee thenceforth.

What we learn from Phule is the strength of Brahman bureaucracy inside the British administration and also the intellectual environment where all of the editors of the papers are Brahmins. The harsh reality, which is the illiteracy of the non-Brahman people, made the whole Dalit movement mostly a peasant movement rather than an urban and intellectual movement from the very beginning. It was not easy to produce thousands of intellectual in one day, but it was possible to talk to crowds and tell them what situation they were in. Because of this fact the political Dalit movement had easily found ground over the non- Brahman masses.

- The work of Phule and his colleagues has to be understood in this context. Phule's own writings reflect its sporadic nature of non- Brahman organizational development: they are unsystematic, sporadic, pictorial rather than discursive, hard-hitting but designed more to shock people into an awareness of the situation than to provide an extensive analysis. And he notes in the introduction to Sarvajanak Satya Dharma he had wanted to write a more thorough book but felt it was more important for the book to be useful to the daily life of the people. Non-Brahman leaders it was more important to speak to the masses than to engage in finely spun analysis.

Politics and the Dalit Movement : Satyashodhak Samaj

Phules movement became an institution when he established 'Satyashodhak Samaj' on 24th September 1873 in order to institutionalise social education, and have a continuous follow up. In order to destroy social and religious slavery, the Satyashodhak Samaj established by Jotirao, emphasised and re-emphasised the following:

- Humans are great by their qualities.
- Incantations, penance, rituals, rebirth- do not have any reality.
- Bhat (Brahmins) or middlemen are not at all necessary for the worship of the Almighty.

Satyashodhak Samaj was a suitable tool for Phule's mass movement to spread the ideals of equality, brotherhood, non-requirement of middlemen in religious matters. Satyashodhak movement did not have the chance to become a political movement until the 1920's. Because most of the time, Samaj was felt short of the support of aristocratic non-Brahmans as well as the support of educated and professional non-Brahmans. Most of the educated non-Brahmans became part of Brahman social classes after they managed to enter the British administration. Even during the 1910's where some of the educated non- Brahmans used the movement for their very political purposes without becoming a member. The elite support did not come from the educated non-Brahmans but it came from the wealthy non-Brahman businessman. With the process of the forming of Indian identity Satyashodhak Samaj slowly disintegrated and later in the 1930's completely dissappeared. And new actors entered the scene as the protector of the lower castes and one of them was Dr. Ambedkar.

Satyashodhak Samaj and Identity

Identity had been defined within caste context in India for the last two and a half millenniums. But within the intellectual environment of enlightement, new definitions had to be accepted. The lower castes and especially untouchables began feeling the need for an escape from the cruel realities created by the Brahmanic social system. They were also trapped in the new situation created by the West where an Indian and Hindu identity was forming against the British imperia. The Aryan theory was not first established in India and it was not for the Indians. It was a tool for some of the new powerfull nations of Europe to legalize their existence and power historically. This need will later give the birth to the fascist and national socialistic ideologies all over the continent. With the Aryan theory it was possible to for the Europeans to claim that their rule over the world was natural and this happened to be a historical fact which was also in close connection to the idea of superiority.

Especially Friedrich Max Muller, a man who spend his whole career for the search of Eastern studies, was one of the most important figure who proved the link between the Sanskrit and modern European languages. Suddenly Europens and Indians realised that the two societies were cousins. The superiority of the Europeans or the British in our case was a fact during the 19th century. And as we have seen most of the Brahmans find their ways into the British imperial society by getting Western education. This feeling was improved with the glamouring Aryan theory linking them directly to the rulers of the country.

- But we have to say that, British Government was not on the side of caste disrcrimination, at least officially. British Government had laid down a policy of imparting education to low castes, one sharply at variance with earlier Peshwa rule. Section 591 of the Education Commissioner's Report said "that the principle has been laid down by the Court of Directors in their letter of 5th May, 1854, and in a subsequent reply to Government's letter dated 20.5.1857.". According to these letters, "nobody should be refused admission to a Government college or school merely on the ground of caste". This principle was reaffirmed in 1863. It was applicable to all institutions which were maintained at the cost of public funds, provincial or local.

Ironically this attitude of British Government should be one of the reasons for the rise of religionist nationalism within upper caste Hindus, where they always strongly opposed the abolishment of the castes. It is interesting to find that all of the Hindu press, excepting only a few non-Brahman newspapers, was critical of the government's action permitting low-caste boys into the public schools.

An overview of the Social Change during the 19th century

It can be said that the reformation of the Indian population was as confusing as its thousand years social structure. But we can say that the first motivation of the reforms came from the need to become like the British imperials. This is very ironic when it is considered that the foreigners or non-Hindus are accepted as worse than even the untouchables being accepted as a polluting existence for the Brahman religion. But history proves that this rule becomes obsolute if the foreigner is an invader capable of displaying his force.

This time the difference was that the new rulers were thinking that the occupied people were backward and in need of teaching. Whether it is true or not this approach was accepted by the occupied nation too. The British rule showed the way for the breaking of some thousand year rituals which were somehow unacceptable to the ordinary people. Sati or widow burning is one of them. And when we remember that Ram Mohan Roy's first motivation was the loss of his sister in one of those rituals.

Equality and justice had always been a reason for the Hindus to change their religion. This can also be verified with the fact that nearly half of the Indian population (including the Muslim states of Pakistan and Bengaldesh) is Muslim. And it is possibly true that most of their ancestors were from lower classes who seeked for equality and justice. Christianity were unable to achieve this status within the Hindu society.

It was for sure that the Western invasion collided with a period where the religion itself was under question at its homeland. The church was under a great pressure which was never seen before. The 16th century witnessed the emergence of new Christian sects other than Catholicism and Orthodoxy. In nearly two centuries religions' importance in the western societies passed away, leaving its place to new ideals. And it is also interesting to see that most of the modern Christian population of India lives around Goa today, the famous Portuguese port where Jesuit missionaries preached Christianity in its medieval form.

British never became neither succesfull in spreading the religion and nor they were interested to do so. The period when the British became the major foreign force in the subcontinent it was the time for new ideas. Equality, justice and nationalism. The first two were also preached by the major religions. But this time the ideals of enlightement carried these ideals especially after the French revolution in 1789. India as we have seen had always been a very complex society with dozens of religions, sects and thousands of jatis.

Most of these social groups can be observed in any society. But in India with the effect of Brahmanism this social groups became concrete and independant entities within the society. So the reactions of these concrete social groups were completely different from each other. The Indian society who accepted the Muslim influence a millennium ago was again ready for a change during the 19th century.

We have also be rightfull to say that Hinduism was also another factor for the society to be effected from the foreign ideals. The loose structure of Hinduism where every clan can take their old deities with them to the religion and where no prophecy or a religious authority exist must have had an important role. Within the borders drawn by these factors and with the immergence of self consciousness as it is defined within 19th century natinalist context, a new Indian society became to be established. The new institutions demanding for reform were in reality western like institutions. And probably first time in history a social consciousness of being Indian was born.

It is much more visible when we look at the big picture of social change in India from the beginning of 19th century to the midst of 20th century. First of all at the beginning the change began with the demands of people who felt pressure under the traditions and religion and also who wanted to be like their British masters. And than we saw more demands especially from the lower castes and a caste consciousness linked to the daily reality of being humiliated by the upper castes. It is also interesting to see that the intellectuals and movements which began with a more liberal mannor, turned into a much more religious one in time. This was parallel to the rise nation consciousness especially against the British. The lower castes who were in favour of abolishment of the religious traditions which put them under two millenniums of pains, were also effected from this process. Because the upper caste movements which began liberally turned into a religious one.

Religion must have been the easiest way to be defined as different from the colonialists. And also Brahmans had no problem with the religion. Some of the problems were already been solved under the British rule (for example Sati). 19th century or simply the British must not be seen as the only way of social revolt against the harsh rule of the Brahmans over the rest of the society. There had been various clashes before. Most of them were between the

Kshatriyas and the Brahmans for the control of the power. But without the help of the lower castes the Kshatriyas probably would not have the chance to stand against the Brahmanic power.

- The more basic opposition, however, was not that between the Kshatriyas and Brahmans who divided power and status at the top of the system, but between the "twice-born" castes (Brahmans, Kshatriyas and Vaishyas) and the Shudras, tribal people and Untouchables, who generally had neither power nor status. These had both a status interest in revolts that promised to negate the caste hierarchy as well "as economic motives for discontent since they were mostly poor peasant and artisan groups. Without a "Shudra" basis, in fact, no "Kshatriya" revolt had a chance of succeeding. Thus for example, the King of Travancore had sought to build up a populist basis for his rule, and the right-left divisions of south India had developed first among middlelevel castes: Brahman and the top Vellarar (the most powerful ruling group) had attempted at first to remain above it but were drawn in later. Similarly, it was in south India, where no "true Kshatriyas" were said to exist and even very powerful groups were considered to be of the Shudra varna, that the strongest movements of cultural revolt existed; here the "Kshatriya-Brahman" and " Shudra-twice born" oppositions tended to merge.

We can say that in the process of Indian social change, religion became a primary step to build a virtually united nation. Later followed the nationalism. Here it would not be hard to find the same pattern, considering the western and middle eastern examples. In that regions, religion was a much more organized institution for thousands of years. So we can say that reformists movements and the parties including Satyashodhak Samaj should also be accepted as some kind of religious organizations gathering masses under their umbrella.

We know that even the Dalit movement, whatever complaints they had about Hinduism, utilized some of the Hindu gods. This shows that religion was important for the people to legalize their movements. Because of this process the Indian nationalism became so much related to the religion as it is today. And this must also be the cause of the Muslim-Hindu seperation where a religion meant a nation.

So two nations were born from one society. The interesting point is the fact that lower castes with their much more rooted opposition to the Brahman religion were never be able to form another nation, although they tried. Here we must remember that beginning with the Phule, Dalit intelligentsia tended to accept themselves as the others, the people who were enslaved during the raids of the Aryans. Because of that belief Phule defined the lower castes as non-Aryans just as Ambedkar.

So during the 19th century they tried to establish a new national identity against the ruling classes. They claimed that during the Aryan invasion which was probably 3500 years ago, the native people of India - who were also a mixture of various races like mongoloids, aborigins etc.- were enslaved and forced to become the foot of the god Brahma.

The reality of these theories are highly arguable as they were mostly depending on the emotional needs for the masses who felt pressure. This was true for the Dalits who were feeling Brahmin pressure, but also true for the upper classes who felt the superiority of the British Empire.

So the Aryan theory was a good tool to be manipulated by each side of the story where the Europeans find a three thousands of historical background to legalize their control over the world, the Brahmins to find a way to overcome the superiority of the ruling British by claiming that they were relatives and the Dalits who find an answer to how they became such a humiliated class for such a long time. Also these efforts of searching for historical links, spent by the various classes of Indian society shows us how a classical society reacts to redefine itself in modern terms. This was the major change and also challenge the Indian society was passing through. All of these arguments about the identity based on religion, caste system and nationalism formed the 20th century India.

Reformation of the Dalit Movement at the beginning of the 20th century

Although Satyashodhak Samaj was still an effective power in the Maharashastra, the province where it all began, it is hard to say that the newly emerging leader of the untouchables, Dr. Ambedkar was effected or get into connection with it. Satyashodhak Samaj was slowly disintegrating when Dr. Ambedkar first appeared. So the intelligent environment from which Dr. Ambedkar had been benefiting was completely different from the environment of Jotirao Phule's one. Being represented in a national congress was not even considered by the Dalits. Phule defined the first Poona political organization Sarvajanik Sabha, as a bath (Brahmin) sabha.

He saw little difference in the Indian National Congress: These cunning Aryabhat Brahmans regard all the world's people as insignificant and hold scorn and envy of them in their minds... Even if these Aryans people establish hundreds of national congresses in counterfeit imititation of the religiously united Americans or French, still I can say with assurance that Shudras and Atishudras will never be members of their National Congress.

And it happened as he said when the first Indian National Congress was established in 1885. In its first session 80% of the Madras delegates and 100% of the Poona delegates were Brahmans, and this dominance continued to be maintained. At that time the Indian Congress was being accepted by the non-Brahman community as the represantative of the upper castes. And they had good reasons to believe this.

Legal Ebolishment of the Caste System

The borders of this study is not enough to define the social politics within the Indian society during the 19th and 20th centuries. But in order to draw a picture of the last century, a method had to be chosen, and in this case we choose to build the subject over the great figures or let's say the corner stones of the lower caste movements who were Ram Mohan Roy, Jotirao Phule and Dr. Ambedkar.

In previous stages we tried to give a brief story of the social changes of the 19th century considering the upper and lower caste relations and also the effects of the colonializm over the country. With the help of the photograhps which we have taken from the antiquity and later 19th and 20th century, we hope that an image of India should be formed within the readers mind. But it must be mentioned that the complexity of the subject causes a need for further reading.

Dr. Ambedkar

The last figure that must be mentioned to complete the greater and historical picture of the position and movements of the lower castes is Dr. Ambedkar. To start the subject wefound it more helpfull to tell the beginning of the story of Ambedkar from an Indian writer, Dhananjay Keer. The manner of the writing will also help us to understand what Ambedkar meant for some Indians. The Ambedkars come from Konkar, a region which provided India with great brains and great fighters, men like Tilak, Karve and Paranjpye. Ambedkar's ancestral village is Ambavade, five miles off Mandangad, a small town in the Rantnagiri District. The family was of some consequence in that village. It enjoyed the honour of keeping the palanquin of the village goddess and naturally the yearly festival was a great occasion for the family to attract the attention of the whole village. Ambadkar's grandfather Maloji Sakpal came of a good Mahar family. Of all the untouchable communities in the fold of Hindu society the Mahars are the most robust, adaptable, intelligent, fighting, brave, virile and leading community.

From the beginning the writer readies us for an epic story. A story which he believes in the heart. It's reflection of how the caste system has entered the Indian mind. The writer tells us that Dr. Ambedkar comes from a good family and even a good caste which is called Mahar. Now we learn that there are more brave, adaptable, intelligent, fighting, virile and leading communities within the untouchables as well.

And this small text also reminds us of a man who was born a leader within his own community with the help of being a member of a good family. Keer continues: The family belonged to the devotional Kabir school of thought. This Bhakti school of thought found consolation in the human attributes like compassion, benevolance and resignation to God. These devotees sought and found moral and spiritual broadening effect upon their mind was that the followers of this Bhakti school had abolished the rigidity of the caste system, as Kabir, the founder of the school, had roundly condemned it. This was one of the reasons why some Untouchable families turned to the Kabir cult. To the followers of the Kabir anybody who worshipped God belonged to God irrespective of caste and birth.

The Second Dalit Generation

It looks like that the soul of resistence which Ambedkar had within was a hereditary from his family. The interesting point about Ambedkar is the job of his father, where he was a member of the British military force. We know that most of the military personnel of the British colonial army was not British at all, but members of the lower castes.

The higher castes preferred to work withing the civil bureocracy rather than the military one. And this must be another clue of the British effect over the Indian society. Because Ambedkar's father was a literate person despite his caste. He usually read the national epics, the Ramayana and the Mahabbarata to his children. He was also able to speak and read in English where he was able to teach his children the language. And within this environment Ambedkar was enrolled to school when he was only five years old.

- There is an interesting case of a similiar battle, though with one important difference. In this event, the persons who carried through the war were Mahars themselves. They were retired British Army personnel. Ratnagiri District was the chief recruiting ground of the British Bombay Army, and a large portion of men enlisting there for service in infantry regiments were from the Untouchable Mahar and

Chambar castes. After completion of their service, or retirement, they settled in some central of favourite village or town with some piece of land, cultivating their crops and bringing up their children, leading a peaceful quiet life. Of such men, a few commissioned and noncommissioned officers settled at Dapoli. This is the place where Dr. Ambedkar, the emancipator of the Untouchables, spent his early childhood and received his primary education.

- Subhedar Major Gagnak and nine other military pensioner, including Ambedkar's father, sent a petition on 1 July 1892 to the president of Dapoli Municipiality asking that their sons be admitted into the Municipial school and taught along with other boys. They stated that this arrangement would induce their boys to study hard and to emulate the example of the boys of other castes in the hope of attaining a high rank in their class.

The environment where Bhim (Dr. Ambedkar) grew shows us the great change within the life of the lower castes thanks to the improvements achieved by the leaders of the 19th century such as Jotirao Phule and also the British rule, although they did not ask for this conclusion. Ambedkar was born in 1891 when the efficiency of the untouchable and non-Brahman movement was on the rise. Ideas and behaviour patterns, very different from those to which the people were accustomed, were thus presented as isolated from religion. The policy of comparative non-interference naturally gave scope for the revolt of the castes that were not quite comfortable under the Brahmin supremacy. Later on, with the incoming of industrial cities, large numbers of peoples congregated in cities of mixed populations, away from the influence of their homes and unobserved by their caste or village people. This is the background of the picture of the contemporary caste.

So we can observe the rise of the second generation of literate Untouchables, where the first generation saw education as a tool to break the unfortunate destiny of their kids. And Dr. Ambedkar was of that second generation who find the chance to get a better education what ever the conditions were. But we have to say that there are no physical links between the schools or other institutions of the non-Brahman movement lead by Phule and the new born Ambedkar. But later Ambedkar would call Phule as his teacher.

Childhood and Education of Ambedkar

Bhim as a child who were genius and full of desire to learn soon realised the fact that he was not an ordinary student. Because he did not belong to the upper castes. He was just an untouchable, nobody desired to touch, speak or even see. He felt the harsh reality of discrimination in every level of his education. Not only by his school fellows, but also from his Brahmin teacher. Bhim and his brother were usually made to squart in a corner of the class on a piece of gunny cloth which they carried to school. The teachers would not touch their note books, nor did some of them even ask them to recite poems or put questions to them for fear of being polluted! When these two boys felt thirsty in the school they turned their mouths upwards and then somebody would kindly pour drinking water into their mouths as if through a funnel.

These examples shows us although most of the upper classes were well educated within the British education system, they felt no pitty to behave the lower classes as if they were beasts. And it is for sure that this behaviours must have sharpened Bhim for his later struggle against the upper classes. The only teacher who treated Bhim well was also a Brahmin teacher.

A teacher who Bhim decided to carry his surname and become famous as Ambedkar. Ambedkar, after finishing his primary education, found support from the non-Brahman Maharaja of Baroda to continue his education in the U.S.A and with this scholarship he left India in 1913.

Ambedkar turned to India in 1923 after nearly ten years of study in the United States and England. He was a highly educated man; his degrees B.A., M.A., Ph.D., M.Sc., D.Sc., Barrister-at-Law are sung in a sort of incantation in one of the Mahar songs about him. He was a highly political person, practical and pragmatic. Still, for personal as well as public reasons, he had to come to terms with the Mahar myths.

At the end Ambedkar became an important figure not only for the Untouchables but also for the whole India as a modern country. By 1930 the British authorities had recognized the right of the Depressed Classes to representation through special electorates which their associations and spokesmen had been demanding since 1917. While the Statuory Commission had already recommended for them reservation of seats in joint electorates, the British Government nominated two of their spokesmen, namely B.R. Ambedkar and R. Srinivasan, to the Indian Round Table Conference which commenced its work in London on 21 November 1930 so as to enunciate their status in the future constitutional set-up of India.

Ambedkar's Ideological Stand

Ambedkar became a respectful person in the eyes of other castes, who became to be a member of the council, which prepared the Indian constitution after the independence of the country. And he was the man who managed to abolish the term of untouchable at least in front of the Law. He was also a reformist who led his community to point of rejection of the Hinduism as a religion and acceptance of Buddhism. After the long struggles with the masters of the Hindu religion the Brahmans, he decided to completely throw away a religion, which simply turned out to be ignoring them as humans. Naturally no account of Buddhism in the Sub-Continent would be complete without mentioning the still extremely controversial figure of Dr. Ambedkar and the Neo-Buddhist Movement which he started with his mass conversion of Dalits or the exuntouchables. Today, more than 90% of all Buddhists in India (only 6.5 millions according to the 1991 census) are the so-called neo-Buddhists converted by Ambedkar, a lawyer by profession, who was one of the founders by modern Indian constitution. This is quite remarkable, considering that from the 11th-12th centuries until the mass conversion (including Ambedkar who officially renounced Hinduism and embraced Buddhism) which took place in October 1956 in Nagpur, Maharashtra, Buddhism had almost completely disappeared in India, its land of birth.86

To understand what was the Dalits were demanding we have to look what Ambedkar says. We believe that there are no clearer examples than Ambedkar's own words to draw the picture of Dalit problem in India.

What Path Freedom

D. B. R. Ambedkar... There are two aspects of conversion. Social as well as religious; material as well as spiritual. Whatever may be the aspect, or line of thinking, it is necessary to understand the beginning, the nature of untouchability and how it is practiced. Without this understanding, you will not be able to realise the real meaning underlying my declaration of conversion. In order to have a clear understanding of untouchability and its practice in real life, I want you to recall the stories of the atrocities perpetrated against you.

The instances of beating by caste Hindus for the simple reason that you have claimed the right to enroll your children in government schools, or the right to draw water from public well, or the right to take a marriage procession with the groom on horseback, are very common. You all know such instances, as they happen before your eyes. But there are several other causes for which atrocities are committed on the Untouchables by the caste Hindus that, if revealed, surprise foreigners.

The Untouchables are beaten for putting on clothes of good quality. They have been whipped because they used utensils made of metal like copper, etc.

Their houses are burnt because they have brought land under cultivation. They are beaten for putting on the sacred thread. They are beaten for refusing to carry dead animals and eat carrion, or for walking through the village with socks and shoes on, or for not bowing down before the caste Hindus, for taking water in a copper pot while going out to the fields to ease themselves.

Recently an instance has been noted where the Untouchables were beaten for serving chapattis at a dinner party. You must have heard and some of you must have experienced such atrocities. Where beating is not possible, you are aware of how the weapon of boycott is used against us. You all know how the caste Hindus has made daily life unbearable by prohibiting your men from entering the village. But very few of you have realised why all this happens. What is the root of their tyranny? To me, it is very necessary that we understand it.

The instances have nothing to do with the virtues and vices of an individual. This is not a feud between two rival men. The problem of untouchability is a matter of class struggle. It is a struggle between caste Hindus and the Untouchables. This is not a matter of doing injustice against one man. This is a matter of injustice being done by one class against another. This struggle is related to social status. This struggle indicates how one class should keep its relationship with another class of people.

The struggle starts as soon as you start claiming equal treatment with others. Had it not been so, there would have been no struggle over simple reasons like serving chapatis, wearing good quality clothes, putting on the sacred thread, fetching water in a metal pot, sitting the bridegroom on the back of a horse, etc. In these cases you spend your own money. Why then do the high-caste Hindus get irritated? The reason for their anger is very simple. Your behaving on par with them insults them. Your status in their eyes is low; you are impure, you must remain at the lowest rung.

Then along will they allow you to live happily? The moment you cross your level the struggle starts. The instances given also prove one more fact. Untouchability is not a short or temporary feature; it is a permanent one. To put it straight, it can be said that the struggle between the Hindus and the Untouchables is a permanent phenomenon. It is eternal, because the high-caste people believe that the religion, which has placed you at the lowest level of the society, is itself eternal. No change according to time and circumstances is possible. You are at the lowest rung of the ladder today. You shall remain lowest forever.

This means the struggle between Hindus and Untouchables shall continue forever. How you will survive through this struggle is the main question. And unless you think it over, there is no way out. Those who desire to live in obedience to the dictates of the Hindus, those who wish to remain their slaves, they do not need to think over the problem. But those who wish to live a life of selfrespect and equality will have to think over this.

CONCLUSION

Unity among diversity is a constitutional motto, but the integration is not an easy task to maintain it. For this, the government will have to go forward with specific programs for marginalized and poor communities. Until and unless, Dalit community, so-called untouchables are not brought into the governance process and can not give the due respect to the Dalit women for participation, national integrity will remain confined to the constitution only. Though the Government has planned various gender friendly programs for women in general, it is an irony that the Dalit women have not been beneficiaries from these all. Still they are deprived of participating in the committees for planning the policies for women and forgotten to have the accessibility in the welfare programs. Women from so-called higher caste family have grasped all the welfare programs and plans.

The government does not care for them. Not only the government, even the political parties do not voice for the Dalit women. Political parties have frequently fashioned their campaigns slogans around the need for uplifting the marginalized sectors, while political leaders, mostly drawn from higher castes offer the promise of equal status and equal rights. But, the political condition of Dalit women is highly determined by the caste and gender discrimination. For the overall development of the country as a whole, there should be a plural participation from all castes, classes, communities and groups from all sectors. Dalit community, which has not any representation in any state level, has to push for representation. Since the Dalit women are triple victims from society, males, and economic and social condition, they should be given specific focus. Government while formulating and executing the programs should not forget to include Dalit women while planning for the reservation policy to women in general. Government should separately determine the quotas for Dalit women and encourage for their education, political participation, representation in public administration and employment. Even there should be clear-cut provision for the representation if any committee is framed. Otherwise, the issue regarding Dalit women will not come into account.

4

Discrimination and Violence against Dalit Women

Dalit women from South Asia are determined to "transform their pain into power". That was the main message of the two day international conference held in The Hague on the 20th and 21st of November 2006. It was the first international conference to discuss the issues of discrimination and violence against more than 100 million Dalit women. In "The Hague Declaration on the Human Rights and Dignity of Dalit women" the participants urged the governments of Nepal, India, Pakistan, Bangladesh and Sri Lanka as well as the international community to support their struggle. In South Asia, Dalits – known as "untouchables" and "outcastes"-have endured caste discrimination for centuries. The situation of Dalit women, one of the largest socially segregated groups in the world, is shocking. Dalit women are among the poorest; they face 'triple discrimination', as Dalits, as women and as poor. The caste system declares them intrinsically impure and "untouchable" and generally they are subjugated by men. Dalit women comprise the majority of manual scavengers, labourers who clean human excrements from dry toilets. Dalit women are targets of extreme violence, including sexual assault and forced prostitution.

VIOLENCE AND IMPUNITY

In the City Hall of The Hague Dalit women presented shocking and heart-breaking testimonials about the violence perpetrated against them and the impunity which followed. Authors of the study "Dalit women Speak Out-Violence against Dalit women in India" presented their findings of a three-year comprehensive study on forms, magnitude and the systematic pattern of violence which is accompanied by equally systematic patterns of impunity. The study revealed that only one percent of perpetrators are convicted in courts.

Physical and sexual violence against Dalit women is not only systemic, but also affects the majority of Dalit women. The study documents how rape, murder, physical assault and humiliation of Dalit women are intentionally used to maintain the oppression of the Dalit community by the dominant castes. Impunity is the key problem that Dalit women face today when they try to seek justice after violence is perpetrated against them. As stated in the Hague Declaration: "Perpetrators enjoy virtual immunity from prosecution as the police, who often harbour caste prejudices, wilfully neglect to enforce the law".

Often, Dalit women have protested and resisted although that has not been recognised and recorded. However, defiance is increasing. "Dalit women today are not merely passive victims; the current mood seems to be not one of mere acceptance, but determined to transform their pain into power", the Hague Declaration empathically states.

The Hague Declaration

In the Declaration the participants of the Hague conference call upon the governments of Nepal, India, Pakistan, Bangladesh and Sri Lanka to support the women in asserting their rights. The governments are called upon to address the failure of the justice system to protect Dalit women and to implement measures to close the vast socio-economic gap between Dalit women and the rest of the population.

The recommendations include: implementing an independent complaint mechanism to address the atrocities against Dalit women; establishing organisations to discuss social, domestic and development issues in their community; taking strong measures to give land to Dalits, which is to be registered in the name of Dalit women (or jointly with men); eradicating practices of manual scavenging and the Devadasi system of ritualised prostitution; allocating sufficient budget to full primary and secondary education of all Dalit girls and ensuring the reduction of pre-natal mortality, infant mortality and maternal mortality among Dalit women.

The participants also urge the governments in South Asia to launch national campaigns for the elimination of caste.

International community should act

The participants in the Hague Conference also call upon the international community, including the UN human rights bodies, the UN organisations, the EU, bilateral aid agencies and NGOs to act upon the recommendations of the Hague Declaration.

In particular they are asked to express their outrage at the caste-induced systematic practices of untouchability and atrocities against Dalit women.

It also calls upon the international community to ensure that, at the latest in 2015, the large 'development gap' (e.g. in terms of poverty) is closed between Dalit women and girls and the 'general population'.

Finally, the ILO is asked propose measures against the systematic violation of the four fundamental labour rights where Dalit women and girls are concerned.

EXISTING POSITIVE ACTIONS FOR WOMEN AND DALITS

There are about 150 existing positive legal provisions and policies for the substantial change of women at large Though, in general, these provisions were made intentionally to upgrade the status of women, only few from so called high caste and class women have benefited to a larger extent only. No impact on the Dalit women is seen so far.

Actions for Women

a) *5% candidacy from women for House of Representatives is mandatory to all political parties.* But the practice has shown that only elite women have succeeded and benefited by this provision. Since personal identity of a candidate rather than of political parties is the attraction, the political parties fear to put candidature from Dalit community.

b) *Reservation of Women in National Assembly:* There is also a provision in the constitution for three seats in the National Assembly of the Parliament. Only the women from so called high caste have got the advantage by this provision. There is not any instance of the Dalit woman as beneficiary of this provision.

c) *Reservation in Local bodies:* In the Local Self-governance Act, there is a provision of the reservation to women for at least one seat in ward Committee. But no Dalit woman benefited by this provision. Similarly there is a provision for the participation of women in the Development Council. Nominal Dalit women have got chance to participate in the Local Councils at the Municipal, Village Development Committee and District levels.

d) *Mandatory Provision for Inclusion of Women:* For the compulsory participation of women in all committees, this provision has been made in various laws i.e. consumer law, local motion pictures, central children welfare, steering committee of local development, breast feeding protection and promotion committee.

e) *Free Education:* The education act obliged all state schools for free education to women. However, Dalit women are not able to have such access due to early marriage and low economic status.

f) *Scholarship:* The scholarship rule has mandated for 20% reservation in scholarship. But none from among the Dalit girls could benefit from this arrangement. Every seat is provided to the so-called higher castes girls and the girls of high economic profile.

g) *Mandatory Plan for a Woman Teacher in Primary School:* The Ninth Plan has obliged every school to nominate a teacher from women, however, no satisfactory impact is seen in favour of Dalit women. This provision is more questionable since the schools are going to be managed locally. But, the social practices inhibit the appointment of a Dalit woman as a teacher to teach children of higher castes.

h) *Relaxation in Age for Civil Service:* The civil service rule (amendment) has relaxed the age limitation for the enrolment for public services to women. Maximum age limit for women to join civil service is 40 years, whereas it is only 35 in case of men. But, there lacks the record of the beneficiary from Dalit women by this provision. Major beneficiaries of this provision of reservation are women from the forward castes.

i) *Women's Bodies to be searched by Women Police:* If the body of woman has to be searched in connection with investigation of a crime, the search has to be conducted by women police without insulting her. Under the existing arrangement, the body of a Badi woman is searched by male police even without prior notice, which is not only objectionable but an insult to the pride of the women folk.

j) *National Commission for Women:* The Commission is established with a view to protecting and promoting the women's rights. But, the composition of this Commission lacks any representation form Dalit women. As such, the Dalit women have not got any positive feeling towards this institution.

Actions for Dalits

k) *Deprived, Depressed and Dalit Community:* His Majesty's Government has established this community with a view to planning and executing the welfare policies for Dalit, but there is no any woman's representation in the composition. The males dominate the committee. This situation is self-defeating as the women from Dalit community have no control over the policy and programmes executed through this body.

l) *National Dalit Commission:* A single Dalit woman was appointed in the commission out of ten members from the Dalit community. There were several claims that there existed potential candidates from the Dalit women for this august body.

m) *Committee for Formulating Reservation Policy:* The Government has formulated a main committee under the chairmanship of Finance Minister and several subcommittees with a view to formulating the model of reservation policy to women, Dalit and *Janajati*. But apparently, there lacks representation of Dalit women in any committees.

Though the government has taken several positive actions for the gender justice Dalit women are considered neither at the time of planning nor in the executing of the policies.

DALIT WOMEN IN INDIA

There are about 250 million Dalits in India. There is meagre improvement in the socioeconomic condition of dalits in the past 50 years. Which that is not enough when compared to non-dalits. Of course, much more needs to be done. The urgent need is to have a national sample survey on dalits. Every fourth Indian is a dalit. There is no proper survey to give the correct number of dalit women in India. They are generally scattered in villages and they are not a monogamous group. About 75% of dalits live below poverty line. Economic backwardness of dalits is mostly due to injustice done to them by the high castes and also due to exploitation. From the time immemorial they worked like slaves, sold as commodities resulting in their social discrimination, economic deprivation and educational backwardness.

EDUCATION

Till some years ago, many dalit women were ill treated and educationally backward inspite of the facilities for free education. The reasons for the high rate of illiteracy among dalit women are many.

The following are the main reasons:

1. Resistance from the family to send girls to schools.
2. Fear of insecurity in villages.
3. Lack of physical facilities like accommodation, school, transport and medical facilities.
4. The girls were forced to take care of the siblings when the parents are away at work.
5. Girls were forced to do domestic chores which prevent them from attending school.

6. Working to earn for the family prevent the girls from attending school.
7. Working with parents to earn their livelihood in beedi factories or other unorganized sector made them illiterate.
8. Because of the sick and unemployed parents girls were forced to work.
9. Many were forced to get married at young age, which stop schooling.
10. Social restriction is that the girls should stop education after marriage.
11. In some areas there are complaints from dalit women teachers of misbehaviors, blackmail and exploitation by the male staff of other high caste people.
12. Distance of schools from home.
13. Irrelevant content of the education system.
14. Fear of alienation of girls from their environment as a result of education are some of the other factors for low literacy level among SC girls. Even if the education improved the marriage prospects of the girls, the minus point is the increase in dowry. Therefore many parents wish to withdraw the girls from schools.

The present positions seems to be better with reference to the rate of literacy among dalits. The literacy rate is 31.48% for boys and 10.93% for girls. Dalits women belonging to the creamy layer of the society are better with good education and socially and economically they are well off like other high castes. They are fully aware of the welfare schemes provided by the Government and their percentage is very low when compared with the total dalit population. In rural areas, the first generation girls from SC needs the attention of Government and other organization. Mostly the teachers of the locality provide information to them about the welfare schemes. In many Dalit association executive position are occupied by male members whereas very poor representation is made by women in their pasts. The women are not properly informed about the Government schemes and there is an urgent need to get a feedback about the welfare schemes where lot of money is spent for the development of Dalits. The funds are not utilized properly for their upliftment. Many of the schemes go unnoticed because they are not popularized properly.

The coaching programmes conducted by the Government for dalit women are beneficial in training many women to compete in the competitive exam. These programmes also do not reach the needy dalit women because they are cornered by the very few creamy dalit women. This should be monitored properly and the schemes should be reached by the most deprived and constantly struggling dalit women. Because these dalit women are neglected by socially advanced communities and also by the better off among the dalits, which leads to an unhealthy socioeconomic condition. There should be some scientific basis to pick up the poorest and they should be equipped with facilities. There are some pre-examination coaching centres giving trainings for dalits which are doing very good service to train them in vocational line, for competitive exam, in medical and engineering field, railway recruitment boards, bank recruitment, etc.

Here are some suggestions for the better implementation of the schemes to dalit women:

1. Competitive spirit should be instilled in the girls.
2. Selection and identification of the talented girls should be done correctly.
3. Identify the candidate at college level for coaching.
4. Result oriented teaching is necessary.
5. Group discussions, quiz, and seminars to instill confidence.
6. Teacher : Student ratio 1:20 or below.
7. Monitoring by the teacher after class hours.
8. Loan facility.

Financial aid for uniform for girls, maps, charts, examination grant, laboratory facilities, library facilities should be provided for them special coaching should be given for meritorious dalit girls to compete for IAS and IPS. Hostel facilities for dalit girls at all levels of education starting from primary school up to higher education should be provided reservation policy especially for girls should be allotted in both admission and employment. There is an increased awareness in recent years among dalit women about their rights and about the Government welfare schemes about higher education. This should be augmented by information technology, which should reach even to the remote rural citizen.

HIGHER EDUCATION

The UGC has given reservation for seats in colleges for SC students 25%, ST 7.5%, which is highly beneficial. Also relaxation in marks for 5% is given to all dalit students in admission. Financial assistance in the form of fellowships is given to dalits. Rs. 3,600/-is given per JRF to continue research studies at the University level. There are special SC/ST cells at the University for effective implementation of the Government orders and to improve the condition of University level dalit students.

There are some of the suggestions for effective implementation of the various welfare schemes for the dalit students.

1. The communication gap between the educational institution and the social welfare department should be reduced.
2. District wise computer database of the male and female dalit students is very essential to provide necessary facilities to them.
3. Pamphlets with details about the welfare schemes should be distributed to the students.
4. Supply of books to the dalit students.
5. Incentive scholarship should be given to deserving and meritorious girls to encourage them for higher education.

GENDER EQUALITY

Female infanticide is more prevalent among the uneducated dalit families. Educational development among SC women is very marginal because only girls were not sent to school because of the responsibilities at home. Therefore the gender discrimination starts at the very early stage in the life of a dalit girl. Normally girl children are retained at home to look after the siblings. Another thing is the compulsory marriage of the girls at very early age after which the education is stopped. Generally in the male-dominated society, polygamy is allowed and more so in many dalit families. Because of this the position of the women deteriorated. Joint family system, polygamy, property structure, early marriage, and permanent widowhood were hurdles for the development of all women in early period. But in the twentieth century, after the Mahatma Gandhien movement to educate women, slowly changes occurred in the position of women. But here, rural women were more blessed than urban women because divorce and remarriage were allowed for them. Mainly Sudras (i.e. low caste people) allowed divorce and remarriage for their women.

OCCUPATION

The occupation of many SC women can be divided in the following heads:

1. Agriculture labourer.
2. Marginal Cultivators.
3. Fisherwomen.
4. Traditional artisans.
5. Leather Workers.
6. Weavers.
7. Scavengers and sweepers.

8. Midwifery.
9. Beedi factories and unorganised sectors.

The Work Participation Rate (WPR) of SC population is said to be for males 22.25% and for females 25.98%.

The contribution of SC women to the economic development of our country is significant especially in the agricultural sector. They are exploited by the higher caste landlords. They are paid very marginal salary for the hard work in the field for the whole day. In leather industries the tanning process is considered to be an unclean job which is done only by socially backward class. Traditional artistes get very more benefit because the middleman exploits them. The condition of scavenger and sweepers is very deplorable and they the most vulnerable sectors among SC. The working condition is very poor and the remuneration is also very poor.

FAMILY ROLE

Because of the girls remain uneducated, they got married very early. Marriage in the high reproductive stage with high fertility rate, children care more. Because of the unlimited family, the burden fell on the young girls which affected their health. They were not able to assist in family matters to their husbands. But now the situation is different. The girls manage to plan their family, educate the children, assist the husbands in family matters and office going and professional girls improve the economic conditions.

On the whole the family becomes socially developed because of the education of the girls. Education among women increased intercaste marriages, which is definitely a sign of development. Government also encourages intercaste marriages among dalits and highcaste by incentives.

GENDER, SEXUALITY, ANTI-BRAHMIN POLITICS, AND THE DALIT HABITUS

Widows are cursing the religion that prohibits a woman from remarrying Those who persecute women shall find themselves in hell The Peshwas created this ignominious treatment of women And for that reason their kingdom was destroyed gopal vithalnak valangkar, *DB*, July 19, 1896, Akhand 5, verse 1–3 Hindu scriptures, especially the Manusmriti, defined both lower castes and women as impure, polluting, and subject to detailed regulation. It is not surprising that Phule and Valangkar equated the plights of these groups. Phule's earliest reform efforts addressed both lower castes and women: he opened a school for untouchable students in 1852 and a home for uppercastewidows in 1854. Placing gender and sexuality at the heart of caste distinctions enabled a powerful critique of the reproduction of caste through the regulation of gender.

Enforced widowhood, an important target of caste radicals' critique, focused on the inhuman treatment of the widow, who was tonsured, subject to severe sartorial codes, prohibited fromwearing jewellery, and forced to observe dietary restrictions to control her passions. Sexual anxieties about the widow were long-standing, but Hindu reformers' and caste radicals' renewed focus on the treatment of widows coincided with the colonial state's efforts to reform the Hindu joint family.

Caste radicals were distinctive and vociferous in emphasizing the importance of caste respectability and sexual purity to the reproduction of Brahminical patriarchy. Thus, when Phule and his wife, Savitribai, opened a home in 1854 for upper-caste widows who faced intimate violence ranging from physical abuse to impregnation, they were criticizing a Brahminical order that sanctioned such practices, even as they were challenging upper castes' capacity to protect "their women." Tarabai Shinde extended their critique in *Stri-Purush Tulana* (A Comparison between Women and Men), written in 1882 in response to the conviction of an upper-caste widow, Vijayalakshmi, of infanticide. Shinde attacked the hypocritical stance of criminalizing women rather than challenging the sexual excesses of men and argued that all men, not merely Brahmins, were implicated in the ill treatment of women. The upper-caste widow also played an important role in Valangkar's critique. He compared the tonsure of widows with cows going to the slaughterhouse and argued that widows were deeply susceptible to sexual advances by "ascetics, mendicants, and priests" who congregated at holy places to take advantage of them. Indeed, an established trope in anti caste polemic was Brahmanism's ideological reduction of women and the lower castes to beasts of burden: their sentience and physicality were inversely related to their value as persons.

Because enforced widowhood exposed the structuring relationship between caste hegemony and control over female sexuality, the practice provided the occasion for early critiques of the caste order and of Brahminical mores in particular. A dialogue between a widow and her father in a Satyashodak *jalsa* (folk drama) uses the widow's physical disfiguration to stage a broader critique of enforced widowhood and to challenge its growing acceptance among non-Brahmin communities where *pat* (second marriages) had previously predominated.

In the first decades of the twentieth century, Satyashodak *jalsas* were the main vehicles for spreading the Samaj's message to the rural populace. Traditional *tamashas,* renowned for their word play and sexual innuendo interspersed with song, typically began with an invocation to Lord Ganapati. The stories centered on the theme of Lord Krishna's dallianceswith his *gopis* (milkmaids). Instead, the Satyashodak *jalsa* invoked the *gana* (the people) as leaders (*pati,* or "the source of rule"). Satyaji's dialogue with Brahmin women on the irrationality of Hindu ritual, discussions about the exploitation of the peasantry, and critiques of the Brahmin-moneylender (*shetji-bhatji*) were popular. The use of coarse and insulting language was standard. Bhimrao Mahamuni from Otur is credited with having staged the first *jalsa* with the support of Shahu Chatrapathi and Krishnarao Bhalekar. Ramachandra Ghadge (Kale, Satara district) started his famous *jalsa* troupe in 1915. Colonial reports indicate the extent to which the Satyashodak Samaj relied on the *jalsa* and other popular cultural forms. A brief note by District Magistrate Satara, dated October 11–12, 1919, recorded: "It was found necessary in April 1919 to issue an order under Sec. 144 Cr. P. C., preventing the religious sermons, kirtans, and 'tamashas' of the Samaj at Karad for two months. District Magistrate reported that the so-called religious 'tamasha' and kirtans of the Satya Samaj consisted of coarse abuse and ridicule of the Brahmans and were rightly stopped." By 1929, more than twenty-nine troupes were performing in southern Maharashtra.

Thus the Satyashodak marriage eliminated the need for a Brahmin priest and emphasized self-respect and equality within marriage. This challenge to the social reproduction of caste through religious exploitation of the non-Brahmin communities, and the sexual regulation of (their) women, inspired Ambedkar, who urged Dalits to perform Satyashodak marriage. He even presided over one in Vidarbha in 1927.65 Similarly, Self-Respect marriages in south India in the movement's heyday (1925–39), took the politicization of marriage to new heights. Self-Respecters, especially their leader, Periyar, or E.V. Ramasamy Naicker, urged activists to perform inter caste and widow remarriages and celebrated them in movie halls and theatres, where they were performed at ritually inauspicious times. By so doing, they staged the theatricality of politics and the significance of sexual politics for radical anti-casteism. The political import of the Satyashodak marriage is reflected by a legal case from Otur in Poona district, a site of radical Satyashodak activism. A Brahmin *joshi* (priest) demanded his traditional fees for performing a marriage even though the Satyashodak marriage had eliminated his role. On appeal to the Bombay High Court, Balaji Patil argued that his fellow caste members had performed his daughter's wedding in keeping with ancestral tradition. His legal representative recognized the novelty of the Satyashodak marriage, however, and argued: "The marriages were performed without any prescribed ceremonies, and no priest as such, was employed. There was no *ganeshpujan* (inauguration of the marriage ceremony through a prayer to Ganesha). There was nothing beyond the placing of garlands on the necks of the bride and bridegroom. There was no distribution of fees (*dakshina*); therefore the village joshis cannot claim any fees. *There is a separate ritual for the Sudras of the defendant's caste. That ritual was not performed*." The 1888 judgment by Justices Sargent and Candy supported the Satyashodaks' argument that because the wedding of Patil's daughter was not performed as a (legally) recognizable non-Brahmin or Shudra marriage, the *joshi* was ineligible for fees. By refusing to sacralize marriage *on the Brahmin's terms,* the Satyashodak marriage positioned itself as an explicit challenge to the social reproduction of caste through the sexual regulation of women. This was of a piece with challenges to Brahmin sacerdotal power and ritually "pure" status in important rationalist texts such as *Svayampurohit* (YourOwn Priest) and Gharache *Purohit* (Household Priest) that empowered non-Brahmin communities to perform religious rituals without Brahmin intervention. Schools for training priests were similarly established in villages, so that rituals could be performed without Brahmin intermediaries.

Though caste radicals were preoccupied with challenging caste ideology by rethinkingmarriage and sexuality, they were by nomeans immune to the extension of novel patriarchal practices into their own households. In the last quarter of the nineteenth century, enhanced regulation of women became a mechanism to resolve anxieties about social status among upwardly mobile, politicized Marathas. Sociocultural practices such as Marathmola percolated down from royal families and landed gentry to young women from upwardly mobile families. This partial segregation of women involved withdrawing their labor and physical presence from public space and became a status marker for Maratha families claiming elite Kshatriya status. Meanwhile, Dalit publicists and reformers underlined the susceptibility of Dalit women to sexual violation according to "custom" and focused on enforced sexual servitude through womens' ritual dedication. Even as Dalit publicists launched a severe critique of the interdependence of sexual compulsion and the material deprivation of Dalit communities, their efforts to modify Dalit intimate relationships also enhanced the authority of male Dalit reformers. The contradictory effects of the social reform of gender by caste radicals can be explained by the fact that Dalit and non-Brahmin political subject-formation increasingly involved the politicization of Dalit and lower-castemen through the reform of family and female subjects. Earlier, colonial paradigms of social reform had intersected with (and enhanced) Brahminical models of caste and sexual purity to produce hegemonic ideologies of domesticity, female enfranchisement, and companionate marriage. They had been vigorously criticized by anti caste radicals, who drew attention to the supplemental relationship of gender and caste and the reproduction of caste norms through sexual regulation. In the first decades of the twentieth century, however, non-Brahmin critiques of the gendered character of caste were muted by emergent forms of caste conflict that increasingly framed the modernization of gender as dependent on the reconstitution of caste masculinity.

An important consequence of the discrete, if mutually entailed, trajectories of gender reform and the politicization of caste by anti caste radicals was that the subject of non-Brahmin and, later, Dalit politics was imagined as male. Let me clarify that my argument in no way refuses the significant public presence of women and the centrality of female labor to the household economy of Dalits and lower castes. As well, bourgeois ideologies of femininity carried a very different valence for stigmatized communities, since coerced sexual labor constituted a key site of collective humiliation. While such developments speak to divergent genealogies of the feminist subject, they also help to explain the specific conditions that set the ground for a masculinist anti caste politics. By the early decades of the twentieth century, Jotirao Phule's resonant narrative of Brahmin invasion and political usurpation was redirected to serve an argument regarding the impure, miscegenated origins of the Chitpavan Brahmins. Maratha masculinity was directly engaged in the resulting narratives, while Dalits—excluded from Kshatriya status—were rendered marginal to the conflict. The emphasis on Dalit and Maratha masculinity was the result of caste radicals' initial emphasis on the importance of gender and sexuality in the constitution of the (political) community of caste. Their divergent trajectories can be explained, however, through caste radicalism's intersections with the institutional contexts of colonial modernity and the discursive logics of an emergent cultural nationalism. My focus is on two things: (1) the manner in which gender and genealogy discursively constituted the difference between Brahmin and non-Brahmin; and (2) how the renewed politicization of caste identities around the axis of gender and sexuality demarcated emergent non-Brahmin and Dalit public spheres.

In Maharashtra, it was said that there were only Brahmins and Shudras in the Kaliyuga (the present, corrupted age). This indicated a Brahmincentric view of the degradation of the all intermediate castes to Shudra status. Constant conflicts over Shudra status were in evidence from the 1700s, if not earlier, and became especially virulent by 1830 with regard to Chitpavan Brahmins' determination to downgrade the Kayastha Prabhus to Shudra status. Butwhowere the Chitpavan Brahmins? Phule had framed them as aliens and interlopers. Valangkar embellished Phule's account: the Konkani Chitpavan Brahmins were Semitic people who had fled the Barbary coast, were shipwrecked off the Malabar coast, married low-caste women from the Konkan region, and became a caste of fishermen. Theywon power and Brahmin status through cunning. Valangkar went further to explain the distinctions between Mahar and Maratha. He described the Mahars as *varnas* of mixed *jatis* who shared the lineage of other Dravidian Kshatriyas—Surya, Chandra, Shes, and Yadu. However, he defined Rajputs and Marathas as Turks who had been sent to annihilate Buddhism and Jainism in India. If Valangkar distinguished the Marathas from other Dravidian Kshatriyas, it is because this was a pronounced theme of Maratha genealogies produced in the early decades of the twentieth century, which sought to redefine Marathas' status as *Aryans* and as Kshatriyas.

Dalits *and* Marathas past felt compelled, however, to engage with the Chitpavan Brahmins' genealogy related in the Sahyadrikhand, a caste origin myth that referenced an act of genocide in the Dasavatara to explain the disappearance of Kshatriyas from the Deccan. In the Dasavatara, the axe-wielding Brahmin Parashurama, an incarnation of Vishnu, is said to have exterminated all Kshatriyas during the Treta Yuga, in retaliation for his father's murder. (Recall that in Phule's account, the Maha-ari had risen against Parashurama twenty-one times, only to be subjugated.) To extirpate his sins, Parashurama tried to perform penance. Unable to find Brahmins in the Konkan, he created the Chitpavan Brahmins by purifying a group of sixty fishermen at a funeral pyre. The Chitpavans were rendered pure *(pavana)* through funereal ashes *(chitta)*.

If this genealogy rendered Chitpavan Brahmins of dubious distinction, it created an even more compromising account of non-Brahmins. The Shudra-Kshatriyas of Kaliyuga, it was said, were the product of illicit intercaste unions between Brahmin sages, *rishis,* and enslaved Kshatriya women. The term "Shudra," in both popular discourse and legal texts, conjured the dishonor of impure origins, a bastard identity born out of bondage, sexual degradation, and servitude. No less than B. R. Ambedkar was impelled by this account of sexual violence to argue that, "[i]n every case, the Kshatriyas are shown to have undergone an abject surrender... [in many stories] the surrender of the Kshatriyas was so to say purchased by them by offering their women to the victorious Brahmins. The stories are all doctored with a view to glorify the

Brahmins and humiliate the Kshatriyas. Who can take such dirty, filthy, abominable and vainglorious stories of reconciliation as true historical facts? Only a supporter of Brahmanism can do so." Indeed, Maratha assertions in the early twentieth century challenged this foundational narrative of sexual violence and caste miscegenation by addressing the *Brahmin's* miscegenated identity.

In order to align themselves with region and nation, Marathas asserted that they were the original inhabitants of Maharashtra and thus true nationalists. To make their case they drew on colonial racial typologies inflected by regional caste conflicts and made sometimes confusing and inconsistent distinctions between Aryans and Dravidians, and Hindus and Brahmins. By the turn of the century, Maratha purity had become a sensitive issue for Maratha activists and elite Maratha families alike.

The latter distinguished themselves from Marathas of uncertain status, referred to by a range of terms—*kadu, akkarmashe* (lit. "miscegenated," "bastardized"), and *kharchi* (semi-legitimate)—and sought to legitimize status through ritual incorporation into varna hierarchy. Marriage advertisements seeking pure alliances between elite, wealthy Maratha families began to appear in the pages of the Kolhapur newspaper *Vijayi Maratha* (Victorious Maratha) and the more conservative, Belgaum-based *Rashtraveer* (Patriot).

Such practices were doubly inflected by the desire to challenge Brahmin hegemony and to claim for Marathas a distinctive Kshatriya identity by aligning *jati* with *varna* status. The net result was a shift away from Phule's tradition of radical egalitarianism and critique of religious orthodoxy toward an embrace of Aryan identity for Kshatriya Marathas, now increasingly represented as Hindus with full access to Vedic rituals in contrast to Brahmins, who were portrayed as being of questionable origin. Notable exceptions to this tendency are Mukundrao Patil, editor of the *Din Mitra* (1910-30), who repeatedly urged an expansive identity for non-Brahmin castes as non-Aryan Hindus ranged against Brahmin domination; and the non-Brahmin activists Keshavrao Jedhe and Dinkarrao Javalkar. They were increasingly confronted, however, by growing Dalit-Maratha conflict as an organized Dalit movement exacerbated economic tensions on a rural field polarized between Dalit laborers and non-Brahmin, especially Maratha, landlords.

Maratha assertions of pure Kshatriya origin positioned themas Aryan originators of Hindu scriptures with a first claim to Vedic authority, and Maratha polemicists urged non-Brahmins to take up the thread ceremony and other Vedic rituals to assert their superiority over Brahmins. This erased the illegitimacy Phule had attributed to the scriptures as signs of Brahmin cunning and made for the Maratha Kshatriyas a central place *within* Hindu history. It also left intact the narrative of the defeat and humiliation of the Dravidian Shudra.

The reconstitution of the Maratha self (and of Maratha masculinity) was thus inherently unstable. At one level it constituted a challenge to Brahmin power (and Brahmin-centric history) across the *longue durée*. However by positing a direct correspondence between the uneven political regimes that produced Maratha as a resonant caste identity in western India and the ritually exclusive *varna* status of Kshatriyas, Maratha assertion relied on a genealogy that denied salience for Phule's imagined collectivity of *shudra-atishudras*. The rewriting of Maratha history left little room for Marathas of questionable status and increasingly rendered alliances between Dalits and Aryan-identified non-Brahmin groups difficult. As debates over caste identity intersected with narratives of sexual violence and structural analyses of the sexual reproduction of caste, complex political tensions between Brahmins, non-Brahmins, and untouchables were also staged. Between 1922 and 1926, an aggressively masculinized counter discourse became a major node of conflict for non-Brahmin challenges to Brahmin superiority.

Ganpati and Shivaji *melas* [festivals], started in the 1890s by radical Hindu nationalist Bal Gangadhar Tilak (1856–1920), had countered Muharram processions by politicizing public space and religion through everyday cultural symbols and historical figures associated with intimate practices of Hindu religiosity. The melas included street marches, singing, and the staging of plays that created a context for displays of anticolonial rhetoric and patriotic fervour. They also accommodated inflammatory anti-Muslim rhetoric and derogation of women and anti-Brahmin radicals.

In turn, Chatrapati *melas* counterstaged Maratha masculinity. Participants wore warrior costumes, carried spears and javelins, sang *mela* songs criticizing Brahmin hegemony, and asserted the true national patriotism of non-Brahmins. The Peshwas were blamed for losing Maharashtra to the British. Insults were common. By 1924, nightly fracases between Tilakites and non-Brahmin activists brought the *melas* under extensive police surveillance and caused the banning of many songs and publications by both sides. The liberal organ, *Servant of India,* noted that the Chatrapati *melas* showed that "they [non-Brahmin activists] could beat the originators of the festival on their own ground, that is, in the employment of indecent language. Their attacks were directed against the very people who introduced this sinister element into the public life of Poona."

This aggressively masculinized non-Brahmin political culture exacerbated caste antagonism through a sexual politics. Popular pamphlets made sexual innuendos about Brahmin women and represented widows as symbols of Brahmin tyranny. They cast aspersions on the sexual purity of Brahmin communities, characterizing them as the illicit offspring of Marathamen and Brahmin women. Brahmins were routinely described as *dasiputras* (colloq. "bastards") in polemical texts, thus reversing the Brahmins' narrative of the Marathas as Shudras and the offspring of *dasis* (enslavedwomen). Indeed, Brahmins complained that one of the taunts employed by the activists was, "the Chatrapati *mela* has come; Brahmin women better run." Gender and genealogy were discursively central to this emergent non-Brahmin public sphere. Non-Brahmin activists emphasized the history of concubinage and Brahmin men's sexual exploitation of lower-caste women (and their own wives) through popular-cultural representations of the Peshwai as a period of sexual debauchery. To suggest that Brahmins were foreigners and the offspring of caste miscegenation threatened the Brahmins' claim to caste purity and, therefore, to ritual authority. Government censorship of "inflammatory" or "obscene" texts illustrates the growing significance of a public sphere of print and performance in exacerbating Brahmin/non-Brahmin conflict in Poona, hotbed of Tilakite activism.

Let us begin with publication of *Deshache Dushman* (Enemies of the Country) in 1925, with an introduction by Keshavrao Bagade. The controversy over the text was preceded by demands that same year that the Poona municipality honor Phule with a statue. The deep-rooted resistance of Brahmins and conservative non-Brahmins—including Phule's relative, Baburao Phule—who accused Phule of being a Christian convert who destroyed Hindu religion, intensified friction and set the stage for a spirited response. The Oriental Translator described the book as "written in the most intemperate and objectionable language; in places the violent fury of the writer has so carried him away that his whirling words are barely intelligible." Bagade admitted that "the language and mode of expressing ideas employed in this book will not please Brahmans." *Deshache Dushman* branded Brahmin leaders as traitors sprung from a stock of foreign invaders of low status and questionable origins. The authors argued that Brahmins were well known for using any means to assert their superiority—from chicanery and cunning to falsifying history. Tilak and Vishnu Shastri Chiplunkar—the latter famous for his vitriolic criticism of Phule and the social reformer Gopal Hari Deshmukh, or Lokahitawadi, in his 1874 *Nibandhamala* (Garland of Essays)—were referred to as enemies of the country "born from the vomit of Brahmans" (in reference to Brahmins' claims that they were birthed from the mouth of Purusa, or "the original man"). Chitpavan Brahmins were generally described as "Satan," "cobras," "sons of prostitutes," and "mother goers." 96 Indeed the litany of complaints against Brahmin patriotism comprised an account of Brahmin treachery, sexual licentiousness, and female exploitation. This text, like others that followed, described Peshwa history as a period of maximal corruption, when Brahmins sold their daughters and loaned theirwives. Shivaji's protection of Brahmin women from the depredation of Muslim men was mentioned in conjunction with Brahmin hypocrisy about the behaviour of their women—"the Bhatmind thinks religion is destroyed when a Shudra is crowned king but cannot comprehend when a Brahmin woman comes jumping from the bed of a Shudra. 98 Brahmins, it was noted, had the vile tendency to "suspect their mother's chastity," "shave women," and to allow widows to throw their illegitimate children on "crossroads eight times a week." At the same time, the Brahmin priest "who calls the non-Brahmins Shudras an enemy is a badmash dacoit [bandit] who casts evil glances at their women." Equating Brahmanism with slavery, the text noted, "it is a sin to give alms to a Brahmin who smokes ganja, drinks wine and ascends the staircase of houses of ill repute. To get marriage solemnized by Brahmins is tantamount to polluting an auspicious occasion [and] writing the horoscope of a future slave generation."

The controversy over *Deshache Dushman* was heightened by a set of parallel publications that challenged Brahmin hegemony and its ritual and material enslavement of non-Brahmins. R.N. Lad, the editor of *Mazur,* and Annabhau Chavan, writer of "The Marriage Ritual of the Bhats According to the Shastras, or Their Foolish Foolishness," were sentenced to nine months rigorous imprisonment for promoting communal enmity. In his piece of June 5, 1926, which described a marriage ceremony that took place in Masur on May 25, Chavan issued a challenge to "the extremely foolish, wicked, mean Bhats in Masur, the daredevil donkeys, the Bhat sons of prostitutes, who seek the evil of the benefactor, who give the form of untruth to truth, and truth to untruth, the cruel Bhats who put the barber's razor on the heads of their mothers and sisters." He called them hypocrites "intent on securing their own selfish ends," who despised Europeans, yet flattered them in "servile ways" and saluted them "by bending down again and again." Chavan argued that Brahmins refused to tolerate the reforms of the Satyashodak Samaj because it challenged them directly. He described Brahmin priests as Golaks, or the illegitimate offspring of "shaved widows," and warned of dire consequences if they cheated non-Brahmins or clamored for "more Dakshina" in the future.

Antagonism between Brahmins and non-Brahmins was at an all-time high in Pune in August 1926—and the writers of *Deschache Dushman* were in jail—when a young Maratha man named Hari Narayan Dhanavade was accused of attempting to molest an eighteen-year-old Brahmin woman named Dwarakabai. An inflammatory newspaper article reported that a witness had seen "the accused in the act of moving his face towards her" when he was dragged away from his victim. Dhanavade maintained that he had been standing in a doorway, far from the incident, when he was set upon by thirty to thirty-five Brahmin youth. Tilak's *Mahratta* editorialized: "It is an insult to the womanhood of Maharashtra.... To the brahmans we have only to say one word. If they wish to live in honour then they must face the crisis with courage, manliness and bravery. They must take every step to defend the honor of their sisters and daughters. They will, we trust, prove equal to the occasion.... it is said that this assault is a most cowardly campaign that is being carried out through some leaders of the non-Brahman party against the Brahman community and their womanhood." The newspaper noted the increased frequency of such incidents in the prior six years in southern Maharashtra, where a concerted campaign to boycott Brahmins had been taking place. The *Vijayi Maratha* challenged this view and noted that "public rudeness to women was originally inculcated by the Tilakites and Brahman Ganapati melas and Tilakite and Brahman anti-feminist movements," and that there was an "old tradition" (among Brahmins) of "composing abusive song against educated women" and "reviling them at will." The paper went on to note that it was non-Brahmin men who had protected Brahmin women when they were abused and set upon by Brahmin men for supporting the Patel (Intercaste Marriage) Bill. In the first decades of the twentieth century, a set of mutually constitutive if deeply contradictory sociopolitical processeswere atwork: emergent forms of upper-caste female mobility and domestic modernity; the heightened centrality of Maratha genealogy and of Kshatriya status for upwardly mobile non-Brahmin families; a long-standing critique of Brahmin hegemony and Hindu history; and finally, a burgeoning anticolonial movement that sought political unity among disparate castes and classes and that took distinctive regional shape. Partha Chatterjee has argued that cultural nationalism revalued the Hindu domestic through women's alignment with the spiritual interior of the nation, even as it gave women a new place in public life and allowed them to navigate the public spaces of work and politics without imputation of sexual impropriety. 108 Chatterjee's argument describes the logic of anticolonial nationalism as *derivative* of colonial categories and *reactive* to the colonizer's discourse about the colonized, so that cultural nationalists could value the domestic intimate even as they sought to transform gendered relations within the family. Chatterjee's account addresses the affective centrality of the domestic sphere—and the Hindu upper-caste woman who symbolized it—for nationalist thought, but fails to take note of the political ambiguity that surrounded this figure. Given the centrality of gender and sexual regulation to the discursive hegemony of Brahmanism in western India, the Brahmin woman had long personified elements of non-Brahmin critique, even as she became the rallying point for a renewed politics of Brahmanism. Here, the historic conflict between Brahmins and non-Brahmins was staged through competing narratives of caste masculinity and differential claims over women.

In contrast to this public, explicitly confrontational, masculinist politics, Dalit reformers' masculinity was predicated on the reform of gender within their community and the defence of community honor against the disdain of outsiders. In 1908, the *Somavanshiya Mitra* published a letter from Shivubai Vallad Lakshman Jadhav-Sonkamble, who identified herself as a *murali*. *Muralis* were young girls from the Mahar, Mang, *kunbi,* and so-called nomadic communities who were married off to the god Khandoba at his temple in Jejuri in fulfillment of a vow. *Muralis* wore a *mangalsutra* of seven cowrie shells and, although human marriages were denied them, as nominal wives of the god they were obli-gated to provide sexual services to men. *Murali* dedication was among a range of regionally distinctive practices involving women of all statuses, which came to be glossed by the colonial state as ritual "prostitution." The lives of dedicated women, however, were more complex. Many remained with one partner all their lives. As temple servants, others acquired property in the form of tax-free *inam* lands.

The legendary Pavalabai was dedicated as a *murali,* though her exquisite beauty and performative skills brought her to the attention of the famous Brahmin *tamasgir* (tamasha performer), Patthe Bapurao, born Sridhar Kulkarni (1866–1948). Pavalabi joined Patthe's troupe and became his companion. Though she was a famous performer, Pavalabai's career mirrored the reduced significance of traditional popular culture to an emergent Dalit politics and the growing presence of a reformist critique of (Dalit) female sexuality. Thus the new performative medium of the Ambedkari *jalsa,*was composed solely of men and reflected long-standing efforts of male reformers to break the association between *tamasha* and the sexual promiscuity of its (female) Dalit performers.

Shivubai's letter was written against this backdrop of male reformers working to abolish stigmatizing practices, especially ritual dedication and sexual servitude. She responded to a letter written by a Mahar *panch* (religious head) castigating *muralis* as social evils whose sexual promiscuity was ruining Dalit men and their families. Shivubai objected that she was forced to do her job by the men of her community. She noted that many women converted to Islam and Christianity to avoid prostituting themselves. Indeed, Shivubai held the men of her community responsible for perpetuating the practice and called for a campaign against fathers who dedicated daughters. Shivubai's indictment of the men who perpetuated the practice was distinctive. Her point was overwhelmed, however, by multiple and overlapping efforts to criminalize the practice. The practice of *murali* dedication was strongest near Jejuri and in southern Maharashtra, where it was associated with a distinctive inheritance practice among the Mahar and Talwar communities. In 1906, the collector of Bijapur argued that "the prevalence of the practice of dedicating girls to prostitution among the Mahars is partly attributed to the fact that the male issue of prostitute daughters are allowed to succeed to a Mahar watan" when a man dies without male offspring. Bomanji argued that even if the practice was customary, "this recognition of illegitimate children should be stopped." What Bomanji failed tomention, however, was that the decision to allow a *murali*'s male heirs to inherit their mother's property had been reached *after a decision to disinherit muralis from directly owning ancestral property*. On February 27, 1857, the collector of Dharwad had "brought to notice the law of inheritance prevailing among Mahars and other low castes that a man dying without male offspring could leave property to a daughter only if she was a 'professional prostitute.'" The collector noted that though it was practiced among "groups comparatively unimportant in numbers and social position," the "loathsome custom" encouraged women to lead a life of "privileged profligacy." The then Revenue Commissioner for Alienations, Sir Barrow Ellis, noted that "though prostitution was not expressly a condition for tenure, it was customary to retain one unmarried daughter to hand down watan to illegitimate offspring." Government Resolution no. 6788, passed on January 22, 1858 barred ownership through illegitimates. Locally, however, the practice was clearly condoned. A complex case from 1873, involving a Talwarki *watan* in the name of "Vianki Talwar," brought up questions of whether a prostitute's adopted son, or her prostitute sister's biological son should inherit her estate. In this case, as with all other cases originating in the Dharwar district, it was decided that inheritance should skip the prostitute and go directly to her male illegitimate offspring. Thus the depiction of the practice of ritual dedication as a form of sexual servitude (and social scandal) was only partially true: *murali* reform gathered steam after female inheritance was stigmatized and Mahar and Talwarmen had become beneficiaries of governing paradigms that privileged patrilineal inheritance.

By the 1890s, various missionary groups had taken up the issue and suggested punishing parents and priests who enforced the tradition and recommended the transfer of dedicated women to orphanages. N.G. Chandavarkar, a social reformer, famous justice of the Bombay High Court and a member of the Society for the Protection of Children, made similar recommendations. By the time the noted Indologist R.G. Bhandarkar sent up a memorial from prominent Indian and European citizens of Poona in August 1906, it was found that an extensive discussion of the *devadasi* issue had already taken place inMadras in 1903.

The figures for dedication in southern Maharashtra for the period 1905–9, when the *murali* controversy reached its height, was as follows: 836 in Belgaum, 911 in Bijapur, and 876 in Dharwar district. The Bombay government's inquiry into the practice encompassed more than four hundred pages of testimony by district magistrates in Bombay, extensive debate on whether *murali* dedication could be criminalized, as well as far-reaching transformations of Hindu law to prevent illegitimates from inheriting—whether male offspring of *muralis* or *dasiputras* customarily entitled to a half share from a Shudra father's estate. The opinion of Dalit male reformers was not solicited, let alone the *muralis*.

Though sidelined by the government, Dalit reformers like Kamble applauded the effort and lobbied for community support. More significant, if rarely noted, is the fact that public attention to the practice of *muralis'* dedication shifted power within the community toward the viewpoint of male Dalit reformers and publicists. The degradation of Dalit women became a powerful issue around which they mobilized to demand gendered respectability through the abolition of customary practice. As much as intervention into *murali* practice was a means to reform the Dalit family, it was also the lever to move power away from figures such as the *panch* and male heads of household and toward Dalit publicists who wielded a normative conception of sexual vulnerability. Debates over ritual dedication— now recast as prostitution—became crucial to the reconstitution of Dalit masculinity even as it secured the social power of publicists, pedagogues, and community spokesmen.

Shivubai's letter launched a furious debate in and beyond the *Somavanshiya Mitra*. Efforts were made in Jejuri to educate families against dedicating their daughters. Shivram Janba Kamble held a meeting in Jejuri where he made a speech against the practice. Muralis like Shivubai held fathers responsible for pushing their daughters into the practice and criticized male customers for creating a market for *muralis*' sexual labor. Butmen castigated muralis for seducing them and breaking up families, thereby assuming *muralis'* "consent" to their dedication. This was tricky given the normal age of dedication and its representation as customary practice. And yet, *muralis* (and their families) were blamed for perpetuating a practice that stigmatized the entire community. Increasingly, Dalit reformers—like missionaries—suggested criminalizing *murali* dedication. A 1909 reformers' petition demanded the registration of *muralis* and the prosecution of parents who performed new dedications. This produced a climate among Mahars that was responsive to criminalization of the practice. By then, the Bombay government had reached a consensus that criminalizing the practice was the most direct means of curtailing it. No new legislation was passed, but a proclamation banning the practice and reiterating the punishment for dedication was issued. Subsequently, the *Somavanshiya Mitra* carried news of two men, Kisan Sadhu Mahar of Jejuri and Mahalu Mahar of Bombay, prosecuted for dedicating their daughter and sister, aged eleven and thirteen, respectively.

Although some *muralis* supported criminalizing the practice of dedication, their primary focus was on redefining their position within the Dalit community. In addition to prosecuting muralis, Dalit reformers like Kamble also promoted *murali* marriage and sexual monogamy as the route to gendered respectability. Shivubai argued that marrying *muralis* acknowledged men's responsibility for the practice, even as it enhanced *muralis'* self-respect and community standing. In fact, on April 18, 1909, the *Somavanshiya Mitra* noted that Shivubai had married the social reformer, Ganpatrao Hanumantrao Gaikwad. Marriage offered protection in a context where men were actively involved in acquiring, dedicating, and frequenting *muralis*. For the women who chose to remain *muralis,* however, emphasis on marriage further stigmatized the practice and pushed it into a zone of shameful secrecy. *Murali* remarriage continued to have great public support. At a meeting of men and women from the *devadasi* and *jogini* communities in Bombay in 1936, Ambedkar addressed women from Kamathipura, the red-light district of Bombay:

The Mahar women of Kamathipura are a shame to the community. Unless you are prepared to change your ways we shall have nothing to do with you, and we shall have no use for you. There are only two ways open to you: either you remain where you are and continue to be despised and shunned or you give up your disgusting professions and come with us.... You will ask me how you are to make your living. There are hundreds of ways of doing it. You must marry and settle down to normal domestic life as women of other classes do and not live under conditions that inevitably drag you into prostitution. As the reform of the traditional practice of *murali* dedication came to be allied with the reform of the Dalit intimate, sexual monogamy and the production of family became appealing alternatives for Dalit men and women to whom this held out a recognizable model of respectability.

The fraught position of female subjectivity "between community and state" is an enduring binarism in South Asian historiography. An adroit colonial move allied women with caste and religious communities and simultaneously castigated communities for reproducing female backwardness and preventing female emancipation. As the relationship between women and community deepened, first in reaction to colonial intervention and later as a form of nationalist glorification, the possibility of gender equality was also precluded. By the turn of the century, uppercaste nationalists had recuperated women as symbols of a modernized "tradition" and relegated them to the inner recesses of community life, arguing that women would be enfranchised from within community rather than through colonial state intervention. An issue taken up largely by Christianmissionaries and later by Dalit reformers, murali reform was distinct from this colonial-nationalist association of women with tradition.

Here, the issue was the overdetermined association of Dalit female sexuality with sexual availability and degraded female value. The ill treatment of the upper-caste Hindu widow by scriptural injunctions is an apt comparison, although Dalit reformists differed in their efforts to create a set of secular associations between femininity and domesticity. As the work of regulating Dalit women continued in more dispersed forms, the degraded status of women was seen to be closely related to the emasculation of Dalit men. Fifteen years after the *murali* issue died down, an editorial by the Dalit activist and thinker B.R. Ambedkar asked why Brahmin and upper-caste women enjoyed an exalted status as mothers when Dalit women's children were subjected to humiliation and denied basic recognition, negating all the desires that a mother might have for her child's well-being. He went on to say, "You have given birth to [us] men, and when we are treated worse than animals, it hurts you." Thus linked to women's degradation, Dalit masculinity was simultaneously positioned as wounded and vulnerable. Importantly, however, the onus was on Dalit women to reform themselves and play a central role in modernizing the community. They had to resignify the gendered habitus: "You should wear your sari in the way that upper-caste women wear their saris. You incur no expense by doing so. Similarly, the many necklaces around your neck, and the silver and tin bangles youwear from wrist to elbow is a mark of identification [*olakhnyachi khun*].... If you must wear jewellery, then get gold jewellery made. If you cannot, then don't wear jewellery. Pay attention to cleanliness!"

What did these exhortations mean for women from a stigmatized community? On one hand, like upper-caste ideologies, they symbolically associated women's status with community status. On the other hand, they emphasized the significance of clothing, jewellery, and the right to ceremonial display as aspects of self-fashioning vigorously policed by upper castes. The right to a new habitus, to good clothing, footwear, jewellery, and bodily comportment—standing erect while speaking, refusing to contort the body in an obsequious fashion—was critical to Dalit self-fashioning. Though discourses of sexuality and of female enfranchisement were caste-specific, the focus on the feminized body—how it was experienced and represented—was central to a range of political processes. Women, marriage, and family remained irreplaceable sites for reproducing caste ideas and practices. Thus emergent forms of a caste specific female subjectivity were directly implicated in the production of a social field where transformations of the non-Brahmin and Dalit habitus could occur, and they deeply affected emergent forms of caste masculinity. The politics of *caste and gender* complicated modes of political participation and of subject-formation associated with masculinization and community modernization. In a very real sense, however, the stage was set for a Dalit public sphere rendered male separate but equal: school, temple, and the dalit self

We all drink water from the same tap, in hotels and Irani stores we sit at the same table and drink tea and eat bread and biscuits. On trains and steam boats we sit with our thighs and shoulders touching.

As a distinctive identity for Mahar Dalits was clarified in the late nineteenth century, so toowere the emerging tensions of village life intensified— conflicts between Dalit and Maratha groups over provision of services, the exploitation of caste labor, and friction between claims to Brahmin proportional representation and anti-casteism increased. The situation made escape from the village highly desirable for Dalits. Indeed, the liberatory potential of machine and metropolis exerted a profound hold on the Dalit imagination and the Dalit modernity that developed in concert with the urbanization of Dalit communities.

Mahar Dalits migrated to cities like Bombay and Nagpur in disproportionate numbers. According to the Indian census, between 1872 and

1881 the number of Mahars in Bombay rose 66 percent. By 1938, almost 92 percent of untouchable workers in the city were Mahars. Mahars performed unskilled labor under difficult and exploitative working conditions—40 percent of them were considered to be performing "coolie" labor, and they constituted more than 45 percent of the total workforce.

143 They were concentrated in particular industries: more than 60 percent worked in the railways or textile mills—the railways were the first and most significant mode of Mahar employment and drew a majority of workers from the Nasik and Ratnagiri districts. Significant numbers worked for the municipality, for factories, and for public works companies such as Bombay Electric Supply and Transport (BEST).

Maharmigrants from Satara comprised the bulk of dock workers and coalminers. Urban migration and urban infrastructure—especially everyday technologies of travel and communication that appeared to shrink, even obviate, social distance—provoked key transformations of Dalit selfhood. *Din Bandhu*'s commentator on urban lifewas clear that modern travel— "sitting with thighs and shoulders touching"—obliterated caste distinctions, because it was impossible to maintain caste taboos or regulate contact in public conveyances. Lower-caste use of steamboats, trains, and trams opened a new dimension where touch was rendered anonymous even as it was secularized. However, these new spaces were in constant danger of being overwhelmed by social pressure to reproduce hidebound Brahminical beliefs and practices, as Valangkar's *abhang* warned.

It is likely that Valangkar's *abhang* was publicizing the Din Bandhu Sarvajanik Sabha, which was formed in 1884 by Krishnarao Bhalaker and others to counter what they considered to be a Brahmin-dominated, exclusivist Sarvajanik Sabha. Valangkar drew on a set of gendered associations between social stigma and public intercourse to challenge Dalits' civic exclusion. Like a woman naturally "shy of her husband and public gatherings" when she was menstruating, Dalits also experienced "shame" and self-revulsion. One was never to see a Mang or a Mahar in public. Valangkar's *abhang* challenged the Dalit's internalization of pollution and proposed that without equality between Brahmin and Mahar, between the excessively fortunate and the excessively stigmatized, there could be no true "public." For Valangkar, the organization of the world through the phenomenology of touch and smell also enabled an extension of stigma from biological bodies to the metaphorical collective of the body politic. In the interplay between literal touch and the imaginative democratization of the body he saw possibilities for self-fashioning and political transformation. Going further, Valangkar also suggested that only with a *caste mind* cleaned of impurities could the Sarvajanik Sabha (a regional precursor to the Indian National Congress) accept the Dalit castes.

Ironically, then, the institutional spaces and amenities of colonial urbanity exacerbated the experience of the caste body by highlighting the irrationality of caste segregation. As Dalit publicists—Valangkar, Kamble, and others—denaturalized the caste order, they also motivated caste Hindus to justify caste distinction in new ways that utilized the regulatory power of colonial institutions to produce new instruments of caste hegemony. Both dimensions, Dalit emancipation and new forms of subjection, were played out in schools and temples.

Access to education was a long-standing demand of Dalit publicists, as it had been for Satyashodak activists. Education was central to self-financing because it demystified the Brahmin trickery at the heart of the continued dehumanization of Dalits and non-Brahmins. There was also the material fact of Brahmin preponderance in colonial administration. Conflicts over access to colonial schooling emphasized the built-in contradictions of colonial education. In 1882, the Hunter Commission asserted the government of India's commitment to untouchable education, reaffirming Wood's Dispatch of 1854, which opened government-funded schools to all castes in response to missionary pressure. The record of government-funded education for untouchables was poor, however. For instance, the first public schools in Poona's Purandhar district opened in 1836, but by 1839 only 17 of 759 pupils came from the untouchable communities. The numbers did not rise significantly in following years.

The most famous case is of the Christian Mahar convert from Dharwar who petitioned the government in June 1856 after being denied admission into the government school. The Bombay government refused to compromise the education of the majority of caste Hindu students at a government school for the sake of "a single individual" by making caste Hindus associate with a Mahar student. Caste Hindus' right to exclusive education was thus reinterpreted as the colonial administration's respect for the religious sentiments of the majority.

The Free Church of Scotland and the American Marathi Mission had supported Phule's Society for the Promotion of Mahars and Mangs, which established schools in Pune between 1848 and 1852. The extensive involvement of missionaries in the field of untouchable education was viewed as blurring the line between proseletyzation and social service, compromising the colonial state's explicit commitment to religious noninterference after the 1857 Mutiny. Colonial officials held missionaries responsible for politicizing untouchables who showed "independence and self-sufficiency," by inciting them to "claima right" evenwhen untouchables themselves chose not to exercise it, thus exacerbating conflict between the majority of caste Hindu students and a few untouchable students.

Conflicts over equal education in the 1880s and 1890s confirmed government fears of unrest. Such an incident had taken place in Rajangaon, in Sirur *taluka,* Pune, in October 1886, when the village *patel* and *kulkarni* twice closed down a school run by the American Marathi Mission, using violence and intimidation to prevent the seven Mahar (and two Maratha) children from attending the school run by Indian teachers.153 A similar report from Satara noted that Mahar boys were not allowed to sit in the school rooms with other boys, and that often a "few miserable Mahar boys are seen seated in the blazing sun outside scribbling on their slates and apparently entirely neglected."154 Or else, as happened in Manmad, Nasik district, in 1884–85, caste Hindus financed an English class through private funds rather than sending their children to the Anglo vernacular school run by the Church Mission Society, which also admitted untouchable students.

Often, the government's anxiety to maintain (and enhance) the population of students attending publicly funded English schools undercut the commitment to education for untouchables. 155 Increasingly, the colonial government faced a spate of petitions as untouchable students—who faced informal boycott by caste Hindus or the active enforcement of segregated education by colonial officials—petitioned for civic inclusion, while the parents of caste Hindu students wished to exclude untouchables from classrooms.

The Bombay Education Department had considerable leeway in deciding issues on a case-by-case basis in this contentious atmosphere.156 As government's general commitment to native education confronted its specific commitment to untouchables' education, a novel resolution arose:Dalit students were placed on the school's verandah at a distance fromboth casteHindu classmates and the classroom, to fulfill the colonialmission of educational access.

Sitting on the verandah obstructed the untouchable students' vision and hearing and left themvulnerable to the adversities of climate. In 1916, Communist activist R. B. More attended classes on the first floor of a school in Tale, in the Mangaon district, sitting on a scaffold erected by school authorities.157 Like the scaffold, the school verandah preserved the illusion of equal education even as it emphasized the liminal status of those Dalit students who had managed to secure a right to government education. Reinterpreting the caste Hindu position as the majority sentiment, colonial officials made the verandah a new technology of segregation that reproduced caste exclusion.

Dapoli, the hub of early Dalit activism, was also a significant site of struggles for equal education. After the Society for the Propogation of the Gospel closed down its primary school, military pensioners petitioned the government on July 1, 1892, to enrol fourteen of their children in the municipality's primary school. After asserting that admitting Dalit children would cause caste Hindu students to leave the school, the Dapoli municipality agreed to open a separate class with a separate teacher if the Mahar and Chambhar pensioners could collect enough boys. B. R. Ambedkar, who attended that school between 1894 and 1896, described how all the Dalit students sat in one room, placing their slates on the ground so teachers could examine them. The children were barred from the common water supply. The right to education, when combined with new practices of segregation, paradoxically *intensified* untouchable students' experience of stigma.

The Dapoli petitioners protested on September 8, 1892, requesting that the students be included in the other classrooms. When their petition was rejected by the Dapoli municipality, the petitioners approached colonial officials, who asked the municipality whether the children could be accommodated on the verandah. The municipality replied that the verandah was not large enough for all the children, but that the Dalit petitioners could pay Rs. 50 to enlarge it, Stalled, the pensioners continued up the bureaucratic line until J. Nugent, commissioner of the Southern Division, told Vishnudas Hari Barve, the chairman of the municipality, that he was required to open the school to the Dalit children.

The municipality responded that equal education should occur gradually in order not to offend orthodox sensibility, and by November 1894 the municipal engineer had not yet approved verandah extension. After threatening repeal of the school's grant, Director of Public Instruction K. M. Chatfield instructed the Dalit children to maintain a safe distance from other Hindu children in the classroom. A visit to the municipal school at the end of 1894 found "the Officers' children sitting in the same class rooms along with the other boys at the distance of three or four feet and receiving instruction with the class regularly." The Dapoli pensioners were said to be satisfied, because "they never wished that their children should mix with the other boys but they wanted that they should receive instruction along with them, separately in the same class rooms, and this is now done." Though the collector of Ratnagiri decided to monitor the progress of untouchable education through quarterly reports, access to schools was a vexing one. Almost a decade later, in 1901, the president of the ADPM sent another petition to the Bombay government, claiming that Dalit students continued to be excluded from the school. As Dalit students tried to enter schools at the turn of the twentieth century, equal right to education was converted into the right to segregated education for untouchable students: caste restrictions were respected due to fear of boycott by caste Hindu students. The school verandah was a new mechanism of exclusion that encompassed overlapping structures of exclusion. One was based on Brahminical norms that replicated caste hierarchies. The other, grounded in liberal language, acquiesced to caste Hindus' refusal of mixed-caste schools as a matter of respect for the opinions of the majority community. Levels of education among untouchable students continued to be abysmally low: less than 0.48 percent were literate in 1911; by 1931, that number rose to 2.9 percent. 168 In response to segregated schooling, Mahar Dalits in Nagpur, Bombay, Poona, and Ahmednagar established separate schools and hostels for Dalit students in the first two decades of the twentieth century, complementing earlier work in Vidarbha and the Central Provinces. Shivram Janba Kamble defended separate schools and argued that because Brahmin schoolmasters perpetuated caste distinctions, schools had to hire Muslim teachers. By 1908, Vithal Ramji Shinde's DCM ran fifteen day schools, six Sunday schools, and four industrial schools in Bombay, Poona, and Ahmednagar. By 1909, the DCM had even reached into Dapoli. In 1916, of 1,600 Depressed Class students, 500 were enrolled in Shinde's schools. Though they were spurred by the failure of government schools to include Dalit students, separate schooling defined a powerful strategy for refashioning the Dalit self.

The Mahar community's growing refusal to countenance socio ritual stigmatization produced new sites of contestation. Like separate educational facilities, efforts to build separate temples reflect an arc of Dalit critique. The economic enfranchisement of an important group of Mahar elites in the Vidarbha region enabled the institutionalization of a separate religious authority for Mahars. The 1877 opening of Empress Mills in Nagpur had provided a new source of livelihood for Mahar Dalits. In addition, a Mahar petty bourgeoisie of *malguzars* (landlords) financed the move into an industrializing cotton economy. This educated elite maintained links with rural areas, endowing schools and hostels and playing a role in shaping early Dalit politicization.

Born in 1864, Vithoba Raoji Moon Pande typified the new Mahar "small scale capitalist" first mentioned in an 1899 settlement report for the Nagpur district. Educated in a mission school and influenced by critiques of caste hierarchy and Hindu superstition, he took advantage of his frequent travel as a cotton trader to act as a *pracharak* (preacher) for the Gorakshan Sabha (Organization for Cow Protection) which had links with the Arya Samaj.

In 1906, Moon Pande established the Antyaj Samaj (Society for the Out castes), renamed the Loyal Mahar Sabha in 1912 and presided over by his close associate, the Reverend G.D. Philips. Before he died in 1924, Moon Pande had requested nomination to the Central Provinces Legislative Council. Like Valangkar, Moon Pande's life coincided with the emergence of the Dalit public and publicists in the crucible of colonial modernity. Unlike Valangkar, however, Moon Pande's challenge to caste discrimination instituted an alternative source of religious hierarchy.

When Maharswere denied use of the Ambal tank at Nagpur's Ramtek temple in 1903, Moon Pandemobilized a large group of Mahars who belonged to *bhajan mandalis* (groups that performed religious music).

They went to the home of the temple owner, Raoji Raghuji Bhosle, who gave Mahars permission to bathe at the Ambal tank on the condition that they stop eating beef and, more generally, desist from unhygienic practices. Bhosle's response typified the upper-caste reformism that rationalized Dalits' degradation as resulting from their stigmatizing practices.

Moon Pande appears to have supported this reform because he held meetings in villages near Nagpur to persuade Mahars to stop eating beef, even demanding that they take a public oath to that effect. Although they did so, it was clear that relations with temple authorities had reached an impasse.

The Ramtek Temple Committee asked Mahars to channel a portion of the fees paid to the *pande* (Brahmin priest) at the *ghats*—for services like shaving or making offerings of *pindadaan* to the ancestors—to the Gorakshan Sabha to fund separate Mahar bathing *ghats* at the temple tank. No Mahar *ghats* were built, however.

Moon Pande responded to the Brahmins' exploitation of Mahars at the Ramtek temple by establishing a separate Mahar priesthood to minister to the community's religious needs. To counter the Gorakshan Sabha's failure to build separate Mahar *ghats,* Moon Pande asked—and received—permission from the RamtekTemple Committee to build a separate temple for Mahars on January 24, 1905. In March 1906, he acquired land for the purpose at a high price. That same year the Antyaj Samaj committee took over management of the new Mahar *ghats,* established an independent Mahar priesthood, and gave Moon Pande *pandeship,* the right to perform rites and receive *dakshina* (charities) from Mahar pilgrims at the *ghats.*

By 1907–08, this parallel structure of religious authority protected Mahar pilgrims from paying extravagant sums for *shraddha* (funeral) rites. Moon Pande's use of Mahars' growing economic strength to assert a positive Hindu identity went further. Alongwith the Reverend G.D. Philips, he collected funds for a separate temple, a Shivalaya, near the Mahar *ghats.* Construction began on October 27, 1920, and was completed in 1924, shortly before Moon Pande's death.

Separate institutions signaled failed efforts at civic and religious equality. They also indexed the changed discursive and political contexts of Dalit self-fashioning. Unlike the establishment of separate schools, Moon Pande's temple and Mahar priesthood reproduced religious hierarchy by legitimizing the priest's role.

Instead of criticizing Hinduism in toto and envisioning a complete excision from Hindu religiosity, Moon Pande's critique of religious exclusion produced a mimetic structure of religious authority, a Mahar priesthood. At the same time, his work underscored the growing economic strength of an emerging Mahar elite whose power as reformers within the community allowed them to challenge the Hindu hierarchy. Moon Pande's actions were radical and reformist, and indicated the ambivalences of Mahar religiosity and the limits to Hindu inclusion. Perhaps more pointed and problematic is them atter of thirteen Mahars who entered a temple dedicated to the god Meghnath.

Shiva, in the village of Washer in Chanda district of the Central Provinces on September 22, 1922. They "slaughtered a goat there, sprinkled its blood upon the idol, put *shendur* [vermillion] on the image and adorned it with flowers." Though staged as religious worship, this incident blurred distinctions between the sacred and the profane because anointing a deity with goat's blood could also be interpreted as an act of defilement. The ambivalence of the animal sacrifice arose from its signifying potential as worship and defilement. If upper-caste Hindus interpreted animal sacrifice as desecrating the temple, it is also true that temples to Shiva, a non-Brahmin god in Maharashtra, would have allowed the practice of animal sacrifice. Was it the sacrifice of the goat (as opposed to the more common buffalo), or the physical presence of Dalit worshippers in the temple that challenged its sacrality? Could the right to worship encompass the right to worship differently, as well as the right of Dalits to worship in a mixed-caste temple?

VIOLENCE BY PRIVATE ACTORS

On January 25, 1998, the Dalit colony of Veludavur village in Villapuram district was attacked by members of seven caste Hindu villages. The attack was allegedly perpetrated by the Vanniya caste and instigated by the Naidars (both backward castes). Tensions began with a government auction of common properties in the village, such as ponds and tamarind trees; the Dalits were demanding their right to participate. The same evening, Vanniyas entered and destroyed 400 Dalit huts. Many of the young Dalit men were in Andhra Pradesh at the time, cultivating sugarcane. Only women, children and the elderly were left in the village, and the women were particularly targeted. A social worker in the village claimed that there were "sexual attempts on many women, but they don't want to talk about it. Many are unmarried or their husbands are away. They fear the consequences if these things are revealed." Over 700 families were displaced as a result of the attack. They took shelter in neighboring villages.

Burnad Fatima of the Tamil Nadu Women's Forum (TNWF) explained the number of cases TNWF had come across in which women were targets of caste clashes:

Any time any caste riots take place, there is immediate action against women and immediate raping. During last year's riots, a forty-year-old woman was gang raped. A seventy-year-old was dragged out of her house and stripped. In Anchipet a handicapped girl was thrown from her wheelchair which was then damaged. Innocent women are butchered, raped, and killed even though they are not directly responsible for any of the riots.

TNWF and People's Watch members went on to describe another attack during the southern district clashes, and the lack of press attention to such cases:

In Nammakal [district] a girl was gang raped, murdered, and then butchered. She belonged to the scavengers community. The men belonged to the weaving community. They cut off her hand and leg and shaved her head. They then cut her head and put a stick into her private parts and then hung her head with the stick. Why are they driven to this extent? Because for them Dalits are nothing. They give more respect to their animals... The papers are censored, they don't name the community, and they don't report the figures.93

A representative of the Rural Center for Women's Development in Tirunelveli district spoke to Human Rights Watch of instances of rape by landlords, other upper castes, and the police, "who always support the landlords... [W]omen never say anything because they are afraid and need employment. Also society would blame them. Even their husband would separate from them.

Punduthai, a forty-five-year-old widow and mother of two, told Human Rights Watch that she had to leave her village to protect herself and her daughter from sexual abuse by Thevar men during the clashes.

In the village, the Thevars entered the house and had sexual intercourse with the Dalit women. They used force and committed rape. My husband died. My daughter is also a mature girl. She is twenty years old.

In November 1997 a twenty-two-year-old Dalit woman spoke up against the debt bondage of her husband and his family (Thevars are the dominant moneylenders and Dalits their primary borrowers). As a result she was brutally beaten and sexually abused by a Vanniya landlord:

Her husband and father-in-law did not go to work for two days. The landlord came and asked why. He threatened and insulted her, and she said, "We are not living here under your mercy." The landlord went wild. He started beating her, he tore her blouse to pieces, touched her breast, hit her in the vagina and rolled her on the ground. There was no one to stop him.

Due to disinterest, ignorance of proper procedure, or their own caste biases, the police failed to register or properly investigate many cases of attacks against women during the clashes. Only with pressure from organized women's and human rights groups has the issue been placed before national commissions. The recommendations of these commissions, however, are not binding under statutory law.

POLICE TORTURE OF WOMEN/CUSTODIAL VIOLENCE

In addition to attacks by members of the upper castes, women are attacked by the police, security forces, and private militias or armies hired by Thevars. Human Rights Watch spoke to many government officials, activists, and villagers in the Tamil Nadu region about police torture and custodial violence against women. C. V. Shankar, director for the Adi Dravida Tribal Welfare Department, of the state government of Tamil Nadu, explained:

We found that women are put in front in both communities and act as a buffer. This has resulted in police action against women. They are taken far away from their homes. Unless they were directly involved in violence, they should not be arrested. In some cases we felt that the arrests could have been avoided.

H. Hanumanthappa, then-chairman of the National Commission for Scheduled Castes and Scheduled Tribes, added:

Once the police start raiding, the menfolk run away. Then they [police] make women the victims. The procedure they adopt is to take the child or wife so that the men come back. They feel that they are the masters of the situation. It has resulted in mass rapes.

The police practice of taking family members as hostages in order to force their relatives to turn themselves in is a common occurrence in Tamil Nadu and other parts of the country. Specific incidents of hostage-taking and custodial violence against women are described below.

Guruswamy Guruammal, a twenty-six-year-old agricultural labourer, suffered a miscarriage as a result of brutal beatings during a police raid on December 2, 1997. She is a resident of Chilaumbotti village of the southern district of Theni andearns Rs. 20 a day (US$0.50). The raid had preceded a planned visited by Dr. Krishanaswamy; posters had been distributed to announce his arrival. On December 2, one such poster was burned by Thevars in the district which led to a Pallar protest and road block. Police raided the village in response to the protests and assaulted many Dalits with their lathis.

At 9:00 a.m. the police lathi-charged the villagers. Superintendent of Police Rajesh Das called me a pallachi, which is a caste name for prostitute. He then opened his pant zip. Sub-Inspector Arivanandam, who is from same community as me, was also there. Rajesh Das said, "Please stand, do not go," and other police scolded me. At 11:00 a.m. the sub-collector came.

Guruammal begged the police at the station to help her. She explained that she was pregnant and in need of medical attention. In response, they called her names and mocked her for making such bold statements the day before. Eventually, Guruammal was transferred to the Trichi jail hospital, where she remained for twenty-five days. After ten days, she had a miscarriage. At the time of the interview, and as a result of being dragged and beaten by the police fists and guns, Guruammal was still visibly scarred on her neck, arms, legs, and abdomen.

She claimed that the police told her to testify that the raid on her village was in search of the illicit brewing of *arrack* (illicit liquor):

They said if you accept the fact that the raid was for arrack, then you will be released. They said, "If you don't say arrack, we will file charges against you." So these are the cases that were filed against me and the fifty-three men.

Although Guruammal was attacked as punishment for speaking up against the police, many other women are punished for alleged crimes committed by their male relatives. Activists from People's Watch and the Tamil Nadu Women's Forum explained the tactics employed by the police:

The police enter houses and attack the women even though they should never search when the women are alone. The police are arresting women if either the husband or son is absconding. They take them into custody and rape them. Three years ago, in a slum nearby, a forty-three-year-old woman lost her husband. Her son was involved in a murder case. She was arrested along with her daughter and daughter-in-law. They were taken to the police station where the police raped the mother in front of the other women. They then brought her home and burned her in her hut.105

The activists also described a new tactic employed by the police of removing women's clothes and beating them from their knees to their shoulders, "because they know that women will not show others these parts."

At a Madras conference on women's rights, held on April 28 and 29, 1995, dozens of Dalit and tribal women publicly came forward to testify about their experiences of custodial rape at the hands of Tamil Nadu police. The conference was sponsored by the Tamil Nadu Women's Forum and Asia Pacific Forum for Women, Law and Development. In many of the statements, women claimed that the police were searching for their male relatives when they first came upon them. Pursuant to Section 160 of the Criminal Procedure Code, police conducting investigations are prohibited from questioning female witnesses at any place other than their residence. Women are often unaware of these laws, and their ignorance is exploited by the police. As she stated at the women's rights conference, Rangammal of Orathanadu village came into contact with the police when her husband was repeatedly arrested for selling arrack. One night, the police came to her house and forcibly took her to the police station.

In the village of Muthaandikuppam, South Arcot district, a husband filed a complaint against his wife, Vasantha, after a misunderstanding between the couple. On the night of March 21, 1994, Vasantha was forced to spend the night in the police station under the pretext that there were no women police available to escort her home. She was "gang raped by four constables and a sub-inspector of the same police station and [then] murdered. They attempted to dispose [of] the body but could not succeed. They spread a rumour that Vasantha committed suicide by hanging from the fan at the police rest room in the police station." Community members, civil liberties groups, and political parties demanded appropriate, severesanctions against the perpetrators. The Tamil Nadu government responded by temporarily suspending the constables involved.

On February 21, 1995, twenty-year-old Poonkothai witnessed the rape and murder of her forty-eight-year-old mother by police who were searching for her brother. The incident took place around 7:00 a.m. when police arrived at Poonkothai's house looking for her brother Murthy: "They blamed my mother [for] hiding the whereabouts of my brother, who is suspected in a murder of a person found dead_ near his house." Despite her mother's repeated denials, the police took both of them, along with Poonkothai's one-and-a-half-year-old daughter, to the Vannarapettai police station.

The police later brought her mother home, stuffed a piece of cloth in her mouth, poured petrol over her, and set her on fire. They left the scene soon thereafter. A neighbour intervened and took the mother to the hospital, where she later died. When Poonkothai's husband approached the police station to file a case, the police registered the death as a suicide. After many NGO protests, the police filed a First Information Report (FIR). Poonkothai's two neighbors, whose sons were also police suspects, and her two sisters-in-law were also taken into custody for several days and similarly tortured. One sister-in-law had just delivered a child.

A report produced by the women's conference stated: "The drama usually played by police is just this. They come in search of the offenders and finding them absconding, whisk away the womenfolk to the police station and outrage theirmodesty." The conference also concluded that atrocities committed on women by the police were increasing.

Renewed Clashes

From October to December 1998, violent confrontations in the districts of Ramanathapuram, Pudukkottai, Perambalur, and Cuddalore signaled that caste clashes had not only continued but had spread to once-peaceful districts. In Ramanathapuram district, Thevars responded to a state-wide Dalit conference by organizing a rally on October 4, 1998. That afternoon, streams of lorries carrying Thevar youths were seen heading toward Ramanathapuram. On the way, several vehicles stopped at roadside villages and Thevars entered Dalit and Muslim hamlets throwing petrol bombs and ransacking houses. Two women were killed. Thevar youths claimed that they were provoked, allegedly by Dalits placing barriers on the road. As news of the attacks spread, Dalits retaliated. Despite all the violence, Koottamaippu—the Thevar coalition sponsoring the rally—was allowed to hold it. Among its demands: the repeal of the Scheduled Castes and Scheduled Tribes (Prevention of Atrocities) Act, 1989.

Dalits and journalists throughout the affected areas have blamed the police and district administration for their failure to effectively respond to increasing tensions in the district arising from publicity for the conference. According to *Frontline,* a bi-monthly news magazine, "The police presence was minimal and vehicles were not being checked for weapons. This was in contrast to the intensive searches carried out by the police when Puthiya Tamalingam [a Dalit organization] held its rally on September 11."

The situation remained volatile in the district for days afterwards. Police were given shoot-on-sight orders for arsonists, while a large contingent of the striking police force was rushed in. Both sides also alleged harassment and torture by the police conducting raids under the pretext of searching for criminals and weapons. According to People's Watch, the death toll on both sides reached fifteen.

On October 7, 1998, three days after the incident, state Governor Fathima Beevi called for an overhauling of the police system to prevent "police excess." The director general of the Bureau of Police Research and Development urged implementation of the National Police Commission recommendations, while the chairperson of the State Human Rights Commission recommended that police personnel should be made to undergo human rights awareness training every six months. None of these recommendations had been implemented as of February 1999.

Just over a month after the violence in Ramanathapuram, caste tensions erupted in Thirunallur village in nearby Pudukkottai district. On November 19, 1998, three Dalit youths were stripped, tied to a tree, and beaten through the night. According to a press report, their "heads were tonsured, and they were also made to roll around the village temple in the presence of a large gathering which included their kith and kin. The next morning they were asked to leave the village." The attack was part of a judgment handed down by twelve members of the all-caste Hindu local village council: the young men were being punished for marrying non-Dalit Hindu girls. Tensions remained high in the village for weeks following the beatings. Not until a month later were the culprits charged and the victims givenpart of their compensation, under the Scheduled Castes and Scheduled Tribes (Prevention of Atrocities) Act, 1989.

On December 1, 1998, in a massive operation reminiscent of the 1995 police raid on Kodiyankulum village, 300 armed policemen entered the Dalit colony at Ogalur village in Perambalur district. Under the pretext of rounding up "anti-social elements," police reportedly entered over 1,000 homes and, using lathis and iron rods, attacked the residents. After causing extensive damage to their homes and property, police arrested sixty-nine Dalits. Among them were thirty-four women, some with babies in their arms and a few who were pregnant. The reported background to the attack was a dispute between the Dalits and the caste Hindus over a piece of temple land and the attempted sexual assault of a Dalit woman by a caste Hindu man in the village; the man accompanied the police during their attack. As of January 1999, the Dalit laborers were still unable to work in the caste Hindu fields and their children were unable to go to school.

Another incident, reported by the news magazine *Frontline,* took place on December 16, 1998. In Puliyur village, Cuddalore district, a mob of caste Hindus (Vanniyas) numbering about 300 raided a Dalit settlement and attacked its residents with sticks and iron rods. Approximately 500 houses were ransacked and thirteen Dalits seriously injured. The day before the attack, a Dalit funeral procession was stopped as it passed a Vanniya house. "In the melee that followed, the caste-Hindu resident was reportedly assaulted by a Dalit, who, it is said, had been slapped a day earlier for smoking in the presence of the caste-Hindu resident." In this case, smoking was a luxury to which the Dalits were not entitled in the presence of a caste Hindu.

TAMIL NADU GOVERNMENT-APPOINTED COMMISSIONS

State governments in India share a common history of appointing judicial commissions of inquiry to quell public outcries against police excesses during large-scale communal and caste clashes. Although these commissions do serve a political function, their findings, if and when released to the public, are frequently in favour of the state. The Tamil Nadu experience is no exception to this rule. As of December 1998 the state was one of five to have established a state human rights commission (SHRC). The commission's investigations into human rights abuses by the police and caste Hindus are, however, blocked if the state first appoints its own judicial commission of inquiry. Like the National Human Rights Commission, state human rights commissions are denied jurisdiction over an investigation if the matter is pending before "any commission duly constituted under any law for the time-being [sic] in force." The state government of Tamil Nadu has exploited this provision by appointing its own commissions of inquiry before state human rights commission investigations get underway. States have little control over the investigations of statutory (human rights) commissions. Conversely, government-appointed commissions almost invariably find in favour of the state and the police. Those findings that go against the state are rarely implemented or made public.

A Tamil Nadu government official explained that judicial commissions' findings "do not become public unless the government tables it with the legislature; findings that are against the state are often not tabled... By appointing its own commissions, the state government does not permit the State Human Rights Commission to do the investigation. It literally ties its hands." The appointment of judicial commissions has become almost routine following caste clashes. The Justice Mohan Commission, for example, was appointed by the state government in July 1997 to look into recurring caste clashes and suggest measures to prevent them, but only "after the state government knew that the State Human Rights Commission was on the job." The Justice Mohan Commission submitted its report in September 1998. In October 1998, Chief Minister Karunanidhi announced that not all the recommendations could be accepted.

In another large-scale clash in Coimbatore in November 1997, Muslims shops and houses were burned down by Hindus, reportedly with support from the police. Before the SHRC could take up the investigation, the state appointed the Justice Gokulakrishnan Commission, and "[a]gain their hands were tied." During the southern district clashes of April to December 1997, police opened fire in two villages and attacked Dalit women in a third. Three commissions headed by three district judges were immediately appointed. The director of People's Watch contends that "it has been the history of Dalit people that every commission of inquiry has gone against their interests." Another activist added that "the retired judges who are appointed always toe the line of the government."

Given proper resources, state human rights commissions stand to play an important role in the protection of human rights. Because their investigations enjoy greater independence from the state than judicial commission investigations, the statutes under which they are formed need to be amended to ensure that judicial commissions cannot be appointed as a means of undermining their powers. Moreover, the mandates of human rights commissions themselves need to be strengthened to ensure that their recommendations are binding and their findings are made public.

THE PATTERN OF ABUSE: SOUTHERN DISTRICT CLASHES

No Dalit has faith in the police establishment... The southern clashes have been attempts of Dalit self-assertion and a reflection of their loss of faith. —

Christodas Gandhi, Tamil Nadu implementation officer for the Atrocities Act 227.

Caste clashes in the southern state of Tamil Nadu have predominantly involved two communities: the Thevars (a backward caste) and the Pallars (or Dalits). As has been the case in other states, Dalits in Tamil Nadu have long suffered from exploitative economic relationships and have frequently been the victims of violence. However, changes since the early 1990s have altered the economic relationship between the Thevars and the Pallars and have changed the contours of the conflict. Having benefited from the state's policy of reservations in education and from the income provided by relatives working abroad, the Pallars have become much less dependent on Thevar employment and have begun to assert themselves in the political arena. The Thevars have responded to this threat to their hegemony with violence. Dalits, too, have begun to fight back.

This chapter examines caste clashes in the state's southern districts between July 1995 and December 1998. Unlike the conflict in the eastern state of Bihar, the violence is often spontaneous and not the result of organized armed movements. Much as in the state of Bihar, however, the police have colluded with the caste Hindus to preserve the status quo and keep Dalits from peacefully claiming their rights. The police, many of whom are Thevars themselves, have conducted raids on Dalit villages ostensibly to search for Dalit militants. During these raids, police have assaulted villagers and detained many under preventive detention laws. Women in particular have been targeted.

According to the Indian government's 1996-1997 annual report for the Ministry of Human Affairs, caste-related incidents in 1996 in the southern state of Tamil Nadu increased by 34 percent over previous years. Out of 282 reportedincidents, 238 took place between scheduled castes and other backward communities. The main caste groups involved were the Thevars, Naidars, and Vanniyas (all backward castes) and the Adi Dravidas and Pallars (both scheduled castes or Dalits). The number of incidents between Pallars and Thevars increased again dramatically at the height of caste clashes in the southern districts of Tamil Nadu from April 1997 to December 1998. The nexus between Thevars, the police, and district officials in the affected areas was repeatedly reflected in violent search and raid operations in Dalit villages, in the forced displacement of thousands of Dalit villagers, often with the aid of district officials, and in the disproportionate number of Dalits arrested under preventive detention statutes during the clashes. Abuses against Dalits continued following a police raid on the Dalits of Gundupatti village in February 1998 and violent clashes between Dalits and Thevars from October to December 1998. According to the state government, at least 251 people died in caste violence between August 1995 and October 1998.229

Clashes in the southern districts of Tamil Nadu have largely been attributed to increased Pallar economic and political autonomy and the backlash against it. Since the mid-1990s, the Pallars have begun to support a new political leadership, unaligned to mainstream political parties, and promoted by two movements: the Dalit Panthers of India (DPI) Tamil Nadu, and the Devendra Kula Vellalar Federation (DKVF) led by Dr. K. Krishnaswamy, a member of the Tamil Nadu legislative assembly. In 1998 the DKVF became a political party and named itself Puthiya Tamalingam. These political movements have provided an organized platform for growing resistance to the still prevalent norms of "untouchability" in the state. Dalits have demanded equal treatment in temple festivals, have refused to carry out ritually demeaning tasks, have demanded access to public water sources, and have claimed an equal share of public goods and village properties. Thevars have responded by "clinging more resolutely to their caste status as a way of affirming their superiority." Government statistics from 1995 revealed that Thevars were the perpetrators in 91 percent of cases involving the coercive enforcement of "untouchability" practices.

Context of Clashes

Between July 1995 and June 1996, clashes between Thevars and Pallars resulted in large-scale destruction of property, loss of life on both sides, and the arrest of many Dalit youths under preventive detention laws like the Tamil Nadu Goondas Act and the National Security Act, 1980.234 In most cases, the usually spontaneous clashes originated over issues of land, the holding of protests and rallies, the use of village resources, or any Dalit attempt to defy the caste-based order. Typically, both sides were armed with stones or agricultural tools.

The cycle of violence began anew in late April 1997 when the government announced the creation of a new transport corporation in Virudhunagar district in the name of a Pallar community member (the Veeran Sundaralingam Transport Corporation, VSTC). Thevars opposed the proposal and, according to press reports, some were heard to remark, "How do you expect us to travel in a bus named after a Dalit? It is a personal affront to our manhood." On May 1, 1997, VSTC was inaugurated; Thevars threw stones at the buses and refused to ride them.

On May 2, Dalit leader Dr. Krishnaswamy was arrested and accused of sparking violence with his "inflammatory speeches." Spontaneous protests erupted as news of his arrest spread through the region. Protesters staged several road blocks and, for the three days that Dr. Krishnaswamy remained in jail, "police resorted to firing, lathi-charges and bursting tear gas shells to control agitating Dalits." Two Dalits were killed by police bullets. On May 7 three Thevars were killed by the police at Sivakasi in Virudhunagar district while protesting the arrest of two Thevar youths.

In protest against police action on Thevars at Sivakasi, Thevars in Mansapuram village attempted to introduce coconut shells at tea stalls for Dalits to keep them from sharing tea tumblers used by caste Hindus. When Dalits resisted, Thevars torched and looted Dalit houses in Amachiyarpatti village. In Rengappanaikkanpatti Thevars vowed to make Dalits "dig pits for the burial of bodies of dominant castes." The entire Dalit population of the village was later forcibly driven out, as Thevars set fire to their homes and fields.

In the months following the renaming of the transport corporation and Dr. Krishnaswamy's arrest, the districts of Theni, Madurai, Virudhunagar, Tirunelveli, and Tuticorin witnessed periodic eruptions of violence and the forced displacement of thousands of Dalits from their homes. Police and district officials treated the situation as a law and order problem, and under the guise of seeking out Dalit militant activists, conducted search and raid operations exclusively on Dalit villages. They arrested and assaulted hundreds of men and women as they looted their homes and destroyed material possessions. As discussed below, women were the primary victims.

A June 1997 fact-finding mission by the People's Union for Civil Liberties (PUCL), the country's largest civil rights organization, concluded that in caste clashes in Madurai district, "Dalits were the worst affected in terms of property loss and physical injuries sustained, like hand and leg fractures, due to violent attack[s] on them"; that police had filed many false cases against Dalits; and that "increased political consciousness amongst the Dalits... regarding their fundamental social, political and economic rights expressed in terms of demands for social equality [and] equitable distribution of resources" played a major role in the attacks against them.

LINKS BETWEEN THEVARS AND STATE AGENTS

The Thevars numerically outnumber other backward castes in the region. The Thevar Peravai (Thevar Front), the most active and organized of Thevar organizations, was until early 1998 led by retired Director General of Police (DGP) Pon Paramaguru. His successor, Dr. N. Sethuraman, was also the general secretary of Moovendar Munnetra Kazhagam, a political party launched by the All India Thevar Peravai in 1998.

During his tenure as DGP from 1972 to 1975, Paramaguru recruited many Thevars into the police force. J. Jayalalitha, leader of the All India Anna Dravida Munnetra Kazhagam party (AIADMK), was considered a "strong Thevar community supporter" during her five-year tenure as chief minister of the state from 1991 to May 1996. Her support included extending influential political and police positions to members of the Thevar community—allowing them to further consolidate their power base. N. Sasikala, Jayalalitha's aide and confidante and a Thevar community member, was also accused of "astutely promoting her caste." Lawyers, human rights activists and the local press have noted that, as a result, a majority of the police force in the southern districts now "hails from [the Thevar] caste and, often, have been unable to overcome their caste affiliations."

According to Dr. Krishnaswamy, though "atrocities against Dalits were institutionalised during the previous AIADMK regime," a 1996 shift in political power to the DMK party, led by M. Karunanidhi, did not result in a "change in the behaviour of the police." Inspector General Vijay Kumar, former security officer under Jayalalitha's administration, was accused by human rights activists of using the police force to engineer attacks on Dalit villages during the 1997 clashes. Activists have also charged that the district collector (local government official) of Virudhanagar district, Rajagopal, a Brahmin native of Thevar-dominated Enjar village, supported the Thevar community during the 1997 clashes: "He committed all sorts of atrocities against Dalits, including lathi-charge and unnecessary shootings." Rajagopal was also accused of forcing Dalits to abandon their houses.

In June 1997 the state government responded to police excesses during the clashes by transferring large numbers of officers out of "sensitive" districts, without meting out any additional punishment. Chief Minister Karunanidhi ordered the transfers after noting "some disturbing trends in the functioning of the lower levels of police during the disturbances, particularly in the southern districts."

Economic context

In recent years the economic relationship between Thevars and Pallars (Dalits) has shifted notably. Like most Dalits in rural India, the Pallars traditionally were employed as agricultural laborers (on Thevar lands) and were paid less than minimum wage. In the early 1990s, Pallars began to enjoy minimal upward economic mobility, which reduced their dependency on

Thevars. Pallars became able to own and farm their own lands or look elsewhere for employment.

A researcher at the Madras Institute of Development Studies attributes increased Pallar prosperity to two factors: The first is the policy of reservations, which has been more effectively implemented in this state, more than other states. Reservations in education frees Dalits from land-based occupation. The relationship between the landlord and the labourer has given way to urban-basedoccupations. The second reason is that many Dalits have been recruited by Gulf countries. They send their proceeds home, and their families are able to acquire land through this process. So feudal dependency has lessened.

Marginal landowners themselves, Thevars have dealt with this new economic threat through caste mobilization: The main backward classes in the state, the Thevars, are opposed to the Dalits. They themselves are not an advanced community. They are landlords but not in a big sense. They are not advanced in education, but still they employed Dalits as laborers. Because of the move away from production sectors, Thevars now can only assert their power through caste pride. So it takes on paper dominance. Before, caste was deployed through land.

The Dalit communities, for their part, have realized the political potential of their somewhat better economic status by becoming more organized in their demands. This has affected state-wide patterns of violence and reactions by state agents. For the first time, the Pallars have begun to resist their traditional mistreatment: politically, by contesting elections, and physically, by responding to violence with violence.

Some Dalit activists have argued that their people's armed response is necessary for self-preservation and economic survival. As Murugeswari, the first Dalit female president of the Kandamanur village council, Tamil Nadu, has stated: While both parties have indulged in violence, there is an essential difference. Dalits are fighting for their rights and Thevars are fighting to retain their hegemony. It would be cruel to equate the fight for livelihood to the arson [sic] to retain power on the basis of birth.

Thevars argue that the Dalits are merely self-interested and provoke the clashes themselves. In an interview with Human Rights Watch, Thevar leader Dr. N. Sethuraman claimed that the violence was being instigated by militant Dalitactivists: the clashes, he asserted, ensured the survival of Dalit organizations and their ability to attract funds from foreign donors. Dalit-oriented NGOs are promoting hatred between the two communities. Foreign Christian organizations fund these Dalit organizations. Their intention is not to eradicate hatred but to perpetuate hatred so that their organization can survive. They induce violence, take photos and get money. They want the clash to continue so they can survive. It is a very negative attitude.

Dr. N. Sethuraman led the Thevar procession through Desikapuram village minutes before the police surrounded the Dalit colony and conducted a violent search and raid operation. The incident is further described below. According to Sethuraman, the practice of "untouchability" has been virtually eradicated in the state. But according to several human rights groups, government reports, and our own investigations, as of February 1998 "untouchability" was still practiced in various forms in most villages where Dalits were minorities. These forms include separate tea tumblers at tea shops and prohibitions on entering places of public worship or wearing shoes in the presence of upper castes.

Sethuraman also claimed that "Thevar minorities are being chased out of their lands and homes," a practice that he termed "reverse untouchability." He went on to add that "the same has not happened to Dalits in a single village." But Human Rights Watch visited several southern district villages where Dalits had been pushed out of their homes by Thevars and, months later, were unable to return. We also visited several villages where social and economic boycotts against Dalits were still in effect and others where murders and large-scale displacement of Dalits had taken place.

Melavalavu Murders

In September 1996, the village of Melavalavu, in Madurai district, was declared a reserved constituency under Article 243D of the Indian constitution. The declaration signaled that the Melavalavu *panchayat* (village council), whichcovers eight villages with approximately 1,000 Dalit families, would have seats reserved for scheduled-caste candidates. In June 1997, a group murder of elected Dalits by neighboring Thevars signaled that constitutionally mandated shifts in legal power to scheduled castes would not be tolerated by caste Hindus displaced from their once secure elected positions.

Several observers have attributed the violence in the village and the resulting tensions to a shift in power relations brought on by the government's mandate of reservation of panchayat seats for Dalits. Dr. George Mathew of the New Delhi Institute of Social Sciences visited the area along with two other researchers soon after the murders. He published his conclusions in an article in *The Hindu*: The murders of the Dalit leaders of Melavalavu Panchayat were clearly because "untouchability" was still ingrained in the social system. The economic conditions in the village were abysmal, but the power was concentrated in the hands of a privileged few. These people had hitherto enjoyed a hold over the common properties such as fish ponds, temple lands and forest produce and did not want to relinquish these privileges to the Panchayat Raj system run by the downtrodden... [T]he violence was basically a result of a shift in the power equations from the haves to the have nots.

The article also noted that the leasing of the twenty-five fish ponds alone would fetch an income of Rs. 500,000 to Rs. 1,000,000 annually (US$12,500 to $25,000). The new *panchayati raj* system put control of such common propertiesin the hands of the panchayat—that is, in Dalit hands—since the 1997 elections. In a separate article, Mathew referred to the killings as a serious attack on the institution of panchayati raj, which has the potential of changing the powerful rural groups. The new panchayats are perceived by the traditional powerful groups as a threat. Melavalavu and similar villages are paying a price for not holding the panchayat elections regularly and strengthening the foundations of democracy.

The case of Melavalavu provides an example of the interaction of social forces, efforts at reform, violent reaction, and impunity. The announcement of reservations in Melavalavu in 1996 led to a threat of "economic sanctions" by the majority caste Hindu community should any Dalit file for the position of panchayat president. The sanction would effectively leave Dalits without employment or access to economic and social services in villages in that area. As reported in the Bombay-based daily, *Times of India*, "They were warned that they would lose their jobs as farmhands and not be allowed to graze cattle or draw water from wells located on 'patta' [unutilized] land held by the dominant castes."

The elections, scheduled for October 1996, were subsequently canceled, as all three Dalit nominees withdrew their candidacy for fear of sanctions against the entire scheduled-caste electorate. When polling finally did take place in February 1997, the election was suspended after several incidents of booth capturing. A thirty-five-year-old Dalit named Murugesan won the presidency in the third round of polling, which took place under heavy police protection and was boycotted by the dominant castes. He was, however, unable to perform his tasks as president: neighboring Thevars physically prevented him from entering his office space at the panchayat building.

Several village residents told Human Rights Watch about violence against Dalit voters during the elections: With police protection the election was held, but at the end of the day upper-caste people entered into the booth and threatened and stabbed one boy and beat both men and women and took away the ballot boxes and threw them into the well. Then again they declared elections after one week. In that one we elected Murugesan. There was heavy police protection. Still the Amblakars [Thevars] boycotted the elections. Then Murugesan was not able to go to the office. Only during the swearing-in ceremony did he go to the office because he had a police escort.

Murugesan's twenty-six-year-old widow, Manimegala, described the threats that her husband had received after winning the presidency: After he was elected he received as many as ten threatening letters from Thevars. He kept them all in his office and showed them all to the [district] collector. Once he showed one to me. The letter said that one day or another we will definitely cut off your head, and they did. The police did not arrest the main culprits.

On the day of the attack, June 30, 1997, Murugesan was returning from a visit to the collector's office to inquire about compensation for houses burned in an earlier incident. Kumar, an eyewitness who barely survived the attack himself, boarded the bus and sat next to Murugesan. The assault, Kumar told Human Rights Watch, was led by a Thevar named Ramar. Ramar and Alagarsamy, the formerpanchayat president, gave explicit instructions to their gang of Thevars to "kill all the Pariahs [Dalits]."

There were nearly forty of them. They were all Thevars. They stabbed Murugesan on the right side of his belly. It was a very long knife. From outside the bus Ramar instructed the Thevars to kill all the Pariahs. Among twelve, six were murdered on the spot. They pulled all six out of the bus and stabbed them on the road with bill hooks more than two feet long. When the attackers noticed his presence, Kumar was chased nto the fields and cut with a bill hook on the back of his neck, his right underarm, and his finger but ultimately managed to escape by fleeing into the plantation fields of a Dalit village. Family members of the six murder victims received Rs. 150,000 (US$3,750) in compensation from the state government under the Scheduled Castes and Scheduled Tribes (Prevention of Atrocities) Act, 1989.15 A total of twelve persons were arrested within a month of the incident. However, eyewitnesses haveclaimed that the ringleaders were not among them. Those arrested were charged under sections 341, 307, and 302 of the Indian Penal Code for wrongful restraint, attempted murder, and murder, respectively, and under Section 3(1)(10) of the Atrocities Act, the act's least serious offense, for name-calling or insulting a Dalit person in a public place.

Kumar claimed that the police had an eyewitness and victim sign papers saying that one of the accused, named Sedhu, was innocent. Human Rights Watch spoke to that witness, a forty-five-year-old agricultural labourer, who told us the following:

A two-member team from the State Human Rights Commission visited the village in early August, five weeks after the killings. Hundreds of women testified to incidents of theft, the burning of Dalit houses, and stone-throwing at night. They also complained of their inability to go to work in the fields, of a lack of police protection, and that most of the men had fled the village out of fear. Karupaia, Murugesan's older brother, organized a march on August 8, 1997 to protest the lack of action on the part of the police. Participants estimated the number of marchers at 3,000, both men and women. They named the principal culprits as Ramar, Alagarsami, Poniah, Baskarar, Andichami, Markandan, Duraipandian, Chandran, Selvam, Alagu, Vadivelu, Karanthamalai, Ranganathan, Chakarmurti, Chockanathar, Sedhu, Rajendran, and Jothi.

When we approached the *taluk* [village block] office, the superintendent of police (SP) and other officials were there. From above the building, a red-colored cloth was thrown down. We were in two rows. A"country bomb" fell in the gap and exploded.20 Everyone scattered. There are iron pieces from the bomb inside Karuppan's leg. Tirumavalavan, the leader of the Dalit Panthers of India who led the procession, was the intended target.

Tirumavalavan proceeded to inform the SP that the people who threw the bomb had descended from the building and were getting away. Many pointed them out, but the police refused to arrest them. The marchers then started throwing stones. The SP ordered a lathi-charge on the procession, and many of the protesters were severely injured. The police arrested a total of thirty-six protesters and charged them under the Indian Explosives Act and under Indian Penal Code sections 147, 148, 323 and 436 for rioting, rioting with a deadly weapon, voluntarily causing hurt, and mischief by explosive substance. They also arrested a member of DPI and held him responsible for setting off the bomb. Tirumavalavan expressed outrage at the police's failure to arrest "the main accused Ramar in the Melavalavu incident," while simultaneously "nabbing a DPI member and holding him responsible for the blast."

On August 9, 1997, the thirty-six people arrested were sent to Madurai jail. They were held for forty-five days. Released on bail, they were required to check in twice a day at the Trichitown police station, over 125 kilometers from the village. At the time of Human Rights Watch's visit, the conditions had been modified to reporting once a day at nearby Mellur police station. According to Karupaia, the arrests were retaliatory:

The police put false cases against us because we organized a procession. They wanted to teach us a lesson. The Section 436 charge [mischief by explosive substance] is still pending. One shop was burned but we did not do it. One hundred Thevars came behind us in the procession and set fire to a shop on the main road. Human Rights Watch spoke to a forty-year-old resident of Melavalavu who was arrested during the lathi-charge:

The leader of DPI and Dr. Krishnaswamy have both charged that the "National Security Act as well as the [Tamil Nadu] Goondas Act were being grossly misused against the Dalits by the state government" and that several Dalits had been kept in preventive custody for many days. In the months following the murders, concerned groups demanding appropriate action by the police organized several protests and marches. On July 10, 1997, members of the Social Action Movement, a grassroots NGO, demonstrated in front of the Madurai collectorate's office in order to highlight the plight of the villagers in the aftermath of the murders. On July 23, 1997, DPI marched to demand the release of all Dalits arrested under the National Security Act in connection with the murders.

By the end of September 1997, more than forty people had been charged in the Melavalavu murders case, while eleven had been formally accused but remained at large. On November 24, 1997, DPI members marched again to urge the government to arrest those absconding in the murders and to demand a Central Bureau of Investigation (CBI) inquiry into the case. Members of the Thevar Peravai, who organized a protest on October 28, 1997, also demanded a CBI inquiry. The then-vice president, Dr. N. Sethuraman, claimed that innocent people had been arrested. When Human Rights Watch spoke to Dr. Sethuraman, now president of Thevar Peravai, about the incident, he claimed it had no basis in caste conflict:

This is not a fight between Dalits and Thevars. There's a lot of proof. It was a personal quarrel between the milk society president, a forward-caste member, and Murugesan, the Dalit president. But they have sorted it out now, and the new president can now perform his duties without any problem. The chief minister says that is a quarrel between Thevars and Dalits, but it is not. We have asked for a CBI inquiry to bring these things out. When Human Rights Watch visited the village in February 1998, the bodies of the six murdered men were still buried in shallow graves in the village center as "a tribute befitting martyrs." The new Dalit panchayat president was again unable to perform his duties, and Thevars—in a concerted campaign to punish Dalits—had ceased to employ Dalits as laborers on their lands. The Thevars also encouraged others to refrain from awarding farm work to Dalits. Many Dalit students were also afraid to go to school for fear of further reprisal.

Human Rights Watch spoke to the new panchayat president, Raja, who was six months into his term. He claimed that the threats from Thevars had continued and that the police protection he received was inconsistent and insufficient to ward off another attack. Five Dalit women, elected members of the panchayat, had also been unable to perform their duties.

The office is in the caste Hindu area. So we have to hold meetings in our TV room here; it is a makeshift office. They are still threatening us. They are watching and following me. Five Dalit women are members of the panchayat. If the elected Dalit women go there, the upper caste would do some harm. If the womeninsist on going into the office, they will hit them. There is one police guard for me. He has a gun, but he puts it inside his bag. He only gives protection. But any other time he doesn't give protection. He has joined the police of the other camp. Everything is paralyzed.

Raja also explained the village's dire economic situation: We got regular employment in their fields. Some Dalits have land, but most are landless laborers. Women received Rs. 12 [US$0.30] for six hours of work from the morning until the afternoon. Men received Rs. 25 [US$0.63] for six hours of work, but they do harder work using bigger instruments. The period after the elections they did not invite us for field work. Now the women work fifteen kilometers away, and most of the men went to Kerala [a neighboring state] and send money back.

5

Struggles and Challenges of Dalit Women

The country is now recording 2-digit economic growth every year and successfully takes quite an important and dominant position in international politics and in the economic arena. The success of India is built up with the international reputation of well-educated human resources, "democratic and stabled" political circumstances, and promises of land, benefits and other resources to the foreign and national investors-which are all based on exploitation of Dalit women. In reality India remains the world leader in maternal mortality, female infanticide and foeticide, deaths due to preventative disease, and other indicators of human development. Even in 2007, in Raitara village of Vanarasi in Uttar Pradesh, a five-year-old Dalit girl is facing imminent death from starvation as the family being slaved in a farm for free labour. Likewise, vulnerable villagers, namely, rural women, meanwhile, get a lot of impacts in the gap between two faces of the country.

Those bad indicators are always appeared in Dalit women. The Dalits and the marginalised are still colonised by the feudal lords the Elites without freedom from caste discrimination. Indians have driven out the colonizers but not the one who are discriminating Dalits. For Dalit women, they are also coerced to be victimised in the patriarchy. Dalit women are bearing the burden of double day caste and sexual division of labour. Dalit women are demeaned and degraded and their body is a free terrain of colonization by men from other community. Dalit women are a deprived section and at the lowest level of economic and educational structures. They are poor, illiterate, sexually harassed, faces state, caste violence and exploited. Doubly, triply or multiply discriminated, Dalit women face a lot of struggles in daily bases otherwise just being overwhelmed with those surges of discrimination up to them. Without being struggling, Dalit women would be just left in despair. This paper, therefore, focuses on struggles of Dalit women.

The paper, firstly, sees Dalit women's struggles. The struggles, however, spread out to wide area of Dalit women's life-too broad to cover just with a paper. The paper, therefore, tries to show a piece of dimensions of the struggle-which helps the readers to understand the overall background of the exclusion of Dalit women-anti-Dalit women's tendency in historical context as well as in cultural context. Secondly, it would be taken up the violation against Dalit women in the culture of globalisation with detailed analysis on their socio economic including rights to livelihood. The violation is now intensifying and internationalised. And lastly, the paper would suggest people's movement based methodology to tackle with multiple discrimination against Dalit women, which can alternated with the course which was set by the top or the others. Also, in throughout the paper, many cases would be presented including nation-wide known incidents as well as local problems of Dalit women.

DALIT WOMEN-THEIR PATHWAY OF STRUGGLES

Discrimination against Dalit Women

Although it is now in modern world, caste discrimination, an age-old practice that dehumanizes and perpetuates a cruel form of discrimination continues to be practiced. India where the practice is rampant despite the existence of a legislation to stop this, 160 million Dalits of which 49.96% are women continue to suffer discrimination. The discrimination that Dalit women are subjected to is similar to racial discrimination, where the former is discriminated and treated as untouchable due to descent, for being born into a particular community, while, the latter face discrimination due to colour. The caste system declares Dalit women as 'impure' and therefore untouchable and hence socially excluded. This is a complete negation and violation of women's human rights. Dalit women are thrice discriminated, treated as untouchables and as outcastes, due to their caste, face gender discrimination being women and finally economic impoverishment due to unequal wage disparity, with low or underpaid labour. According to the Hindu caste hierarchy, there are four castes namely the Brahmins (priestly caste), the Kshatriya (warriors), the Vaishyas (traders) and the Shudras (menial task workers).

Below this four-tier caste ladder there is another rung of peoples, who are called the untouchables (Panchamas). Among the untouchables, the status of women is further eroded and closely linked to the concept of purity. This is what the rigid, fundamentalist Hindu promotes through continuation of caste system, imposing the Brahminical values to maintain the caste system. The creation of a number of Hindu religious books including the *Manusmriti,*

Atharva Vedas, Vishnu smriti, and many others like these and their strict compliance by the Brahmans (upper priestly Hindu caste), led to a society in which equality between men and women was far from existent (Agarwal: 1999). Dr. B.R. Ambedkar, an architect of the Indian constitution, also makes it very clear in his article titled "The rise and fall of Hindu woman" that the root cause of suffering for women in India are these so called Hindu religious books. Books like the Manusmriti divide people into a stratified caste system and promote inequality between men and women. According to the *Manusmriti,* women have no right to education, independence, or wealth. It not only justifies the treatment of Dalit women as a sex object and promotes child marriage, but also justifies a number of violent atrocities on women as can be seen in the following verses: A man, aged thirty years, shall marry a maiden of twelve who pleases him. Or a man of twenty-four a girl of eight years of age.

If (the performance of) his duties would otherwise be impeded, he must marry sooner. (*Manusmitri* IX.94) By a girl, by a young woman, or even by an aged one, nothing must be done independently, even in her own house." (*Manusmriti* V.147) Her father protects (her) in childhood, her husband protects (her) in youth, and her sons protect (her) in old age; a woman is never fit for independence. (*Manusmriti* IX.3) Even the killing of a Dalit woman is explicitly justified as a minor offence for the Brahmins: equal to the killing of an animal (*Manusmitri*). If the killing of an untouchable was justified as a minor offence, you can imagine the treatment they received throughout their lives. In a male dominated society, Dalit women suffered unimaginable oppression, not only through caste, but gender too, from which there was no escape.

The laws in the *Manusmriti* and other Vedic scriptures close all economic, political, social, educational, and personal channels through which Dalit women could be uplifted. The horrendous Laws in the *Manusmriti* were incorporated into Hinduism because they were favourable only to the Upper castes, which form the majority of India. Even today, in modern times, we see the severe oppression and exploitation of Dalit women. The Laws of the *Manusmriti* have a devastating effect on the level of education reached by Dalit women. The caste discrimination inherited by birth leaves Dalit women facing multiple oppressions that violate their economic, political, social and cultural rights. The most deprived section of the society comprises of Dalit women who are the poorest, illiterate and easy targets for sexual harassment. The women face not just caste violence inflicted on them by the dominant castes, but also state violence.

Dalit Women's Struggle in Hindu Culture

Culture, meanwhile, regardless of its history-traditional culture or modern culture-reflects positionality of peoples collectively with rules, values and norms. Culture is dynamic changes never static with identities and shared experiences. Family, religion, and education system used to be the main elements of culture. Culture is influenced by media. Rituals are always carried out by people, which are reinforcing the meanings of life. The traditional culture which is locally interacting, reconstitutes against this the cultural imperialism which is institutionalized which is the identity of cultural power. Culture of the Oppressed is to resist the culture of the dominant to bring freedom. Traditional culture has continuity of people's lives and respects moral codes adopted by people. The stories of the oppressed revealed through symbols and practices. People's culture is a culture of multiplicity which is dominant over other culture. This involves a political structure which is decentralized sensitive to local culture. The alternative cultural politics leads to cultural and social change. India is, essentially, home for many cultures mutually enriching contact with each other. Indian culture has come from Dravidian culture.

Indian culture is a living force. It has a significant role in moulding the culture of Asia. The Hinduism History which has continued degrading Dalit women through dogmas and concept of purity, then, affects culture which can work as a catalyst for progress of Dalit women's living environment. With Sanskritization which is hinduization a dominant model, the ideals and beliefs of the Brahminic practices are imposed on Dalits to adopt a life style with untouchablility practices. Sanskritization is an alien faith to Dalits, the spirituality of Dalits is replaced by Sanskritic spirituality. The Dalit life is incontinuation, that is, of dead and living are the integral spirituality of Dalit culture. Brahminical culture endangers Dalits' identity and integrity. It enhances and annihilates Dalit culture instead of enriching the culture.

The culture is reflection of resistance from the past to the present and moves to shape a blueprint for the future life which becomes a flowing stream. There is continuity of collective life in Dalit culture. In addition, modernization introduced consumerism and market economy which has destroyed ethos, value system, celebration, and affirmation of the culture of the people, particularly the culture of Rural Dalits. Traditional culture is a way of living and producing for life, to sustain life. But through imperialistic modern culture, the mode of production is set only for consumption. It is called as neo-colonization of traditional culture which is not the people's culture.

Meanwhile, what would be the question of duties of a wife? Who is the head of the family? Wives are devoted to their husbands and afraid of even mentioning the name of their husband. Barren woman considered to be "*amangalam*", bad omen and inferior to others, to be a curse to the society. Puberty is viewed as 'flowering' stage in a girl's life, as pleasurable. Fertility, women are referred to mud waiting to receive seed. Woman in marriage are framed to be obedient and submissive wives. Motherhood is expected to be nurturing, fearful, good wives and bearers of worthy sons. Sexuality of fertility is socially permissible and sexual acts such as homosexual, lesbian behaviours are considered to be deviant, perverse and abnormal. Society allows multiple forms of sexual behaviour to co-exist practically but not socially. Erotic literature such as Kamasutra hints at the existence of homosexual desire and love.

Hindu Temple Sculpture

Diverse sexualities are present and celebrated in Hindu temple sculpture. Pro-life existence of non-normative sexual culture is significant. They reveal the norms that a society lives by, to be constructed rather than given, clearly authorized by systems of patriarchal power. Madurai Meenakshi, Queen of the city, becomes bride given away every year in marriage. Marriage ceremony is the history of female domestication and husbandry authority. Although it has been praised diverse of sexuality of the "human beings" at the one side of Hindu concept, Fundamentalist, Hinduism excludes plurality of the people even in sexuality.

Particularly, lower caste, labouring women, who are Dalit women-are treated as the sexual "property" of the men of the all caste. The other caste women are treated as good and lower caste Dalit women as bad women because of Dalit women social status is low, subordinated that is why they are made to be sexually available to other caste. Dalit women are marked as natural and fit victims of violation, contrast to upper caste women who are considered to be pure and custodians of chastity. Chastity of upper caste women could be taken up as big issue in their "culture" because of being submissive wives who is called *pativiratas*. The lower caste women are considered not to be chaste. Sexual purity is anticipated caste purity which is honoured by the society. Dalit women follow the Rituals more than the Dalit men. Dalit women associate with earth. They put the earth on the forehead, the mixture of water and mud strained that water is given to babies. They are related directly with the earth which is the life source. Worshiping the trees, decorating trees with *Kungumam,* turmeric that is worshiping old trees and rocks with the decoration. Cultural programme of festivals is only moment for the Dalit women who get into trance (or being "possessed" so to say). It is the only time they express their inner feelings and speak against other caste men, husbands, and demanding arak the local alcohol, chicken, good food, and behave like goddess. Before transplanting, the seeds are germinated in pots and Dalit women carry them by singing songs. Dalit women worship the nature for better and more food to be produced. Dalit women's dances are *Kummi,* and following to them they have *Kulavai*-wherever they work they sing. To show the closeness with the nature, they sing songs about their forefathers, mothers, the children and they abuse the landlords through their songs. After the hard work in the day during the night they sit together and chat with each other.

They use lot of proverbs while talking and fighting. They tease each other and their blood related men from their kin who are about to be married with them. They relate with each other, and while calling the person they will not use the name but the relationship. They sing when a baby is born, when a girl attains puberty and also *Oppari* death. These practices we never find with women of other caste. Dalit women are very strong and they give birth to more children. Dalit women work equally with the men, that is, why they oppose male domination and prove that they are stronger than the men.

Dalit women work hard to survive. They are very open-minded, innocent, and not exploiting others but exploited by others. They have good characters. Dalit women, everyday, relate themselves with people in four ways. 1) With their family members, children, husband, 2) With the traders who buy their products, 3) The other caste landlords who give them work, and 4) Relate with distant relatives during marriages, deaths. Now beyond this the new effort is that Dalit women attend conferences, meetings, workshops and training programs which allowed them to meet with many Dalit women. Dalit women are illiterates. They know only work related to land. They have not achieved even as one persent politically. They remain only us voters. They have no chance of learning about the country, the other ethnic groups and languages. Not all the Dalit women are member of the movement as well as in the political party.

They are not involved in politics. Dalit women leadership is also controlled by the men. Dalit women have their own language. They preserve their language of their land. They have their own justice that is they do not have permanent enemies amongst themselves. For many years they follow the Rituals of the land. They are different from other caste women because they do not depend on their men like others. They work equally with men. When the men were taking the spade, Dalit women are ready with their basket to take mud. Every work it is both Dalit men and women work equally. Dalit women are workers, and they are not slaves to their husbands. Dalit women have very strong resistance power which has to be sustained. Dalit culture was destroyed after the invasion of Aryans. Dalits lived through the dominant Brahminical culture. Sanskritization of Dalit culture, based on pure and impure concept was thrust on the oppressed, downtrodden communities especially on Dalit women. Dalit culture was silenced and destroyed. Dalits through a war, resistance gave life to the culture that faced the death by the dominant culture. Dalit culture is liberation, freedom, solidarity, equality, a culture of resistance towards freedom. Dalit culture is preserved through various forms of theatre which is revolutionary, disturbs and leads to action which is political action.

Perform Dance of Dalit Women

Dalit women perform dance which is devoted to Mathamma the Kulathaivam. The dancer is, however, almost exploited as being expected to dance in an erotic way. This is religious sanctioned prostitution. The month of June (*Anni Matham* in Tamil Calendar) is the temple festival for five days.

The temple is built, festival conducted, the 'Car' is held in front all by the other caste. Out of five days the Mathammas, Dalit girl children are given to the goddess believing those children will be cured by the healing power of goddess. Once the child is cured, she is married to the goddess and named after her. She becomes a powerful replica of Mathamma. Later on she is mocked and treated as a public property. In public places she is teased and her children born are face lot of humiliation in the school by other children.

Mathammas socially and economically exploited by the community. She lives on her own without the support of families. A Dalit woman, becomes a dancer, then sexually exploited ends her life with nothing but left out with diseases. The dominant brahminical culture from which the Devadasi system is extended to Dalit community is prevailing Dalit women.

Tamil Nadu Dalit Women's Movement (TNDWM), meanwhile, faced harassment even from Dalit men in the community for exposing the issue of Mathamma. The Dalit movement with patriarchal norms started publicly attacking leaders from TNDWM "individually". They are accused, through wall posters, public meetings and black mailings. TNDWM faced harassment confronting the caste and patriarchal nature of the communities which is also influenced by Hindutva ideology. Hindutva Ideology perpetuates hatred towards other religion and maintains the culture, the exploitative dominant culture through caste.

THE CONDITION OF DALIT WOMEN

The difficult lives of Dalit women are perhaps best revealed by studying the social, economic, educational, health and political conditions of Dalit women, which are outlined below.

Social Condition: Untouchability

Though outlawed since 1963 and made punishable by the Constitution of the Kingdom of Nepal in 1990, untouchability is still practised. Thus, Dalits are treated as socially untouchable even in a democracy. This can be observed around the periphery of the Kathmandu Valley and in the rural areas. Even in public places, such as schools, Dalit students face discrimination. The entire Dalit community is exploited and discriminated on the grounds of caste, but women, as noted earlier, are further victimised. Untouchability related to women is practised in many ways that affect all Dalit women every day.

For example, when Dalit women fetch water from public water taps, wells, etc., they suffer from mental as well as physical assaults. Moreover, by traditional cultural practise, women usually are the member of the family that worships in the temple; but in Nepal, Dalit women are not allowed to enter the temples nor are they allowed to enter the house of upper caste people. Meanwhile, intercaste marriage is socially disapproved, and Dalit women are the principal victims of this system. If a girl from an upper caste family marries a lower caste boy, for instance, then she is accepted by the boy's family. However, when a marriage takes place between an upper caste boy and a lower caste girl, problems occur as she is not accepted by her husband's family. Subsequently, she is mentally and physically abused and abandoned in many cases.

Economic Condition: Exploitation

Most Dalits have their own traditional occupation, but they are economically exploited. It is estimated that more than 50 percent of the total population of the country lives below the absolute poverty line. Dalits, due to their history of discrimination, exploitation and abuse, constitute a large proportion of this number-approximately 90 percent of the total Dalit population of four million people. Since women have no economic power in the family, it clearly indicates the economic condition of Dalit women. These women have to work hard as labourers to earn a living, but they receive very little in return. Moreover, payment is mostly in kind, and their pay does not justify the intensity of the work. There is no doubt that Dalit women are more economically exploited than their upper caste women counterparts.

Education Condition: Illiteracy

The literacy rate of Dalit women is very low in comparison with high caste women. The present literacy rate of men is 66 percent, and the education rate for women is 30 percent. However, the literacy rate of the Dalit community is 16 percent; and for Dalit women, the literacy rate is only 7 percent. Among two million Dalit women, there are hardly 10 to 15 graduates and postgraduates. Ignorance, absolute poverty, caste and gender discrimination can be considered as the explanation for such statistics.

Health Condition: Lowest Life Expectancy

In Nepal, the life expectancy of women is lower than that of men (Nepal is one of the three countries in the world where women live less than men). Compared though to the so-called "upper caste people," the health condition of Dalits is very miserable. For example, a very backward Dalit caste-the Mushar of Terai-has a life span of 42 years against the national average of 55 years. Moreover, gynecological diseases, like a prolapsed uterus, are very common among Dalit women. They do not know much about birth control and spacing and become pregnant every year. Furthermore, because of illiteracy and ignorance, they live in filthy and unhygienic conditions which further deteriorates their health. The children of Dalits are also severely malnourished. As Dalits do not have easy access to clean drinking water in most places, they are compelled to drink polluted water and thus suffer from various gastrointestinal diseases. In this environment, both the mortality and fertility rates are high.

Political Condition: Non-Representation

Nepalese society is patriarchal, and the involvement of women in public life is not encouraged. This social prohibition applies to politics too. Thus, although Nepali women comprise 52 percent of the country's population, their representation in politics is among the lowest in Asia, i.e., as low as 5 percent. This is in spite of the 1990 Nepalese Constitution in which there is a mandatory provision that 5 percent of all candidates put forward by the country's national parties should be women. However, there were no mandatory rules for women to be represented in local government. In 1997 though, 5 percent of the seats were reserved for women in local government, and yet this rule cannot embrace Dalit women. Dalits are about 20 percent of the total population, but Dalits are not represented in national-level politics. Presently, there are four nominated parliamentarians in the National Assembly, but there is none that have been elected to the Lower House of Parliament. If the representation of men is so negligible, then one can easily imagine the political participation of Dalit women.

Sexual Exploitation: Trafficking

Because of poverty, ignorance and illiteracy, Dalit women and young girls are compelled to be involved in prostitution. One of the Dalit castes-Badi-is regarded as the prostitute caste.

In addition, there is the trafficking of girls. Most of the Dalit girls taken by the brokers are trafficked to Indian brothels. In addition, many women working in carpet factories, hotels and government and private offices are sexually harassed and exploited.

Because of the untouchability problem related to caste, Dalit women are deprived of the opportunity of working in the moneymaking professions, i.e., opening teashops and restaurants. Their time is spent on earning subsistence wages, and they do not have time to think about improving their condition.

Solutions

We feel very uncomfortable in reporting that very few efforts have been made by the government of Nepal to eradicate the problems of Dalits in general and of Dalit women in particular.

In recent years, particularly after the restoration of multiparty democracy, the women's movement has gained momentum with the emergence of many women's organisations and leaders. Unfortunately, none of these women's organisations have taken the issues and plight of two million Dalit women seriously.

This is why we established an organisation dedicated to the rights and emancipation of Dalit women. As mentioned above, there is a serious lack of consciousness among the entire Dalit community about their fundamental human rights. Therefore, they accept all forms of discrimination and exploitation as God's grace to them. Meanwhile, the outside world has been silent about caste exploitation and discrimination.

In recent years, we, a few educated Dalit women, have come forward to move the issue forward. We intend to influence the government, donor agencies and international non-governmental organisations (NGOs), enabling them to realise the harsh reality of Dalit women and to direct resources for the upliftment of these downtrodden women. We also plan to agitate at the local level against caste discrimination and violence and to join hands with other like-minded organisations. The vast problems of Dalits and Dalit women cannot be solved through the efforts of one or two organisations though. Therefore, we strongly feel that all national forces should join hands together. In this spirit, we would like to offer the recommendations below.

(1) Various programmes should be launched to uplift the living conditions of two million Dalit women.

(2) Scholarships should be provided from primary to higher education to all Dalit girls.

(3) The practice of untouchability in all public places, like schools, water sources and teashops, should be punished with immediate effect.

(4) All laws and acts which discriminate against Dalits and Dalit women should be rescinded immediately, and a law should be formulated and enforced to discourage the practice of untouchability.

(5) Intercaste marriage between Dalits and non-Dalits should be promoted and protected.

(6) There should be reserved seats for Dalit women in appropriate constitutional bodies, and these seats should be reserved for Dalit women in elections from the local to the national level.

(7) The government should abide by the U.N. International Convention on the Elimination of All Forms of Racial Discrimination.

(8) Dalits and Dalit women should be represented in the National Human Rights Commission.

(9) A separate commission at the national and the international level should be formed to identify the problems of Dalit women and to make recommendations to resolve these issues.

As for national and international NGOs, it is recommended that they consider the steps that follow.

(1) A series of in-depth studies should be undertaken about Dalit women.

(2) All NGOs should declare Dalits as one of their target groups of development and should formulate specific programmes to improve their lives.

(3) All human rights organisations should network with Dalit organisations and expose the human rights problems of Dalit women at the national and international level.

(4) The government of Nepal should be pressured to implement all of the U.N. conventions on human rights.

(5) International NGOs especially should give priority to Dalits and Dalit women in employment and involve them in the formulation of plans and programmes for the Dalit community.

SUSTAIN DALIT WOMEN'S STRUGGLES

Civil Society's Challenge?

Having faced the deprivation of human rights of Dalit Women, what kinds of actions have been taken by the civil society? In order to achieving "uplifting" or "development" of peoples in disadvantage class, Development NGOs as well as international institutions emphasize recently "rights based approach". The United Nations Development Programme has set so-called Millennium Development Goals in order to "monitor" the implementation of the goal for human development. But those are neither our approach nor our goals. As it can be seen in Dalit women's situation, people are struggling for their livelihood, and the movement should reject those meaningless mercies from the top. The movement, in fact, pursues "struggle based approach" and "People's Goals". The "Right based approach" is a language of donors. This makes movements isolated in each cells. People's movements are compromising not confronting. We should rather keep up the "Struggle based approach", which leads movements to bring changes in people's lives. The peoples around so-called 'civil society', therefore, do not share the problem with Dalit women. The civil society is narrowing down by becoming fundamentalists under the name of "rights based approach". At the citizens' forum for celebrating 60th years of independence, which was taken place at Bangalore, for example, there are a lot of oppositions to serve beef cutlet as a choice of the meal service. As the reality, however, there are people who have beef. Inclusiveness is important and not to exclude efforts of various initiatives. There is a need to join hands to stay with the people in multiple struggles against multiple discriminations and exploitations.

Dominant Culture

Supporting of Dalit women by providing services: children's day care centre, and urgent scholarship is of course one of our struggle against dominant culture of globalisation. Likewise, SRED and TNDWM also directly support the struggles for the victims of culture of casteism and patriarchy: such as Mathammas. Our approach to Mathamma begins with their name and status. Mathammas refused to be called as Mathammas. The first change with in them is to have new names, and to remove the 'Sacred Pottu Thali'. The movement of Mathammas: Mathamma Liberation Movement was formed primarily to stop the practice of giving the Dalit girls to Mathammas. During the festivals, Mathammas from the movement were vigilant that no woman, no Mathamma dancing is taking place publicly. Now the temple festivals dress up men as women and the dance continues. In Kaverirajapuram during temple festival the leaders stopped Mathamma dance with the help of police.

But the movement found that it was the wrong strategy as it created incredible views from the villagers from other movements. The Mathamma movement is, now, visiting villages where Mathamma temples are, and conducting meetings, cultural programs, explaining the hurdles they went through by themselves. They keep persuading by saying that 'Stop the practice of Mathammas'. Mathamma leaders from the movement contested in election with many threats and boycotts. They, however, claimed equal status, and went through all the procedure of the election which itself is an empowering process challenged the system, the community and the men in the villages. Devi, the leader of the movement who was contested, explains her experience in the election as follows;

During the election campaign, those who are against me strongly said: "why do you nominate yourself for the election? You are Mathamma and who will vote for you?" But I didn't accept any words in the remarks. I did not win this time, but it was brilliant experience. There are a lot of problems that Mathammas are facing. If I become a ward member, I will give the rights for the mathammas and totally I would like to stop this practice. I will make employment, education and housing, and all basic needs-I will try to get them through government.

They stopped dancing of exploitation but started to dance to liberate others because she is to be liberated. Now, some of them have leadership and empowerment training with the support of Yasuda literacy foundation of Buraku Liberation and Human Rights Research Institution. With the training, the women gains more force to struggle against the dominant culture.

Kollathur women are also challenging to the huge dominant entity by empowering themselves in the movement. They organised Kollathur Dalit Women's Sangam, and are fighting in the struggles in legal process as well as in their livelihoods. They keep embracing a slogan: "Close the Aqua Farm". Globalisation emphasises efficiency and competitive culture. Thus it appears that for the majority of Dalits and poor, globalisation has meant further deprivation. The struggles against globalised economy are also, for Dalit women, struggle against culture of dominant casteism and patriarchy.

Dalit Women's Challenge

SRED, thus, extends the area of activities in various levels: from local to international level. For local level, if there are caste based oppression against Dalit women, immediately stay at the side of the people to protest against the oppression. In Rangapuram village, Dalit children are not allowed to go to school because the Non-Dalits blocked the way to go to school. SRED immediately sent fact finding mission of people's movement, such as Tamil Nadu Dalit Women's Movement, and made a petition to make a safe road to school-going children. When making a petition, police forces was sent from many place to the district educational office of Kancheepuram, and they immediately arrested unlawfully activists of Dalit women. This year, at last, the new road for children was successfully launched at the village. In Anandapuram, village, without the bridge over the river, Dalit children are not able to cross the river in rainy season to go to the school.

Dalit mothers, meanwhile, who work in the field, definitely need the place to send children whilst they are working. Since 2004, SRED launched Dalit day care centres, to provide space for children to play, to sing, to paint, to learn and to prepare for the formal school. Primarily the centres are used for day care centre, which enable Dalit women who have to go to the field to leave the children at safer place. After this day care centre, they will go to primary school. The centres are, however, used for multi-purpose.

Working children can get education after work in evening class. The centres are playing crucial role for school going children as the safer place after school for doing further learning. Some times the centres are used for meeting purposes. At Anandapuram, with the warm support from Nagano branch of Buraku Liberation League, successfully established a centre. But meanwhile, have limitation of the budget to launching the centre for many villages, therefore re-arrange meeting room to Day care centre. Actually Sred staff members are doing secretary work just by hearing children's voice, and also frequently have a discussion where there are a lot of paintings and learning materials for children. In the community based work, found out that the similar situation to other children, namely, Irulas, Tribal people as well as quarry workers. When families remain as bonded labourers, when parents have to take children to quarry work place because of lack of finance to prepare for their study, families migrate seeking for their work. Children's rights to education are denied. The centres and the programmes in the centres are particularly designed by paying attention with caste-free environment, and children are ensured to be away from any discriminated thoughts, practices, and behaviours. Dalit communities, particularly girl children, face difficulty also in higher educations.

Just only with falling to financial difficulty affected by Tsunami, Dalit girl students were sent back to their home without continuing the second year of the course whilst they managed for the first year of the course. Even getting the best scores at the twelfth grade, Bharati, a Dalit girl faced difficulties to find appropriate scholarship schemes and resulted to give up their education (nursing course). SRED collects supports for those Dalit girls and help them to continue their higher education.

Asian Rural Women's Conference

Apart from the community and grassroots based challenge for overcoming the difficulty surged up to Dalit women, the SRED and Tamil Nadu Dalit Women's Movement are trying to organising forums on rural women. Amongst Dalit women 81.45% lives in rural area.

The globalisation, meanwhile, affects firstly the vulnerable sectors in rural area, where, obviously, Dalit women are working. But also, the rural women in other community, such as Irulas Tribes, Narikuravars, Dhobis, and fisherfolks are suffering in the similar situation. Not only in India, but also, there are many rural women who are struggling in current political economy of globalisation. The concerns on international trade, international agro-business, and patents to traditional seeds are all rural Dalit women's agenda as well as women from other community. Actually, Dalit women flew to Hong Kong to take an action at the 6 ministerial meeting of WTO to protest against promotion of pesticides and genetically modified foods. The forum, Asian Rural Women's Conference, which is taking place on 6-8th March, 2008 in Arakkonam/ Chennai, India, is putting together marginalised women in the region who are against imperialist oppression. By asserting dignity of rural women, which cannot be seen in any other rights-based documents, many marginalised women in the region create the power to struggle.

The conference will develop a unity of analysis from the experiences of rural women and the situation of women in the context of a globalised world. Last July, some Indian women's organisations gathered at our office, and conducted National consultation on rural women, which of course include latest developments on rural Dalit women. On 31 July to 2 Aug, presenters from some Asian countries gathered in Manila, and have issued rural women's declaration. Of course caste based discrimination was clearly mentioned in the context of the struggle against patriarchal globalisation. Meanwhile, the Manila conference did not have any Japanese participants, particularly from Buraku community. It would be grateful for Dalit women to share the issue with Buraku women in March for "Rights, Empowerment and Liberation", which is the main slogan of the conference. Asian Rural Women's Conference would also be the occasion for cultural expression of oppressed rural women.

Dalit women are using '*Thappu*', the drums, to show that drums can be beaten up by women not only by men. Drum beatings are to give life to the Dalit culture which was killed by the Brahminical culture. There are Dalit women's dances as well, such as *Kolatam, Oyilatam, Karagattam, Thappatam, Paraiyattam,* which all accompany with the drum music.

The drums have languages that the Dalit women beat all rituals. *Parai* the drum is beaten by *Paraiyer* is the myth and the *parai* was treated like the Dalits as 'untouchable' by the dominant culture.

The Dalit women revived the beating of *parai* and revolted against the dominant culture by giving new, revolving meaning to *Parai*. Dalit women beat drum to oppose the domination which is systematic, structural and multiple. Beating drum is to destroy the ideology of domination. Beating drum is to beat up the monoculture and to bring inter-culture of the oppressed, downtrodden, the broken, people together towards liberating humanity, transformation to achieve Equality, Freedom, Justice for a 'Humane' society through cultural and social society. Dalit women in Tamil Nadu are ready to drum out the globalised patriarchal fundamentalism, which produces casteism and gender discrimination, with the solidarity of other minority women.

CONTEMPORARY OPPRESSION AGAINST DALIT WOMEN

At Special Economic Zones (SEZs)

At present, 134,000 hectors of lands are set 67 multi-product SEZs in India (Financial Express, 30 Aug 2006). Although the land owner might receive the compensation for the land acquisition as the SEZs, the peasant Dalit women are facing the peril of the livelihoods by losing their job as well as being evicted from the land. For Dalit women, "trickle-down effect" theory, in which people can expect "trickled" benefits dropped down from the country or big companies' economic growth, is just a mirage, not a reality at all. The alienation is creating widespread discontent amongst farmers and common people all over India. The state, meanwhile, behaves as an agent of the corporation. The state government, which is essentially responsible to the citizen not only becomes advocates of the corporations but also acts as corporations. The state government itself takes away the land, especially agricultural lands, coastal lands with the coastal regulation zones, salt pans, and forest lands for SEZs.

The land taken for SEZs, meanwhile, only 35% is used for industry and the rest for non-industrial purposes: recreation centre-and housing. Although people are raising their voice, the oppression from the state government is intensified. In Nandigram, West Bengal, 17 villagers were shot to death with the protest against government taking away lands for corporation; chemical hubs of Salim group. Out of 17 killed 12 are Dalits. The people of Nandigram have lived in daily fear of retaliation when the Citizen's Committee entered to the district. The mission found that women were extremely apprehensive, begging the mission to spend the night with them. The state, however, is not restoring land rights and titles to landless Dalit women.

Land given to SEZs promoters is more than 1000 hectors which obviously violates Land Reform Act. SEZs will not create employment for local Dalit women but it will push away Dalit women because SEZs employs skilled and educated workers. Communities, especially Dalit women in unorganised sectors, will not be employed in SEZs.

In Tuticorin, Tamil Nadu, for example, another Nandigram is about to be occurred. Even though there are vociferous protests against the Tata's titanium dioxide plant to be situated at Sathankulam of the district, there are a lot of oppressions from the ruling party to the pantchayat leaders to urge them to accept the project. Also, even before the pantchayat leaders accept the project, the state government made an agreement with the company for establishing the Rs 2,500-crore titanium dioxide project. Negligence of local people voices in the politics and economy in SEZs definitely erodes the livelihood of the most vulnerable groups in the region, the Dalit Women. Besides of land conflict occurred by SEZs, the insecurity of women is intensified. Those who work as manual labourer in big factories are mostly poor women, such as Dalit women. When returning from the factory to their home late at night, women need to worry about their safety. In Ulundurpettai taluk of Villupuram district, there were 3 rapes – one was Dalit woman, and other women were from other community.

All are workers in big factories, and attacked on the way to go home from their workplace. SEZs are not only taking away the land, political rights, and dignity, but also depriving of Dalit women's opportunities for self-improvements, such as educations. In northern Tamil Nadu, where Society for Rural Education and Development (SRED) develops various community-based activities, it has been introduced between Chennai and Kancheepuram. From all over India and foreign countries-e.g. Reliance Group which runs many business all over India, Nokia, Hyundai, and Samsung-have invested to the zones and established huge factories along with the super highway which connects Chennai, Kancheepuram, and Bangalore. The establishment of SEZs firstly affects peasant landless Dalit women by displacing them from the lands without any compensation. They employ not only skilled workers, but also manual labourers from Dalit villages, mostly young women for manual works. Buses with the company logo are waiting for Dalit young girls early in the morning in front of the Dalit villages. Dalit girls are encouraged to go for work with SEZs than continuing for higher education. Dalit girls cannot have opportunities to learn any skills, even as "on the job trainings", and would face the unemployment as "uneducated woman" when the economy goes bad. Very recently, the Swiss based international lingerie company-Triumph has decided to invest to the area in order to establish key factory for underwear business throughout of the Subcontinent. The key of the final decision of investment was the quality of traditional technology in Garment industry, which Rural Dalit Women have conserved for many years in order to sustain their rural life (The Indian Express). Meanwhile, they are planning to sell those women's underwear for 400-1000 Rupees which is almost impossible price for local Dalit women, whereas the provider of the skills would face of insecurity.

At Dalit Women's Workplace

The political economy of globalisation erodes livelihoods of Rural Dalit women, who even luckily live far away from the Special Economic Zones. The agriculture sector has been transformed into the easier money making industry, such as floriculture and horticulture. Agriculture is turned into floriculture where small farmers would be eager to see cash everyday. Dalit women and school-going Dalit girl children are employed to pluck flowers for extremely low wages. Dalit Women and Dalit children are working in the fields where hazardous agro chemicals and pesticides are sprayed which affected the health of the Dalit women and Dalit children. The studies conducted on the impact of floriculture on the health of Dalit women in Santana Gopalapuram were on half an acre of land there are 10 workers: both men and women.

According to the villagers, floriculture has been around for last 20 years, but in the last 5 years, it has intensified and more farmers are moving to floriculture. Earlier they used to grow groundnut and rice. Women specifically mentioned that they have to get up early and finish household work before going to pluck flowers. They work from 6am in the farm and they can eat only after 10 am at the earliest. Also, due to constantly bending and plucking of flowers for almost 6 hours for low wages, at a stretch, there is chest, back and leg pain. Pesticides are sprayed almost when they are on the field, and smell persists for 3 days or more. Women are suffering from excessive white discharge, rolling feeling in the stomach, hysterectomy, and even tumour in uterus. Floriculture affects also the rights to education of Dalit girl children.

Dalit girl children are employed in order to pluck the flower before going to school and after the school. Dalit girl children are not able to recheck what they have learnt in the school and this turns into potential factor of drop-out. Of course with the health problem with pesticide, Dalit girls are failed to access to the school as well. Even some of the family members fell down with diseases caused by the pesticide this affects children's rights to go to school. In Kollathur where the agricultural lands were taken away for aqua farm for exportation which is located by the Buckingham Canal, at the backwater area of east-coast of Kancheepuram District, Tamil Nadu, is a Dalit village. Dalits have worked for cultivation of cashew nuts, prawn and fish catching in the backwater. In 2004, a Chennai based entrepreneur, F. Bartholome has obtained the license from the Aquaculture Authority and opened an industrial prawn farm called Chinna Aqua Farm. The farm came up on agricultural land, right alongside backwaters. The farm discharges untreated effluences from the farm which salinated agricultural lands and the backwaters. The Aqua farming in India was promoted by the government in 90's for one of the international business strategies of the country without thinking about the environmental impacts.

Soon after, in 1996, the Indian Supreme Court has regulated the use of coastal area for environmental reason, including creeks and backwaters which polluted water bodies. Running the farm without registration and permission shall be a criminal offence, but in practice, Bartholome's farm, for example, successfully got the license although it violates the regulation which stated in the law due to the lack of seriousness in the implementation of the law and due to corruption. Kollathur aqua farm is located on agricultural land whereas agricultural land should not be used for Aqua farming. Bartholome himself is also connected strongly with politicians. Ironically even after the inclusion of regulations, the production of prawns in the area for the exportation is increasing. The land has been transformed from traditional agricultural lands for people's food to money making products for exportation.

And now, with the toxic waste the Aqua farm cause loss of agricultural production which affects directly the daily food production of the Dalit villagers. Also, prawn catching and mussels collection by the Dalit women was totally affected with the pollution. This causes food insecurity as well as livelihood insecurity to Dalit women. The toxic waste polluted not only plants and animals but also human beings, mostly Dalit women who work in the field and with the toxic polluted back waters directly. Women got itching, skin disease and dimming of eyesight. Ground water has been salinated, and Dalit women lost adequate water for agriculture as well as for drinking. Not only endangered the livelihood by losing their work, but also women had to suffer from the physical pain by the disease, and from no money for the medical cost for treatment. The Dalits of Kollathur village are suffering from impacts of the pollution directly and indirectly due to the false cases many villagers who struggled against the farm were beaten up and charged.

Just in the last two years, more than 40 young men from this village of 4000 attend court cases four times in a month; need to pay a lot of cost for legal procedure; cost for advocates as well as transportation cost to the court. The increasing vulnerability in rural traditional life encourages not only industrial transformation but also migration. At Thirumalpur of Vellore district of Tamil Nadu where women earn only Rs.12.50 as wage for half-a-day's labour for agriculture work forced them to migrate to neighbouring State to earn more than Rs.50 per day. The Dalit women leave their children with their elders. Both men and women migrate they are made to stay in big halls or in schools. The women migrant workers sleep in one corner and their husbands as well as other men in other side vice-a-versa. They have no privacy they rely on near by pump sheds, lakes and ponds to bathing and washing their clothes, which are very insecure places. Every time they migrate from their village for a maximum of 20 days. The contractor employs them with an assignment to carry out harvest in 20 acres of land. After taking his commission of 30%, the contractors pay the rest to the workers. Women lose freedom and dignity in bad working conditions when they migrate.

6

Discrimination and Caste Exclusion of Dalit Women

In India, exclusion revolves around the societal interrelations and institutions that exclude, discriminate, isolate and deprive some groups on the basis of group identities like caste and ethnicity. It is caste-based exclusion which forms the basis for various anti-discriminatory policies. Historically, the caste system has regulated the social and economic life of the people in India. The organisational scheme of the caste system is based on the division of people into social groups (or castes) in which the civil, cultural and economic rights of each individual caste are predetermined or ascribed by birth and made hereditary.

The assignment of civil, cultural and economic rights is therefore unequal and hierarchical. The most important feature of the caste system, however, is that it provides for a regulatory mechanism to enforce social and economic organisation through the instruments of social ostracism (or social and economic penalties), and reinforces it further with justification and support from philosophical elements in the Hindu religion. The caste system's fundamental characteristics of fixed civil, cultural and economic rights for each caste, with restrictions on change, implies "forced exclusion" of one caste from the rights of the other caste, or from undertaking the occupations of other castes.

Exclusion and discrimination in civil, cultural, and particularly in economic spheres such as occupation and labour employment, are therefore internal to the system and a necessary outcome of its governing principles. In the market economy framework, occupational immobility operates through restrictions in various markets such as land, labour, credit, other inputs and services necessary for any economic activity. Labour, being an integral part of the production process of any economic activity, would obviously become part of market discrimination. This implies that the caste system involves the negation of not only equality and freedom, but also of basic human rights, particularly of low-caste untouchables, thus becoming an impediment in personal development. The principles of equality and freedom are not the governing principles of the caste system. This is because the underlying principles of the caste system assume particular notions of 'human rights'. Unlike many other human societies, the caste system does not recognise the individual and his/her distinctiveness as the centre of the social purpose. In fact, for the purpose of rights and duties, the unit of Hindu society is not an individual. Even the family is not regarded as a unit in Hindu society, except for the purposes of marriage and inheritance.

The primary unit in Hindu society is caste, and hence the rights and privileges (or lack of them) of an individual are on account of him/her being a member of a particular caste. Also, due to differential ranking and the hierarchical nature of the caste system, the entitlements to various rights become narrower and narrower as one goes down the hierarchical ladder within the caste system. Various castes get artfully interlinked and coupled with each other in a manner such that the rights and privileges of the higher castes become the causative reasons for the disadvantage and disability of the lower castes, particularly the untouchables. As Ambedkar observed, a caste does not exist in a single number, only in plural.

Castes exist as a system of endogenous groups that are interlinked with each other in an unequal measure of rights and relations in all walks of life. Castes at the top of the order enjoy more rights at the expense of those located at the bottom. Therefore, the untouchables located at the bottom of the caste hierarchy have much fewer economic and social rights. Since the civil, cultural and economic rights (particularly with respect to occupation and property rights) of each caste are ascribed, and are compulsory, the institution of caste necessarily involves forced exclusion of one caste from the rights of another. The unequal and hierarchical assignment of economic and social rights by ascription obviously restricts freedom of occupation and human development.

Social Exclusion

Social exclusion is the denial of equal opportunities imposed by certain groups of society on others, leading to the inability of an individual to participate in the basic political, economic and social functioning of society. Amartya Sen draws attention to various meanings and dimensions of the concept of social exclusion.

He draws a distinction between situations where some people are kept out (or left out), and where some people are included (forcibly) on deeply unfavourable terms. The two situations are described as "unfavourable exclusion" and "unfavourable inclusion". Sen argues that it is important to distinguish between 'active exclusion' — fostering of exclusion through deliberate policy interventions by the government or by any other wilful agents (to exclude some people from some opportunity), and 'passive exclusion', which works through the social process in which there are no deliberate attempts to exclude, but nevertheless may result in exclusion from a set of circumstances. Sen further distinguishes the "constitutive relevance" of exclusion from that of "instrumental importance".

In the former, exclusion or deprivation have an intrinsic importance of their own. For instance, not bring able to relate to others and to take part in the life of the community can directly impoverish a person's life, in addition to the further deprivation it may generate. This is different from social exclusion of "instrumental importance", in which the exclusion in itself is not impoverishing but can lead to impoverishment of human life. Mainstream economists have further elaborated the concept of discrimination that operates particularly through markets.

Caste Exclusion's Forms and Discrimination

Caste/untouchability and ethnicity-based exclusion reflects in the inability of individuals and groups like former untouchables, adivasis and similar groups to interact freely and productively with others and to take part in the full economic, social and political life of a community. Incomplete citizenship or denial of civil rights (freedom of expression, rule of law, right to justice), political rights (right and means to participate in the exercise of political power), and socio-economic rights (economic security and equality of opportunities) are key dimensions of impoverished lives (Jonas Zoninsein, 2005). Caste and untouchability-based exclusion and discrimination can be categorised in the economic, civil, cultural, and political spheres as follows:

Firstly, economic exclusion can be practised in the labour market through denial of jobs; in the capital market through denial of access to capital; in the agricultural land market through denial of sale and purchase or leasing of land; in the input market through denial in sale and purchase of factor inputs; and in the consumer market through denial in the sale and purchase of commodities and consumer goods.

Secondly, discrimination can occur through what Amartya Sen describes as "unfavourable inclusion", through differential treatment in the terms and conditions of contract, one of them reflecting in discrimination in the prices charged and received by discriminated groups. Discriminated groups can get lower prices for the goods that they sell, and could pay higher prices for the goods that they buy, as compared with the market price or the price paid by other groups.

Thirdly, exclusion and discrimination can occur in access to social needs supplied by government or public institutions, or by private institutions in the fields of education, housing and health, including common property resources like waterbodies, grazing land and land for common use.

Fourthly, groups (particularly untouchables) may face exclusion and discrimination from participation in certain categories of jobs (the sweeper being excluded from household jobs) because of the notion of purity and pollution, and may be restricted to so-called "unclean" occupations.

In the civil and cultural spheres, untouchables may face discrimination and exclusion in the use of public services like roads, temples, waterbodies, and institutions delivering services like education, health and other public services. In the political sphere, untouchables could face discrimination in the use of political rights, and in participation in the decision-making process. Due to physical (or residential) segregation, and social exclusion on account of the notion of untouchability, they may suffer from a general societal exclusion. Since there is a societal mechanism to regulate and enforce the customary norms and rules of the caste system, untouchables generally face opposition in the form of social and economic boycott, violence, and such acts as a general deterrent to their right to development. Caste and untouchability-based exclusion and discrimination are essentially "structural in nature" and comprehensive and multiple in coverage, involving the denial of equal opportunities.

Empirical Evidence of Caste Exclusion and Discrimination

The question is why dalits and adivasis, categorised as scheduled castes (SCs) and scheduled tribes (STs), have poor access to resources that directly and indirectly determine the level of income. Why their ownership of agricultural land and non-land capital assets is low compared with non-SC/STs. Why unemployment rates are high compared with non-SC/STs. Why daily wage earnings of SC/STs in non-farm activities are lower compared with non-SC/STs. Why literacy rates and education levels are much lower when compared with non-SC/STs. We first need to look at the evidence on discrimination in civil, cultural and political spheres provided by official data, besides an all-India study and four regional studies. These include an all-India 2000 ActionAid study ('Untouchability in Rural India' by Ghanshyam Saha, Satish Deshpande, Sukhadeo Thorat, Harsh Mander, Amita Baviskar and research and other regional staff, Delhi), a study on Karnataka (1973-74 and 1991), Andhra Pradesh (1977), Orissa (1987-88) and Gujarat (1996). The all-India study presents evidence from 11 states. The studies based on village surveys bring out the actual magnitude of the exclusion, discrimination and atrocities against dalits.

Economic Exclusion and Discrimination

Conducted in 555 villages across 11 Indian states — found that discrimination in labour markets operates through exclusion in hiring, and unfair or low wages. In about 36% of the villages, SCs were denied casual employment in agriculture. In about 25% of villages, SCs faced discrimination in wage payments. SCs received daily wages at a rate that was less than the market wage rate, or wages paid to non-SC workers. Belief in the concept of purity and pollution also impacted hiring of SC labourers — in about one-third of villages SCs were excluded from employment in the construction of houses. In the case of other markets, the study observed discriminatory treatment of SCs in access to irrigation water and public and private services.

In a little more than one-third of the villages, SCs were denied access to water for agriculture. In case of agricultural land, selective evidence from some states brings out the restrictions placed by the high castes on SCs in the purchase of private agricultural land, and use of public land for agriculture and housing. In the case of access to common property resources like grazing land, fishing ponds, and other resources, SCs faced exclusion in about one-fifth of the sample villages. The notion of pollution and purity reflected in the exclusionary and discriminatory behaviour of higher castes in the consumer markets — in the sale and purchase of consumer goods, particularly milk, vegetables and other such goods. In 35% of the villages surveyed, SCs were not allowed to sell any kind of goods at village-level markets. In about 47% of villages, SCs were not allowed to sell milk to village cooperatives and private buyers.

The survey data also reveals some isolated evidence of exclusion and discrimination in the sale and purchase of consumer goods like bakery products and vegetables. Such restrictions compelled SCs to go to small towns and other nearby marketplaces where their caste identity was not so obvious, or was hidden. Micro-level studies such as those from Andhra Pradesh (Venketeswarlu, 1990) and Karnataka (Khan, 1995) provide some evidence on economic discrimination in occupation, employment, wages, and the credit market as well as in other economic spheres. The Andhra Pradesh study observed that SCs faced restrictions in efforts to change their occupation.

Similarly, the Karnataka study revealed that nearly 85% of SC respondents continue to be engaged in their traditional occupations, with only 15% able to make a switch-over. The Orissa study (Tripathy, 1994) observed discrimination in land lease, credit and labour markets in rural areas. Nearly 96% of untouchable respondents in one village and all untouchable respondents in the second village were discriminated against in wage payment, with 28% in one village and 20% in another facing discrimination in payment of rent.

For urban areas, Banerjee and Knight (1991) observed that "there is indeed discrimination by caste, particularly job discrimination" and that "discrimination appears to operate at least in part through traditional mechanisms, with untouchables disproportionately represented in poorly-paid dead-end jobs... Even if discrimination is no longer practised, the effects of past discrimination could carry over to the present. This may help explain why discrimination is greatest in operative jobs in which contacts are more important for recruitment, and not in white-collar jobs in which recruitment involves formal methods." Such economic discrimination had obvious impacts on the earnings of SC households, and reflected in the incidence of high poverty among them.

The Right to Food

In terms of scale, caste discrimination afflicts more than one out of three fair price shops and more than one out of three government schools serving midday meals. In terms of geographical spread, it is unquestionably a nationwide problem — from 24% in Andhra Pradesh to 52% in Rajasthan, to a vast majority in Uttar Pradesh and Bihar, respondent villages from every state reported problems of caste discrimination and exclusion in the midday meal scheme. Likewise with the FPS, no state is free of discrimination — from 17% in Andhra Pradesh to 86% in Bihar. For instance, every state reports a substantial percentage of dominant caste public distribution system (PDS) dealers practising caste-based discrimination in the distribution of PDS goods, for example preferential order of service by caste, or hierarchically segregated timings for dominant caste and Dalit customers.

While the problem is nationwide, its degree varies considerably from state to state. Where higher percentages of midday meal cooks and organisers are Dalit, and where a higher percentage of midday meals are held in Dalit colonies, a lower incidence of caste discrimination in the scheme is reported. In Andhra Pradesh, where indicators of Dalit participatory empowerment and access are relatively high (49% of respondent villages have Dalit cooks, 45% have Dalit organisers, and 46% are held in Dalit localities), reported caste discrimination in the midday meal scheme stands at 24%. In Tamil Nadu, where the same empowerment and access indicators are lower (31%, 27% and 19%, respectively), reported discrimination stands at 36%. And in Rajasthan, where the indicators are alarmingly low (8% Dalit cooks, 0% Dalit organisers, 12% held in Dalit colonies), reported discrimination was extremely high at 52%. A similar pattern emerges in access to fair price shops, where higher proportions of Dalit dealers and FPS held in Dalit colonies correspond with lower proportions of reported discrimination and 'untouchability' practices.

Civil and Political Spheres

Macro-level Evidence: During 1999-2001, an average of 28,016 cases per year were registered by untouchables in the country under the Anti-Untouchability Act of 1955 and the SC and ST Prevention of Atrocities Act. This comes to about three cases per 100,000 population and included restrictions on access to temples, wells, taps, tea stalls, restaurants, community baths, roads, and other services. The ratio of such cases was highest in Rajasthan (9.3), followed by Madhya Pradesh (7.7). The ratio was about three cases per 100,000 population in Orissa, Karnataka, Gujarat and Andhra Pradesh. The break-up of crimes against untouchables for the year 2000 include 526 cases of murder, 3,497 of grievous hurt, 290 cases of arson, 1,000 cases of sexual assault, and 11,587 cases of other offences. During a nine-year period between 1992 and 2000, a total of 252,370 cases of crime, including cases of discrimination and atrocities, were registered by untouchables.

Evidence from Primary Surveys: First, the results of the most comprehensive study based on an intensive survey of 555 villages in 11 states across India. In this section, we consider the practice of discrimination in the "secular public sphere", including access to water sources, public thoroughfares, transport, and other village-level services and amenities like tea shops, barbers' or watermen's services, and so on.

Out of all the villages surveyed, complete denial was observed in a little less than half the villages — 48.4% in terms of access to public water/drinking places, 36% in terms of access to shops, 26% in terms of the use of restaurants/hotels, 21% in terms of entry to health centres/clinics, 9.2% in terms of public transport, and 3.2% in terms of entry to cinema halls/recreation facilities, etc.

In the case of individual service-providers also, the denial was more than apparent. Out of all the villages surveyed, denial of barber services was reported in 46% of the villages, washerperson services in 46% of the villages, carpenter services in 26% of the villages, and potter services in about 20% of the villages. While complete denial of access to particular water sources (well, tank, tubewell, etc), village shops, health clinics, transport used for public purposes, services offered by washerpersons, carpenters, tailors, potters, etc, is the most evident form of social exclusion, what is more common is the imposition of differential treatment in access to these and other public services, which takes various forms. This was observed in one-third of the villages in the form of separate seating arrangements and a separate set of cups at tea stalls/restaurants for untouchables. Similar forms of discrimination were observed in purchases from shops, entry into public transport, and treatment at private health clinics, etc.

Discrimination Story of Karnataka

The Karnataka study for 1973-74 is based on a fairly large sample of 76 villages, 38 urban centres and 3,330 households. Of the total households, 73% are untouchables (Parvathamma, 1984). A little more than half the untouchable respondents were not allowed to draw water from the public well in the village. The magnitude of the problem was less severe in urban centres, but even in urban areas 15% of respondents reported restrictions on the use of public waterbodies. The practice of untouchability was more widespread in terms of access to the village temple and access to high-caste houses. More than 60% of untouchables were not allowed into the village temple. A little less than half the dalits were not allowed free access to the local village teashop. In urban areas, the discrimination was much less (only 6%). In essential services, the practice of untouchability was widespread. A little more than half of the respondents did not receive the services of a barber and washerman in the village. In urban areas, access improved considerably. In public services like postal services, health and education, the practice of untouchability was much less. Almost all had access to postal services, but half of the respondents faced some kind of discrimination insofar as postmen avoided entering Dalit residential areas. Generally, discrimination in services rendered by government doctors and nurses and the village school was less. Still, in the early-1970s, one out of 10 persons among the scheduled castes was not allowed inside the village shops. One out of 10 persons among the scheduled castes could not wear clothes or ornaments of their own choice without being harassed.

Nearly 20 years later, another study was conducted in Karnataka taking 941 respondents from 52 villages and from most of the districts (Khan, 1995). In the political sphere (that is, sitting together or drinking tea in the village panchayat office), the discrimination was much less. Otherwise, not much had happened in the two decades since the previous study was carried out. About three out of four respondents were denied entry into the village temple and also denied participation in religious processions. Social mixing or relations across caste barriers were also not allowed. Most people among the untouchables did not have free access to the water taps of the high castes, and three-fourths of them had no access to the village tank.

Discrimination Story of Orissa

The Orissa study covered 65 untouchable respondents from two villages (one small and one large) in 1987-88 (Tripathy, 1994). In both villages, the settlements of untouchables were separated from those belonging to the upper castes. An overwhelming majority — 80% — of respondents in the small village and 70% in the large village were prohibited from drinking water from the public well and public tubewell. In the large village there were separate pulleys in wells for the untouchables. At village community feasts and marriages in both the villages, the former untouchables were treated unequally. The same is true of temple worship, barber services, washerman services, priest services, etc. Sixty-four per cent in the large village and 100% in the small village were treated unequally in the village meeting. Eighty per cent of the respondents in both villages did not have access to teashops; 70% in the large village and 80% in the small village faced unequal treatment or discrimination in getting services from grocery shops. Their small number, poverty and fear (in the small village) discouraged the dalits from contesting elections. But dalits had free access to schools and hospitals in both villages.

Discrimination Story of Gujarat

The Gujarat study was conducted in 69 villages, in 1996, to observe changes in the practice of untouchability (Shah, 1998). The study examined 17 spheres of village life. The practice of untouchability in the seating arrangement of students in village schools was negligible and non-SC students mingled freely in the school. Non-SC teachers do not discriminate against SC students, but they are not easily accessible to SC students outside the school boundary. Not all schools have the facility of drinking water for students. Where it exists, all students take water from a common vessel. Nearly 10% of village schools have teachers belonging to SCs. None of them complained that their colleagues discriminated against them in school. However, except in south Gujarat, these teachers do not get accommodation in the high-caste locality of the village. They either commute from their village or the nearby town, or they rent a house in the SC locality. Almost all villages are covered by state transport. Except in 7% of the villages, untouchability is not observed whilst boarding and sitting in the bus. Open or subtle untouchability is practised at panchayat meetings in 30% of the villages.

The seating arrangement in panchayat offices is common for all members, but there is a tacit convention whereby certain seats are marked for SC members. Though tea and snacks are served to everyone, separate plates and cups are reserved for SC members, and they are stored separately. In most village temples, 75% of SCs are not allowed to enter beyond the threshold, though they may worship from a distance. Many villages with large numbers of dalits have constructed temples in their localities to avoid confrontation. In 46 villages, SCs had separate water facilities near their localities. In the remaining 23 villages in which untouchables take water from a common source, SC women take water after the upper-caste women. In seven villages (11% of the sample) SC women are not allowed to fetch water from the well. They have to wait till the upper-caste women pour water into their pots. The upper-caste women shout at them constantly and humiliate the SC women: "Keep distance, do not pollute us!" Most tailors do not practise untouchability.

However, in most cases, they do not alter the used clothes of SCs. Nearly one-third of potters observe untouchability while selling pots to SC clients. Most barbers (nearly 70%) refuse their services to SC males. The extent of untouchability has remained almost intact in the sphere of house entry. Except for a few villages, SC members of villages do not get entry beyond the outer room of the houses of high castes. Even in villages where the young folk do not believe in physical untouchability, and who serve tea to SC guests in their houses, entry into the dining room is not encouraged. The practice of untouchability has considerably reduced in some public spheres that are directly managed by state laws, such as schools, postal services and elected panchayats. The practice of untouchability on public roads, restricting free movement of SCs, has considerably declined although it is too soon to say that dalits are not discriminated against in the public sphere.

ACCESS TO JUSTICE

A number of anti-discrimination statutes and other legal provisions exist as legal safeguards against caste and untouchability-based discrimination. As mentioned earlier, the primary piece of legislation designed to provide a measure of protection to people from scheduled castes and scheduled tribes and to enforce their rights are the Anti-Untouchability Act, 1955 (in 1979 it was re-named the Civil Rights Act) and the Scheduled Caste and Scheduled Tribes Prevention of Atrocities Act, 1989. There are limited studies that examine the effectiveness of these legislations and access to institutions of justice. However, available evidence indicates that these legislative provisions are highly underutilised. SC/STs also suffer from discriminatory access to institutions of justice such as the police and the judiciary. Studies indicate that the scheduled castes/tribes face insurmountable obstacles at various levels from village-level functionaries like sarpanchs to the police, public prosecutors and other functionaries who are extremely non-cooperative and discriminatory.

This is essentially reflected in denial of justice to SC/STs. Official data on civil rights cases shows that of the total number of cases registered in 1991, only 1.56% were convicted. The conviction rate came down to .60% in 1999 and .85% in 2000. This shows that the conviction rate in cases relating to civil rights violations and atrocities was less than 1% and close to 0%. Analysis of 100 documented cases of atrocity during 2000-2003 in Andhra Pradesh throws some light on the reasons for the low conviction rate. The case studies indicated "a disturbing trend of subversion of the rights of dalits to justice and compensation under the law once an atrocity takes place" (Agrawal and Gonsalves, Dalit Human Rights Monitor 2003). The study observed negligence and collusion at the stages of registration, chargesheeting and investigation, at seeking justice before the law in the courts and in giving compensation. About the role of the judiciary, Dalit Human Rights Monitor 2003 observed: "If the low conviction rate under the Act is any indication, the judiciary has responded poorly to the Act. Judiciary delay and dilution of the scope, applicability and meaning of the SC/ST Act has resulted in denial of justice to the dalits".

THE INTERFACE OF CASTE AND GENDER

Assessments of human development at the aggregate level hide gender differences. Women belonging to marginalised groups suffer triple deprivations arising out of lack of access to economic resources, caste and gender discrimination. SC and ST women constitute perhaps the most economically deprived section of Indian society. Most of them don't own agricultural land and work as wage labourers. In 2001, about 57% of SC and 37% of ST women respectively were agricultural wage labour in rural areas, as compared with 29% for non-SC/STs. In urban areas, 16% SC and 14% ST women were daily wage labourers as compared with only 6% from non-SC/STs. Only 21% of SC women were cultivators compared with 51% for STs and 45% for non-SC/STs. SC/ST women also faced differential treatment in wage-earning, particularly in urban areas. In 2000, SC and ST women casual labourers received daily wages of Rs 37 and Rs 34 respectively, compared with Rs 56 for non-SC/ST women; the national average was Rs 42. Besides this, a large number of SC women are engaged in so-called 'unclean' occupations, like scavenging.

Because of their association with these occupations, the women face discrimination in the social and economic spheres. Lack of educational development is another important problem. In 2000, the literacy rate among SC and ST rural females (aged 15 and above) was 24% and 23% respectively, compared with 41% for non-SC/ST women. The literacy rate among SC women in urban areas was 48%, compared with 54% and 70% for ST and non-SC/ST women respectively. The dropout rate among SC and ST women is also relatively high at every stage of education. The high dependence on casual labour, with relatively low earnings, among SC and ST women induced a high degree of deprivation and poverty among them. The gender break-up of poverty is not available.

However, the high degree of deprivation is reflected in other indicators of wellbeing — under-nutrition and health. About 65% and 56% of ST and SC women respectively suffered from anaemia compared to 47.6% of non-SC/ST women. In 1998-99, 21.2% of SC and 26% of ST children under four years of age suffered from malnutrition (based on weight-for-age). Of these underweight children, 54% of SCs and 56% of STs were severely undernourished. There is a significant difference between SC and ST children and non-SC/ST children, 13.80% and 41.1% of whom are malnourished and undernourished respectively. While the Government of India has adopted the national goal of reducing the present infant mortality rate (IMR) to 60 by 2000, the SC's IMR, child mortality and under-5 mortality is 83.00, 39.50 and 119.3, respectively. Compare this with 61.8, 22.2 and 82.6 for non-SC/STs, respectively.

Similarly, IMR, child mortality and under-5 mortality are 84, 46.3 and 126 among STs. About 72% of births to SC women and 81% of births to ST women took place at home; the corresponding figure for others is 59%. Because of their lower social status, sexual exploitation of SC/ST women is also high. There are some caste-related social customs and religious practices in Hindu society that exploit only women from Dalit communities. One of these customs is devdasi or jogini, involving religious prostitution imposed on unfortunate girls who are married to a village god and then become the subject of sexual exploitation by upper caste men in a village. A primary survey estimates the number of joginis in six districts of Andhra Pradesh at 21,421. There are similar practices in states like Tamil Nadu, Karnataka and Maharashtra where Dalit women are designated devdasis or devotees of god.

THE OPPRESSION OF SHUDRAS/DALITS IN INDIA

The caste system is as old as the Hindu religion itself, in fact, it even predates Hinduism by some centuries. One important thing to know about the caste system is that it was brought into the Indus Valley from the outside by a tribe of semi-nomadic people called the Aryans (the "Noble Ones"), who originally inhabited the steppe country of southern Russia and Central Asia and entered India, through the Indus Valley, around the year 1500 BCE.

The Aryans had a linear sense of time and had a structured caste system with three sets of castes (warrior caste on top, followed by a priestly caste, and then everyone else) and a plethora of mostly male gods, the language that the Aryans spoke was Sanskrit which latter became the basis for Hindi. When the Aryans invaded the Indus Valley the people of the Indus Valley had a religion with no caste system, a circular sense of time (hence the Hindu concept of reincarnation, etc.), and a pantheon of female goddesses.

The fact that the outsider Aryans introduced India to the caste system and was a warrior-centred culture that had a reverence for male gods is one of the reasons why scholars, such as Kalpana Kannabiran argue that "patriarchy is in fact the basis of the caste system and that the patterns of hierarchy, power and authority which characterise the caste system are derived from earlier forms of gender-based oppression."

When the Aryans first invaded the Indus Valley they called the Indus Valley people (Indians) Dasa (Sanskrit for dark-skinned) and the three-tier caste system was morphed into a four-tier caste system called the Four Varnas (which means color); Brahmins, the priestly class were now on the top, Ksatriyas, the warrior class were now below the priests, then their was the Vaishyas, skilled labor, and the Sudras, unskilled labor.

Outside of the caste system were the non-Vedic peoples and the Dalits (the untouchables). Originally the lighter one's skin color was the higher up in the caste system one was (with the Aryans obviously being at the top of the system) and the higher up in the caste system one was the more "pure" that person was (purity was of a huge concern of the Indus Valley people with many ritual and private baths having been excavated).

The majority of the people in the Indus Valley fell within the lower castes which can be seen today since 77% of Indians comprise these lower castes (as well as Dalits, scheduled castes/scheduled tribes [SC/ST], etc.). What this mini-history lesson shows us was that the concept of caste is a concept that was brought into India by outside forces (the patriarchical and warrior culture of the Aryans) which then incorporated itself into the civilization of the Indus Valley people through the Vedas (specifically the Rig Veda).

The Aryans and Brahmins needed a system to keep themselves on top and the majority of the dark-skinned Indus Valley people at the bottom, the caste system was the perfect way to do this, and in fact this had been the case until around 500 BCE when the traditions of the Vedas and the Brahmins began to be attacked by Hindu ascetics.

From around 600 BCE to 200 BCE there was an incredible Vedic development in the Hindu tradition (a philosophic development) which can be described as the "democratization of Hinduism." Out of this philosophic development came the Upanisads (upanisad implies "sitting at the feet of the teacher," Upa=down, Ni=near, and Sad=sit).

The Upanisads were focused on attaining the mystical knowledge that would free a person from "re-death" or punarmrtyu. The Brhadâranyaka Upanisad placed emphasis on the knowledge of the cosmic connection underlying ritual. "When the doctrine of the identity of atman (the Self) and brahman was established in the Upanishads, the true knowledge of the Self and the realization of this identity...substituted the ritual method." Asceticism started becoming more widespread (which was one the factors leading to the creation of the latter Upanisads) in reaction to the rigid doctrines of the Brahmin and of the Vedas.

What's important to note as that even though these ascetics were critical of the Vedas and scathing in their critiques of the Brahmins they were still very much Hindu in nature (in fact, they probably didn't consider themselves anything else, all though the term Hindu wasn't around then) and their philosophical teachings and thought derived from the Vedas.

These ascetics denied that only Brahmins could receive bliss and escape reincarnation and stated that through giving up the world and all desires anyone, whether Dalit or Vaishya, could attain psychic security, or rather, liberation through the attainment of unification with Brahman. Out of reaction to this the Brhamins devised a doctrine called the four asramas (abodes) which dived the life of the "twice born" into four stages" which would keep asceticism in check by confining it to middle-aged males. On top of these ascetics came leaders who led offshoots of Hinduism and breakaway sects such as Siddhartha Gautama (the Buddha) and Vardhamana (Mahavira, the great teacher of Jainism).

These two leaders rejected not only the pleasures of the world, but more importantly, they rejected the claims of the Brahmins and the ritualistic Brahminic schools who claimed authority and superiority over other Hindus and Indians by claiming to be pure and to have the right to perform traditional rituals and sacrifices, as well as having the rights to interpret their meanings.

While the Buddha rejected Hinduism (as well as religion) all together, Mahavira kept to the central aspects of Hinduism while abandoning the rituals that allowed the Brahmins to dominate all aspects of life. Mahavira stated that through one's own efforts one could attain liberation and freedom from rebirth, short of the Buddha, this was one of the most complete rejections of the Brahmins (and in turn their belief in ritual purity and caste) that anyone could have ever articulated.

All of this now brings us to today and to the subject of the liberation of Dalits and to the subject of my final blog in this series, a Hindu Liberationist perspective on the plight of Dalits and of their liberation from caste oppression. What disturbed me about the student protests against the further admission of lower caste and SC/ST students was that these high caste students had the wrong premise that the oppression of lower caste and SC/ST peoples was the "correct" form of Hinduism and the only form that should be practiced (all though I do recognize that some of these students could have been playing the "caste card," claiming caste privilege in order to protect their privilege in society).

Yet we have seen in the ancient history of Hinduism that caste was an outside concept placed upon the Indus Valley people by an outside tribe of semi-nomadic pastoralists, this shows us that the concept of caste didn't grow "organically" from Indian soil but was imposed from the outside, and hence, the shedding of caste ideology and caste oppression would in a sense mean the shedding of outside Aryan domination against the Indian peoples, of course many high caste Indians still adhere to their Aryan roots and view their Brahmin status as a source of pride, not something to overcome in order to help out their lower caste and Dalit sisters and brothers.

Despite the seemingly set in stone concepts of caste in the Rig Veda many Hindus over the preceding centuries fought back against the Brahminic elite and questioned the writings of the Vedas, especially the writings on ritualistic purity (a major concept in caste ideology) and on the "privileges" of the Brahmin caste.

Whether it was the radical Siddhartha Gautama, who renounced Hinduism, or Vardhamana, who used acetic concepts of Hindu thought to criticize the present day establishment, thoughtful Hindus and the ever evolving Hindu religion never laid down and accepted the perverse policies of the Brahmin and their constant quest for power.

Because of this we can see that Hinduism was never a monolithic religion that accepted the Vedas sayings on caste and ritual as blindly as present day Hindu nationalist BJP (Bharatiya Janata Party) and RSS (Rashtriya Svayamsevak Sangh) supporters would like us to think.

History has shown us that a thoughtful and pious Hindu can be one who rejects certain ideas of Vedic thought that are oppressive and evil and history has also shown us within the Hindu tradition there has always been an ever evolving struggle for freedom against the Brahminic caste in the realm of the physical and the realm of the spiritual, such as reclaiming concepts of freedom from rebirth and attaining liberation by being joined with Brahmin.

With this in mind I will now actually tackle (in part VI, the final part, of this series) the problems of the caste system and the oppressions Dalits have faced over the centuries (especially the 20th century and now) and how Dalits will be the ones to actually bring about change in this present day situation and how Dalits are the only ones to bring about their own salvation (not from outside help from people such as Gandhi or someone like myself) and how the Hindu religion plays a role in this, and how it can play a liberating role instead of the role of oppressor.

INCOME GENERATING SCHEMES FOR SC, ST, OBC, MINORITIES AND WOMEN

Govt of India at the Centre, took up the task of the Nation as whole, with all seriousness, after Independance. Govt set up a Planning Commission at the Centre, amidst many opposition, resentments and criticisms. The Party in Power, Congress appeared to be fully committed for the Development of the Nation, Welfare of the Society as a whole, and all Sections of the Society. That appeared to be inevitable in a Democracy, and a Republic. Moreover, the Congress Party during the Freedom Movement and after, had been in all Public Statements, championing the cause of the Weaker Sections like the SCs&STs, Minorities, OBCs and Women. And Special Provisions had also been made in the Constitution, for the Development of the Poor and the Weak in the Country. Further, many specific Provisions have been incorporated in the Constitution for the Welfare, Development and Protection of different Weaker Sections of the Society, like SCs, STs, Minorities, OBCs and Women. The Constitutional Promises and Guarantees, and Legal Protections for the SCs&STs were followed by the Congress Govts, with Reservations in Services.

This has helped a good number of them in different regions to participate in different spheres of National Activities, Development, Administration and Governance, where Reservations have been allowed to operate. The Scientific Socialistic Development and Justice oriented Modern Vision of Jawaharlal Nehru, the first Prime Minister of India, and his choice to go in for Planned Development through Five-Year Plans, laid a great emphasis in Developing all the Weaker Sections. In addition, Special Programmes and Schemes were also taken for the Welfare, Growth and Development of many SCs, STs, Minorities, OBCs and Women from amongst them, as well as other Women. These helped, to improve the standards of the lives of the Weaker Sections, in a Nation where they were otherwise marginalised, neglected and oppressed, depending on the situation.

NEED FOR DEVELOPMENT OF THE WEAKER SECTIONS - THE SCS STS OBCS AND MINORITIES

The SCs STs OBCs and Minorities, have been forced to remain as the Weaker Sections of India, and the Women confined or oppressed to be the most and multiply exploited sections of the Country, for nearly four millenniums.

This bad situation, can not and should not continue anymore. Definitely not in the Twenty-first Century of the third millennium, in an age of fast travel and mass communication. There is a need for the Govts to do something special and tangible, to free and liberate the Weaker Sections, from the cobwebs of oppression, marginalisation and backwardness. They have to be uplifted to the levels of normal human-beings of the World.

The Then Prime Minister Jawaharlal Nehru's Views

The need to Develop the Weaker Sections, and the sensitivity with which appropriate Policies have to be adopted, can be better appreciated by what Jawaharlal Nehru, the then Prime Minister of the Nation, wrote on 9th Oct 1958 regarding Development of the STs. We can not allow matters to drift in the Tribal Areas, or just not take interest in them. In the World of today, that is not possible or desirable. At the same time, we should avoid over-administrating these areas, and in particular, sending too many outsiders into Tribal Territory. It is between these two extreme positions that we have to function. Development in various ways there has to be, such as communications, medical facilities, education and better agriculture. These avenues of Development should, however, be pursued within the broad framework of the following five fundamental principles;

1. People should Develop along the lines of their own genius, and we should avoid imposing anything on them. We should try to Encourage in every way their own Traditional Arts and Culture.
2. Tribal Rights in Land and Forests should be respected
3. We should try to Train and Build up a team of their own people to do the work of Administration and Development. Some technical

personnel from outside will, no doubt, be needed, especially in the beginning. But we should avoid introducing too many outsiders into tribal territory

4. We should not over-administer these areas, or overwhelm them with a multiplicity of Schemes. We should rather work through, and not in rivalry to, their own social and cultural institutions
5. We should judge results, not by statistics or the amount of money spent, but by the quality of human character that is evolved.

The above reflects the special sensitivity with which the then Prime Minister, approached the issue of Tribal Development. We should have by now developed adequate strategies for the Development of Scheduled Castes, OBCs, Minorities and Women. Special Strategies should have been evolved for the Women from SCs&STs, OBCs and Minority Communities, who suffer the most in the Country. Special steps should have been taken, particularly for the SC&ST Women, who were subjected to multiple exploitations as –

1. poor and helpless people
2. SCs&STs
3. at times as Minority Community SCs&STs, and
4. top of them all as easily vulnerable Women

Sadly, even today there are no special Cells in the Planning Commission even for the 260 million plus SCs&STs. How then can we really hope that, the Weaker Sections of the Country will ever be developed? The Development of the Weaker Sections have to have a bearing on their Occupation, Problems, Requirements, Needs and Aspirations.

Problems of the Weaker Sections

1. Lack of Income Generating Assets and Resources
2. Lack of Regular Income
3. Lack of Access to Finances
4. Non-availability of regular Employment
5. Low Wages
6. Indebtedness
7. Shortage of Food and Fodder
8. Difficulties in getting Water
9. Landlessness
10. Homelessness
11. Sickness, lack of timely Medical Aid and adequate Health Care

12. Illiteracy Ignorance and Superstitions
13. Cheating by middlemen and Contractors
14. Oppression of their Communities
15. Suppression of the promising and developing individuals and families
16. Discrimination
17. Non-Payment of proper Wages

General Occupations of the Weaker Sections

1. Cultivators
2. Marginal Farmers
3. Seasonal Agricultural Labourers
4. Employees in Household Industries
5. Home Services and Repairs
6. Public Services like Security and Scavenging
7. Leather Workers
8. Skilled and Unskilled Workers
9. Producers of Handicrafts
10. Process Units
11. Petty Manufacture
12. Domestic Helpers
13. Casual Workers
14. Other Workers

Strategies and Approach for Planning Development

1. Market Induced Plans
2. Trickledown Theory
3. Financial Assistance to Individuals
    a) Loans for specific Projects
    b) Bridge Loans to facilitate Financial Assistance
    c) Govt Subsidies as Incentives
    d) Govt Aid as help
    e) Grants to special Programmes
4. Promotion of Co-operatives
5. Encouraging Community Development
6. State Intervention at Community Level
7. Pro-Active Target Groups oriented Schemes

Requirements of the Weaker Sections

1. Literacy
2. General Education
3. Professional Education
4. Health Education
5. Residential and Ashram Schools
6. Book-Banks
7. Freeships for primary education
8. Scholarships for higher studies
9. Fellowships for study abroad
10. Special Hostels for SCs, STs, OBCs, Minorities for Boys
11. Special Hostels for SCs, STs, OBCs, Minorities for Girls
12. Admissions into general Students Hostels of the Colleges and Universities
13. Skills Training Centres
14. Coaching Centres for Civil Services and Banking Exams

There is a need to address these basic problems first and fully. Therefore the Programmes and Schemes being designed developed evolved and implemented, should address these problems appropriately and fully, not casually in passing or incidentally.

Weaker Sections Development Programmes

All Development Programmes can be classified as –

1. LONG-TERM PROGRAMMES
   a) General Area Development Programmes
   b) General Community Development Programmes
   c) Special-Group Oriented Plans
      i) Tribal Sub Plans for STs
      ii) Settlement of Nomadic and de-notified Tribes
      iii) Improving the Working Conditions of Sweepers
      iv) Improving the Working Conditions of Flayers and Cobblers
      v) Special-Component Plans for SCs
      vi) Development of specific Backward Classes like Gold-Smiths, Weavers, Fishermen etc
   d) Socio-Economic Programmes

e) Human-Development Programmes
   i) Upgradation of Skills
   ii) General Education and Employment
   iii) Professional Education
   iv) Management Training
   v) Entrepreneurship Training to set up Industries, set-up Business etc
   vi) Loans to start Economic activities

2. SHORT-TERM PROGRAMMES
   a) Training to impart Skills
   b) Financial Assistance to set up Rural Development Programmes
      i) Cottage Industries
      ii) Mini-Economic Activities
3. EMERGENCY PROGRAMMES
   a) To meet crisises
   b) To meet disasters and natural calamities
4. POVERTY ALLEVIATION PROGRAMMES

Development Approach

1. Individual oriented
2. Community centred
3. Cluster approach
4. Saturation approach
5. Integration approach

NEED FOR POVERTY ALIEVIATION PROGRAMMES

The present Govt and the PM had publicly shrunk away to slip out of all Political and Community Responsibilities. They want to wriggle out of the Social Contract with the People and Society for Human Development. That includes General Education of the Children, employment, health care, environmental hygiene, housing and transportation. These and the growing Corruption in Public Services, have left the Govts short-strapped of funds. Hence, they are no more in a position to take up and find money to finance time bound tangible Developmental Programmes for Welfare Schemes. Hence, the Govts are forced to take up just a little bit of Poverty Alleviation Programmes, to keep the people satisfied a little.

Govts' Efforts to Develop Weaker Sections

General and overall Developmental Planning in the Country, was launched in 1951, in the form of Five-Year Plans. When the Five-Year Plans could not be finalised due to Political and other Considerations, Annual-plans were adopted. All these Plans, took into consideration the need to Develop the Poor and the Weaker Sections. It kept in view the concerns of the first Prime Minister of India, which was subsequently evolved as the Policy of the Govt and Planning Commission. The First Five-Year Plan, during the years of 1951-56 believed in Trickle-Down Theory.

It envisaged that Programmes under various sectors of Development would benefit all sections of Population including the Weaker Sections of Society. But sadly, this reliance failed and the expectations were belied. Benefits of Development never reached the poor and the weak, for obvious reasons. Hence, Special Programmes for the Backward Classes were formulated, especially and separately under the Backward Classes Sector, with a very Small Backward Class Division in Planning Commission, New Delhi. The Special Requirements of SCs&STs were particularly taken into account. The Second Plan over the years 1956-61, was formulated with the promise to ensure that, Economic and Social Benefits of National Development would accrue to the Backward Classes also, and to the relatively much marginalised and less privileged SCs&STs. These were expected to bridge the gaps between the dominant castes and the weaker Sections on the one hand, and lift the neglected SCs&STs at least to near the levels of the Other Backward Classes. The important component of the Second Plan, were separate Tribal Development Plans, with respect and understanding of their Culture and Traditions. This was based on the Philosophy of Panchsheel for Tribal Area Administration and Development enunciated by the first Prime Minister of the Nation.

During the Plan, 43 Special Multi-Purpose Tribal Blocks were opened, which later became Tribal development Blocks for about 25,000 Tribals as against the normal 65,000 per Block. The Third Plan of the Years 1961-66 and the three Annual Plans during 1966-69, advocated Greater Equality of Opportunities, and reduction in the Economic Disparities and differences in Income and Wealth in the Society. Its thrust was towards even distribution of wealth, reduction of inequalities in the community, and levelling up the economic power of most sections of the society. The Fourth Plan of 1969-74 envisaged, the Basic Goal of Rapid Increase in the Standard of Living of the People, through measures which also Promoted Equality and Social Justice.

In 1971-71, six pilot-projects were set up in Andhra Pradesh, Bihar, Madhya Pradesh and Orissa, with a separate Tribal Development Agency for each Project. The Fifth Plan during the Years 1974-79, was a watershed for the STs.

In the Year 1975-76, Tribal Sub-Plan was launched, by keeping aside Plan Funds for the Development Scheduled Tribe Areas with exclusive allocations for specific and separate Programmes and Schemes for STs Welfare and Development. This approach, and its success was appropriately copied and adopted for the Welfare of SCs in the subsequent Plans. The Annual Plan of 1979-80, saw the launching of the Special Component Plan for SCs so that they could also receive their due share of Plan Allocations and Benefits of Development from various Developmental Sectors. This facilitated convergence and pooling of available resources and Plan Allocations from every Sector to Develop the SCs in proportion to the SC Population in the Society. The Sixth Plan 1980-85 continued with the SCP for SCs which became a significant feature of the Five-Year Plans, along with TSP for the STs.

These facilitated monitoring and evaluation of the Development of both SCs and STs. The Seventh Plan 1985-90, saw the strengthening of SCP and TSP, with the flow of funds from the State Plans, Central Plans and Special Central Assistance (SCA) and Institutional Finance, facilitating enlargement of infrastructures and expansion of their coverage to benefit more SCs&STs. In 1989, National SC&ST Finance Development Corporation (NSFDC) to provide loans to SCs&STs for taking up gainful and profitable self-employment productive activities, and business was established. The Eighth Plan 1992-97, aimed at bridging the gap between the Development of the Weaker Sections and others, by the beginning of the Twenty-first Century.

The Ninth Plan 1997-2002 was said would Empower the Socially Disadvantaged Groups to become agents of Change and Development by themselves. It was expected to create an enabling Environment Conducive for SCs&STs, Minorities and OBCs to exercise their rights freely to enjoy all privileges, and lead a life with confidence and dignity at par with the rest of the society. Disparities were to be removed, exploitation and suppression eliminated, protection provided to the disadvantaged groups of Weaker Sections, such that benefits of Development would *reach the unreached* through Equitable Distribution and Social Justice. These it was said would facilitate the weaker sections not merely as beneficiaries but also as participants in the Planning and Implementation of the Developmental Process. It was expected that funds would also flow to Women of the Weaker Sections, for their Development.

However belied till-date, were all the Promises to the People about –

1. Social Empowerment
2. Economic Empowerment, and
3. Social Justice

During the Year 1997, at the time of the 11th Lok Sabha, five Office Memorandums, affecting the Reservations in Employment of not only SCs&STs but also the OBCs were introduced.

The unkindest cut of all, came during the 12th Parliament, when this Govt brought out the sixth OM. It remains to be the most dangerous of all the Black Anti-Reservation OMs. It deprives the SCs, STs and OBCs who come up on top to be in the merit list, their position in the merit list, if they had otherwise availed of any concessions as SCs/STs/OBCs. This one, without any provocation or Court Judgement whatsoever.

Importance of Income Generating Schemes

The World is now wise to believe in the Chinese Proverb – *It is better to teach an hungry individual to fish, than give a fish to eat, least the individual may come back again for the next fish.* Therefore it is good to introduce people to Income Generating Schemes, to take up their life and future in their own hands, than help them with food or doles or any other form of financial or material assistance.

DEVELOPMENT OF SCHEDULED CASTES AND SCHEDULED TRIBES

The basic need of the SCs&STs was to end their forced Segregation by the Caste System. The best Strategy that could be considered was Reservations for SCs & STs. Reserving the dues of SCs & STs to SCs & STs, was the only way to ensure their proportionate share in all walks of life.

As a result of Baba Saheb's Struggles, and his demands in the First and Second Round Table Conferences in 1930-32, the British agreed to provide some Reservations.

Political Reservations for SCs & STs

Of these only Political Reservations, though time-bound are compulsory and inescapable, being a firm Constitutional Provision. This opened the way for the SCs & STs to participate in the Governance of the Country, directly to some extent possible, and force the Govts to take the Problems of SCs & STs seriously, and Plan for their Welfare and Development.

However, there are no Reservations for SCs in the Upper Houses in the Centre and the States. As a result, the Representation of SCs & STs in the Upper Houses are still poor. There is a need to introduce Reservations for SCs & STs in Rajya Sabha in Parliament, and Legislative Councils in the States.

RESERVATION IN EMPLOYMENT FOR SCs & STs and to OBCs at the time of making Appointments.

Reservation in Employment, though without any time-limit, is only an enabling Provision in the Constitution, that also in Public Services. It is therefore left to the discretion of the Bureaucrats, Governments, Parliament and Legislative Assemblies. This was the Most Effective Programme for the Development of SC&ST Communities.

Reservation in Employment is a means for Community Participation in the Governance of the Country through Administration, its Executive Functions, and Decision making roles for day to day business of the Govts. It should not be-as it is often prone to – mixed with the Development of any Individual or family. It should not be seen just as a means of Employment, for getting a respectable and regular income as wages pay and allowances or salary every month. Yes, Employment of the Individuals are incidental to reservations in services. From 1990, Reservations for OBCs at the time of making Appointments had been introduced. It was challenged vehemently in all Political Fora, in every possible manner in Society, in the educational Institutions, and in the Streets. Hence the Govt of India, mad compensatory Reservations in favour of the poor amongst the dominant castes. In spite of this, the decision of the Govt in introducing Reservations for the OBCs in the matters of Appointments was challenged in the Supreme Court. The Supreme Court finally in its Judgement in 1992, upheld the Reservations for OBCs, at the time of making Appointments. But, they set aside the compensatory Reservations for the Poor amongst all other Dominant Sections of the Society.

Employment of an individual, is the best and direct method of Developing the Individual, family, the larger family associated with the person to a large extent, and the section and area of the community from where the individual hails, to a certain extent. For, it helps to provide a decent and regular income over a period of 30 to 40 years, depending upon the age of the individual at the time of recruitment and employment, and type of job employment and retirement age. And it provides encouragement, facilitates guidance and incentives for others around to study and seek better and higher employment. Therefore, it is suggested that SC & ST Institutions, should directly employ SCs & STs as much as possible, as it is in the case of other Minority Institutions.

Reservations Available

Today Reservations for the SCs & STs are available in –

1. Political Reservations in Parliament (Lower House of the People-Lok Sabha) and the State and UT Legislative Assemblies (Lower House of the People)
2. Reservations in Employment
3. Reservations in Education
4. Reservations for Economic Development
5. Some Reservations in Housing

Need for Reservations in Private Sector

It is sad that today, with Liberalisation and Privatisation of even Govt Sector, Banks, Public Sector Enterprises, the Job Opportunities where the SCs & STs can reasonably hope to get a fair-play in the selections, or get jobs at least through Reservations in Employment, have shrunk.

The present Govts, are in a hurry to Privatise. It helps the Private Sector, to walk away with the Govt Enterprises at throw away prices, fixed by some private appraisers again to the advantage of the private sector.

And, it has not built any Safety-Clauses to protect Reservations in Employment, in the PSUs being Disinvested or sold off, or even protect those SC & ST Employees working already in the PSUs. There is an urgent need for these.

There is a need to evolve Reservation in all establishments, that make use of the Natural Resources of the Nation, like Land, Water and Man Power, even if they bring in their own money to the extent of 100%

Sabotaging Reservations

At present, Reservations in Services are under threat. They are being directly attacked by various Unions, dominant caste Welfare Associations, private individuals and even by some individual Advocates. While some of the staff and employees manipulate the existing Reservations, particularly the Rosters meant to identify the Vacancies to be Reserved for SCs, STs and OBCs, even senior officers are not free from these prejudices. At the slightest opportunity, they change the Reservation Policy, Rules and Orders, to the disadvantage of SCs, STs and OBCs. There appears to have emerged, an unholy understanding between the dominant castes advocates, officials of the courts, judges and senior officers, to Sabotage Reservations in Services.

Reservation in Education for SCs & STs

Reservation in Education, is only part of the Directive Principles to the State in the Constitution. Therefore the same is left to the sweet will and purely for the political considerations of the Govts in Power at the centre and in the States or Union Territories. Again due to Liberalisation, and opening of Education to Private Entrepreneurs and Business People, admissions has become difficult and costly, cost of Education had gone prohibitively high, and the quality of education in most private educational institutions has become worthless turning out unemployable and unsuitable graduates. On the other-hand rich dominant castes have managed to buy their way into these private institutions to virtually purchase their professional degrees and mange even well paid jobs thereafter, leaving the SCs & STs in the lurch. Now, there is a big hostile threat to the Education of the SCs & STs, and all other Weaker Sections, including the Minorities, OBCs and Women from the SCs, STs, Minorities and OBCs. The strategies being silently adopted are –

1. Intervention through Courts and direct Administrative Orders behind the back of Parliament, without any discussions to deny Admissions in Medicine, Engineering, Science, Post-Graduate Studies, Specialities and Super-Speciality Courses
2. Prohibitive Increase of Fees including Library Hostel and Examination Fees
3. Privatisation of Education that charge very very high fees and heavy admission charges in black
4. Passing out Doctors Engineers etc, without proper teaching and training, due to lack of Teaching Faculty, Laboratories and Workshops, leaving them unsuitable for good jobs
5. Turning out Doctors Engineers etc in thousands, that there is wide-spread unemployment and under-employment even amongst them

The main aim of many dominant castes, and thrust of their thinking plans and actions is to keep the Weaker Sections, still jobless, without adequate income, helpless, hopeless, weak and dependent.

Reservation in Economic Development for SCs & STs

Reservation in Economic Development, is again only part of the Directive Principles to the State in the Constitution. As a result the Schemes and Programmes are so lob sided, and practically serve no purpose. Fifty-five years of Independence could not develop any SC or ST really as an entrepreneur or as Industrialist or Business-Person.

The SCs & STs today lag far behind the others, though by way of Education and Employment in Public Services they might have developed much better in the past. That, thanks to the Statesmanship, Vision and Policies pursued by Baba Saheb, Babuji, Jawaharlal Nehru and Indira Gandhi. Today, with all round unrestrained liberalisation and privatisation without any human face had increased unbridled corruption in every sector. This makes all the more difficult for the SCs & STs to get any loans or plans cleared through even Govt Departments, without paying speed money and bribe. And most SCs & STs can not afford to pay any. As a result, even most educated and well-experienced SCs & STs are finding it difficult to make use of any Economic Development Programmes meant for SCs & STs.

Bibliography

Ahir, D.C.: *Dr B.R. Ambedkar: Buddhist Revolution and Counter-Revolution in Ancient India,* B.R. Publishing, Delhi, 1996.

Ambedkar, B. R.: *Annihilation of Caste: An Undelivered Speech,* Arnold Publishers, New Delhi, 1990.

Anand, J. H.: *Dalit Literature is the Literature of Protest,* Dalit Solidarity, Delhi, 1995.

Anandhi, S. *Contending Identities: Dalits and Secular Politics in Madras Slums,* Indian Social Institute, New Delhi, 1995.

Bari, S.A.: *Gandhi's Doctrine of Civil Resistance,* Kalamkar Prakashan, New Delhi, 1971.

Benjamin, Joseph: *Scheduled Castes in Indian Politics and Society,* Ess Ess Publications, New Delhi, 1989.

Beteille, Andre.: *Caste: Old and New,* Asia Publishing House, Bombay, 1969.

Blunt, E. A. H.: *Caste System of Northern India,* Oxford University Press, London, 1931.

Brown, Judith M.: *Gandhi and Civil Disobedience,* Cambridge University Press, London, 1977.

Fiske, A.: *The Untouchables in Contemporary India,* University of Arizona Press, Tucson, 1972.

Gandhi, M. K.: *The Removal of Untouchability,* Navjivan Publishing House, Ahmedabad, 1954.

Ganesan, L.: *Relevance of Reservation,* Valentina Publications, Madras, 1991.

Gawali, P.A.: *Society and Social Disabilities under the Peshwas,* National, New Delhi, 1988.

Ghurye, G. S.: *Caste and Class in India,* Popular Books, Bombay, 1950.

Gorhe, Neelam: *Social Development and Dalit Women,* Gyan Pub. House, New Delhi, 1995.

Gurukal, Rajan: *The Formation of Caste Society in Kerala,* Rawat Publications, New Delhi, 1994.

Hutton, J. H.: *Caste in India: Its Nature, Function and Origins,* Cambridge University Press, London, 1946.

Jogdan, Prahlad G.: *Dalit Movement in Maharashtra,* Kanak Publications, New Delhi, 1991.

Jogdand, P.G.: *Dalit Women in India: Issues and Perspectives,* Gyan Pub., New Delhi, 1995.

Kamble, J.R.: *Rise and Awakening of the Depressed Classes in India,* National, New Delhi, 1979.

Lokhande, G.S.: *Bhimrao Ramji Ambedkar: a Study in Social Democracy*, Intellectual Publishing House, New Delhi, 1977.

Mann, K.: *Tribal Women in a Changing Society*, Mittal Publications, Delhi, 1987.

Moffatt, Michael: *An Untouchable Community in South India: Structure and Consensus*, Princeton University Press, NJ, 1979.

Naidu, A. Nagaraja: *Caste and Land in Colonial South India*, Rawat Publications, New Delhi, 1994.

Omprakash, S.: *Development of the Weaker Section: Problems, Policies and Issues*, Uppal Publishing House, New Delhi, 1989.

Paranjpe, A. C.: *Caste, Prejudice and the Individual*, Lalvani Publishing House, New Delhi, 1970.

Shetty, V. T. Rajshekar: *Dalit Movement in Karnataka*, Christian Literature Society, Madras, 1978.

Silverberg, James: *Social Mobility in the Caste System in India*, Mouton Publishers, The Hague, 1968.

Srinivas, M. N.: *Caste in Modern India and Other Essays*, Asia Publishing House, Bombay, 1962.

Tripathi, R. S. and Tiwari, P. O.: *Dimensions of Scheduled Caste Development in India*, Uppal Publishing House, New Delhi, 1991.

Tripathy, R. B.: *Dalits: A Sub-Human Society*, Ashish Publishing House, New Delhi, 1994.

Venkateshwarlu, D.: *Harijan-Upper Class Conflicts*, Discovery, New Delhi, 1990.

Webster, John: *The Christian Dalits: A History*, Indian Society for Promoting Christian Knowledge (ISPCK), Delhi, 1994.

Index